◁ W9-BKV-454

OECD *Economic Surveys*
Electronic Books

The OECD, recognising the strategic role of electronic publishing, will be issuing the OECD *Economic Surveys*, both for the Member countries and for countries of Central and Eastern Europe covered by the Organisation's Centre for Co-operation with Economies in Transition, as electronic books with effect from the 1994/1995 series -- incorporating the text, tables and figures of the printed version. The information will appear on screen in an identical format, including the use of colour in graphs.

The electronic book, which retains the quality and readability of the printed version throughout, will enable readers to take advantage of the new tools that the ACROBAT software (included on the diskette) provides by offering the following benefits:

❑ User-friendly and intuitive interface
❑ Comprehensive index for rapid text retrieval, including a table of contents, as well as a list of numbered tables and figures
❑ Rapid browse and search facilities
❑ Zoom facility for magnifying graphics or for increasing page size for easy readability
❑ Cut and paste capabilities
❑ Printing facility
❑ Reduced volume for easy filing/portability

Working environment: DOS, Windows or Macintosh.

Subscription: FF 1 800   US$317   £200   DM 545

Single issue: FF 130   US$24   £14   DM 40

Complete 1994/1995 series on CD-ROM:

FF 2 000   US$365   £220   DM 600

Please send your order to OECD Electronic Editions or, preferably, to the Centre or bookshop with whom you placed your initial order for this Economic Survey.

OECD
ECONOMIC
SURVEYS

1994-1995

UNITED STATES

ORGANISATION FOR ECONOMIC CO-OPERATION AND DEVELOPMENT

ORGANISATION FOR ECONOMIC CO-OPERATION AND DEVELOPMENT

Pursuant to Article 1 of the Convention signed in Paris on 14th December 1960, and which came into force on 30th September 1961, the Organisation for Economic Co-operation and Development (OECD) shall promote policies designed:

— to achieve the highest sustainable economic growth and employment and a rising standard of living in Member countries, while maintaining financial stability, and thus to contribute to the development of the world economy;

— to contribute to sound economic expansion in Member as well as non-member countries in the process of economic development; and

— to contribute to the expansion of world trade on a multilateral, non-discriminatory basis in accordance with international obligations.

The original Member countries of the OECD are Austria, Belgium, Canada, Denmark, France, Germany, Greece, Iceland, Ireland, Italy, Luxembourg, the Netherlands, Norway, Portugal, Spain, Sweden, Switzerland, Turkey, the United Kingdom and the United States. The following countries became Members subsequently through accession at the dates indicated hereafter: Japan (28th April 1964), Finland (28th January 1969), Australia (7th June 1971), New Zealand (29th May 1973) and Mexico (18th May 1994). The Commission of the European Communities takes part in the work of the OECD (Article 13 of the OECD Convention).

Publié également en français.

3 2280 00481 3416

Table of contents

Boxes

Tables

Figures

BASIC STATISTICS OF THE UNITED STATES

THE LAND

Area (1 000 sq. km)	9 373	Population of major cities, including their metropolitan areas, 1992:	
		New York	19 670 000
		Los Angeles-Anaheim-Riverside	15 048 000
		Chicago-Gary-Lake County	8 410 000

THE PEOPLE

Population, 1994	261 000 000	Civilian labour force, 1994	131 056 000
Number of inhabitants per sq. km	27.9	*of which:*	
Population, annual net natural increase		Employed in agriculture	3 409 000
(average 1986-91)	1 854 600	Unemployed	7 970 833
Annual net natural increase, per cent (1987-92)	0.75	Net immigration (annual average 1987-92)	771 833

PRODUCTION

Gross domestic product in 1994		Origin of national income in 1994	
(billions of US$)	6 738.4	(per cent of national income[1]):	
GDP per head in 1994 (US$)	25 818	Agriculture, forestry and fishing	1.9
Gross fixed capital formation:		Manufacturing	17.9
Per cent of GDP in 1994	14.6	Construction and mining	5.1
Per head in 1994 (US$)	3 757.0	Government and government enterprises	14.5
		Other	60.6

THE GOVERNMENT

Government purchases of goods and services,		Composition of the 104th Congress 1995:		
1994 (per cent of GDP)	17.4		House of Representatives	Senate
Revenue of federal, state and local governments,				
1994 (per cent of GDP)	31.5	Republicans	233	54
Federal government debt held by the public		Democrats	201	46
(per cent of GDP), FY 1994	51.7	Independents	1	–
		Vacancies	–	–
		Total	435	100

FOREIGN TRADE

Exports:		Imports:	
Exports of goods and services		Imports of goods and services	
as per cent of GDP in 1994	10.7	as per cent of GDP in 1994	12.1
Main exports, 1994		Main imports, 1994	
(per cent of merchandise exports):		(per cent of merchandise imports):	
Food, feed, beverages	8.2	Food, feed, beverages	4.6
Industrial supplies	22.6	Industrial supplies	15.6
Capital goods (ex. automotive)	40.1	Capital goods (ex. automotive)	27.3
Automotive vehicles, parts	11.2	Automotive vehicles, parts	17.5
Consumer goods (ex. automotive)	11.7	Consumer goods (ex. automotive)	21.6

1. Without capital consumption adjustment.
Note: An international comparison of certain basic statistics is given in an annex table.

This Survey is based on the Secretariat's study prepared for the annual review of the United States by the Economic and Development Review Committee on 11 September 1995.

•

After revisions in the light of discussions during the review, final approval of the Survey for publication was given by the Committee on 5 October 1995.

•

The previous Survey of The United States was issued in November 1994.

Introduction

1994 was a very good vintage for the US economy: real GDP expanded by some 4 per cent; over 3¹/₂ million jobs were created; the unemployment rate dropped 1.3 percentage points; real disposable income per capita jumped by nearly 2¹/₂ per cent; the federal budget deficit fell a further percentage point of GDP; and consumer price inflation was only about 2³/₄ per cent. Obviously, while such outcomes are highly satisfactory, they cannot be counted on to repeat themselves. Indeed, a major concern in 1994 was to avoid a build-up of excessive momentum which would have fuelled higher inflation. To this extent, the significant deceleration in economic activity since the beginning of 1995 has been welcome, and the elusive goal of a "soft landing" may well have been achieved. The slower growth has meant that the unemployment rate stopped falling before excessive wage pressures developed and forced much higher interest rates in order to safeguard low inflation rates. Yet job creation continues, real disposable incomes are still rising, the downward trend in the budget deficit is being maintained, and it even looks as though the persistent rise in the current account deficit may have come to an end.

The short-term outlook is always problematic at such potential turning points. Some observers foresee continued slow growth attributable to earlier interest rate increases, an inventory overhang, a debt-burdened household sector, major spending cutbacks at the federal level and weak demand for US exports from the United States' three main trading partners. Alternatively, others predict a return to robust growth, as interest-sensitive spending components have shown recent renewed strength. The Secretariat's view is that moderate real GDP growth should resume in the second half of this year. Interest rates are not especially high in real terms and have come down significantly at the long end, but neither are they as low as in 1993; inventories are by no means lean but are probably excessive in only a few sectors; the trend increase in household indebtedness has

1

persisted, but net worth continues to rise as a result of strong appreciation of financial asset prices, and delinquency rates remain low; underlying export growth is strong and likely to stay strong once the Mexican and Japanese economies begin to recover and fundamental US competitiveness gains manifest themselves. Until a final budget agreement is reached it is difficult to ascertain how much of an impact lower federal spending may have over the short term, especially as tax cuts may offset some or all the contractionary effects. Accordingly, using 1987 price weights year-on-year real GDP growth is expected to average 3 per cent this year (implying about 2¼ per cent or a fourth-quarter over fourth-quarter basis) and about 2½ per cent in 1996; corresponding figures on a chain-weighted basis would be about ¾ percentage point less. An uptick in inflation is projected to continue, but to be very limited in magnitude. The current external deficit should be fairly steady in relation to GDP: a bit higher in 1995 and then marginally lower next year as competitiveness gains begin to feed through and the economy's cyclical position comes more into line with those abroad. The economy's recent performance is discussed in Chapter I. Chapter II first takes a more selective look at some aspects of this business cycle and how it compares with preceding cycles going back to around 1960 so as to inform the assessment of the likely future course of the economy. Its likely trajectory over the next 18 months is then described.

Monetary tightening continued into early 1995, but the abruptness of the slowdown in activity and the consequent reduction in inflation pressures led to a small cut in short-term interest rates in July – a move anticipated by a strong bond-market rally already underway. Chapter III examines the evolution of interest rates and money and credit aggregates over the past year. It focuses especially on the reasons for the rapid flattening of the yield curve and for the first-half weakness in the dollar, despite attractive interest rate differentials.

The budget deficit of the federal government has been a major concern of the Committee's for a very long time. In the light of the election last year of a new Congress apparently committed to balancing the budget, Chapter IV takes a detailed look at the longer-term outlook for federal finances should existing policies be maintained. It goes on to outline the rationale for deficit reduction and then scrutinises the various proposals to eliminate the deficit and how some changes to the budget process might influence outcomes.

Besides a greater emphasis on deficit reduction the current Congress has been intent on implementing a wide variety of structural reforms, many of which move away from policy decisions taken in recent years by rolling back the tasks of the federal government. A few have already become law, but most are still working their way through the legislative process. Chapter V surveys these proposals in the areas of labour and financial markets, agriculture, the environment and regulatory policy. It also describes important developments on the external trade front, both in terms of continuing bilateral and multilateral frictions and initiatives for future liberalisation.

The education system was the subject of a detailed analysis in the previous Survey of the United States. This Survey follows up with a study of the system of adult education and training, particularly with a view to clarifying its role in improving the lot of those at the low end of the skills spectrum. The widening distribution of wage and other income makes this a vital policy question, and institutional design and government initiatives are seen to be key. Conclusions drawn from this and the other sections are presented in a final chapter.

I. Recent economic trends

Overview

The US economy picked up steam in 1994, its fourth year of expansion (Figure 1), despite fiscal consolidation and monetary tightening. Labour and product markets tightened significantly as the unemployment rate fell to 5½ per cent by year end, and the manufacturing capacity utilisation rate reached its highest level since the 1970s. But the effects of rising interest rates in 1994 as well as the repercussions of the Mexican peso crisis induced an inventory correction and a noticeable slowdown in the growth of output in the first half of 1995. As the effects of the transitory factors wane and the impact of lower long-term rates begins to manifest itself, the economy is expected to reaccelerate back towards its potential growth rate in 1996. Notwithstanding tight markets, price and wage increases remained subdued in 1994 and picked up only moderately over the first half of 1995. With the economic slowdown having eased much of the mounting pressure on labour and product markets, the outlook is for only a slight further acceleration in inflation. The current account deficit widened throughout 1994 as US domestic demand grew more rapidly than that of trading partners; with the reversal of relative demand prospects, the deficit should begin to narrow in 1996.

Demand and output: robust growth and then a noticeable slowdown

In 1994 the economy expanded at its most rapid pace since the current expansion began in the spring of 1991 – indeed the fastest in a decade – led by double-digit growth in business fixed investment, a pickup in stockbuilding and a surge in exports. Overall growth in output was tempered by continued retrenchment by the government sector and further import penetration. However, by the

4

Figure 1. **CYCLICAL INDICATORS**

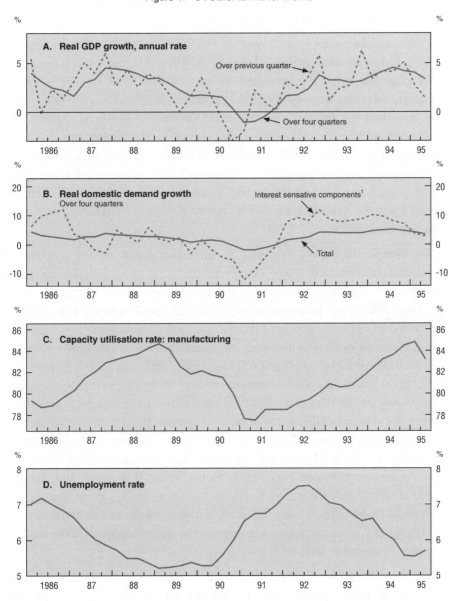

1. Consumption of durables plus residential investment.
Source: Department of Commerce, Federal Reserve Board and the Bureau of Labor Statistics.

end of the year an easing of demand began to appear, first in the housing sector and then in consumption, particularly of durable goods.

Private consumption was buoyant in 1994, advancing at a 3½ per cent rate. Real disposable income grew just as quickly, despite the tax increases and transfer cuts that were implemented as part of the 1993 budget agreement (OBRA93), reflecting wage gains from stepped-up employment growth as well as strong growth in proprietors' income and interest and dividend income.[1] But consumption growth slowed sharply, beginning in December and continuing through April 1995. Meanwhile employment and income continued to advance strongly through the first quarter, and the saving rate rose nearly a full percentage point (Figure 2). However, in the second quarter consumption rebounded and real disposable income fell, in part due to heavy April tax payments, driving the saving rate back down.

The rise in the saving rate was an important factor in the slowdown in demand and has puzzled many observers. Initially, the weakness in private consumption was widely viewed as a pause from the torrid 20 per cent annualised growth rate in durables purchases during the fourth quarter. But its persistence has led to a search for other explanations, and concern about over-indebtedness has surfaced especially because consumer instalment credit advanced at a 13 per cent clip in 1994, its largest increase since 1985, and total debt rose 8 per cent.[2] Unlike businesses, consumers have done little deleveraging during the recovery; indeed, debt-to-disposable-income ratios have reached new highs. However, the rise in liabilities has been accompanied by an increase in the value of asset holdings, despite the relatively poor equity and especially bond market performance in 1994, and net financial wealth and total net worth have risen. In theory, the rise in debt can play a role to the extent that assets and liabilities influence demand independently. But, with consumer debt service requirements as a share of disposable income still well below its peak, and delinquency rates on mortgage and instalment credit at low levels, the evidence of debt-burdened households is mixed at best.[3]

The housing sector is arguably the most interest and cyclically sensitive component of final demand. Residential investment held up well in 1994 (Figure 3) despite the run-up in interest rates, presumably fuelled by an above-average rate of income growth and possibly by a ''buy-in-advance'' motive, as surveys indicated that consumers thought it was a good time to buy before

Figure 2. **FACTORS INFLUENCING CONSUMPTION**

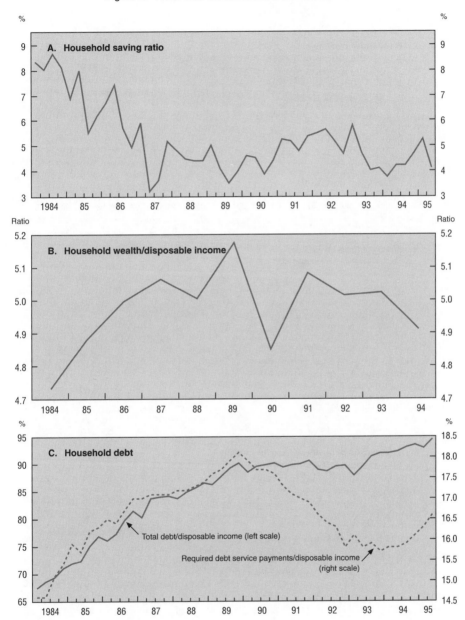

Source: Federal Reserve Board and OECD.

7

Figure 3. **DEVELOPMENTS IN INVESTMENT**

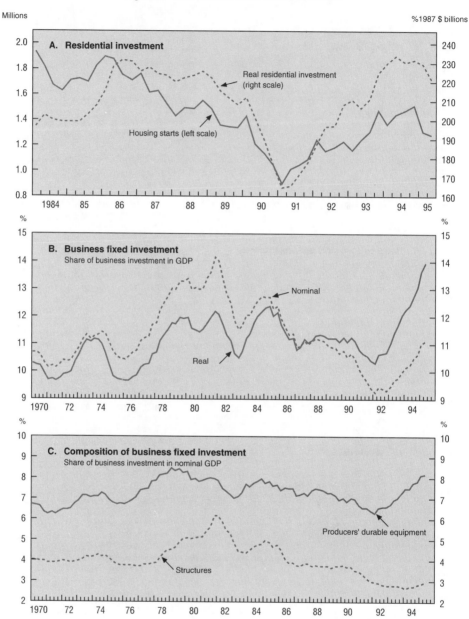

Source: Department of Commerce.

interest rates rose further. Indeed, housing starts averaged nearly 1.5 million units, 13 per cent above the 1993 rate and probably somewhat above long-run or trend needs.[4] Thus, even without the rise in rates, stock adjustment reasons would have pointed to a decline in starts as the desired stock was reached. Both of these factors together led to a sharp slowing in housing starts during the first half of 1995. The sharp fall in mortgage rates over the winter and spring began to give some support to housing only at the end of the second quarter when a pickup in sales of new and existing units and then starts occurred; its effect on construction activity began to emerge in the third quarter.

Non-residential fixed investment soared in 1994, posting its largest increase in a decade and is headed to the longest run of consecutive quarters of real growth recorded. As 1994 wore on and through the first half of 1995, the expansion became increasingly investment led (see Chapter III). The faster pace of investment has translated into a pickup in the growth of manufacturing capacity, helping to ease capacity constraints. Much of the strength in business investment has been in information processing and related equipment which grew at a 24 per cent annual rate in 1994. This sector has benefited from rapid productivity gains, especially for computers and peripherals whose prices have been falling at double-digit rates. This has created problems for interpreting the national accounts data because, with current methodology, sectors whose prices are rising more slowly than average will be weighted too heavily; thus, beginning late this year major methodological changes will be implemented and a new chain-weighted real GDP series will be emphasised (see Box 1). The extent to which relative prices of investment goods have fallen is evident in the contrasting performance of nominal and real investment shares of GDP (Figure 3). Investment in the form of non-residential structures, about one-quarter of business fixed investment, rose in 1994 for the first time since 1990; it had been hampered by over-building that occurred in the 1980s, encouraged first by incentives included in tax laws in the early 1980s which were removed by the 1986 tax reforms and then by aggressive bank lending in the late 1980s.

In 1994 stockbuilding made its first significant contribution to growth since early in the cycle. Stocks had been growing more slowly than sales throughout the expansion, especially at the manufacturers level. This came to an end in 1994 as firms apparently reacted to the rapid pace of demand, lengthening delivery lags and the growing risk of rising prices. Then the sharp fall-off in

Box 1. **Impending US national accounts revisions***

The Bureau of Economic Analysis (BEA) will make a comprehensive revision to the national income and product accounts at the end of 1995, the first since 1991. One major change will be to replace its fixed-weighted index as the featured measure of real GDP with an index based on chain-type weights; both measures will continue to be available, however. Chain-weighted indices use weights from adjacent years rather than from a single base year. The chain-weighted index is superior for comparisons of economic activity over long periods of time when production patterns and relative prices are changing because it allows for regular updating of output and price weights. When fixed-weighted real GDP is recalculated using more recent prices, the products that have experienced relatively small price increases receive less weight (because prices are the relevant weights). Such recalculations typically reduce measured GDP growth because products for which price increases are smallest are often those for which output grows most rapidly (computers and related equipment in particular), as purchasers switch demand toward them. Use of chain-weighted volume indices will minimise this ''substitution bias''. This problem is particularly important in the US case because of its use of a hedonic-pricing approach to the deflation of computer expenditures – a practice which is followed in only a few other OECD countries. The BEA notes that, while on average for the 1985-92 period there was no evidence of significant substitution bias, and GDP growth outcomes measured by fixed weights and chain weights were about the same, in 1993 and 1994, real growth estimated by the fixed-weight measure was 0.6 percentage point higher than by the chain-weighted measure, and during the four quarters ending in Q2 1995 the average gap widened to 0.8 percentage point. One disadvantage of the chain-weighted index is that the components of real GDP will not add up to the total and nominal GDP will not equal the product of chain-weighted real GDP and chain-weighted prices; but implicit deflators will continue to assure the latter identity. On the other hand, use of chain weights will eliminate the revisions to historical growth rates caused by a change in base year. In addition to adopting the chain-weight measure as its featured index, the benchmark revision will move the fixed-weighted measure forward to 1992 weights, make definitional changes such as incorporating government investment accounts and bring in other adjustments to reflect new data and new depreciation and capital stock estimates.

----

*   This box draws heavily on material included in Landefield and Parker (1995) and Lasky (1995).

demand from softening retail sales, particularly for cars and light trucks, and the Mexican peso shock (see below) resulted in an unwanted accumulation of goods which brought about an abrupt inventory correction in the second quarter. Indeed, the slowdown in the automobile sector alone, in reaction to weakening sales and bulging stocks, is estimated to have reduced GDP growth by over 1 percentage point at an annual rate in the second quarter of 1995.

With fiscal consolidation and robust economic growth, the government sector net lending position improved significantly. On a national accounts basis, the federal deficit fell from 3.8 per cent of GDP to 2.4 per cent and the cyclically-adjusted balance improved by 1.0 percentage point (Table 1). The state and local surplus remained at 0.4 per cent of GDP, while its cyclically-adjusted counterpart deteriorated by about 0.1 percentage point. The improvement of the federal finances reflects the spending cuts and tax increases that were implemented as part of OBRA93. Tax receipts as a share of GDP rose by 0.5 percentage point. Expenditures rose a scant 2 per cent over a year earlier as nominal government consumption[5] and agricultural subsidies fell, and the growth of transfers was trimmed. In real terms, federal consumption has now declined 13 per cent since the 1991 peak, with sharp cut-backs in defence and meagre increases in non-defence categories (Figure 4). Indeed, in 1994 real non-defence spending edged down as employment contracted, in part reflecting the implementation of the National Performance Review [see last year's Survey, OECD (1994e)]. During the first semester of 1995 these broad trends have continued; taxes as a share of GDP have edged up and expenditure growth has remained subdued, except for a further pickup in interest payments, reflecting the higher short-term interest rates.

Table 1. **Government net lending**

Percentage of GDP, national accounts basis

	1960-69	1970-79	1980-84	1985-89	1990	1991	1992	1993	1994
Federal	-0.2	-1.7	-3.6	-3.5	-2.9	-3.5	-4.7	-3.8	-2.4
State and local	0.0	0.8	1.1	1.0	0.5	0.3	0.4	0.4	0.4
Social security[1]	0.5	0.8	1.1	1.2	1.1	1.1	1.1	1.0	1.0
Other	-0.5	0.0	0.0	-0.2	-0.6	-0.8	-0.7	-0.6	-0.6
Memorandum:									
Cyclically adjusted net lending									
Federal	n.a.	n.a.	n.a.	-3.3	-3.2	-3.2	-4.3	-3.6	-2.5
State and local	n.a.	n.a.	n.a.	1.0	0.3	0.5	0.6	0.5	0.3

n.a.: not available.
1. Essentially employee pension funds.
Source: Bureau of Economic Analysis and OECD.

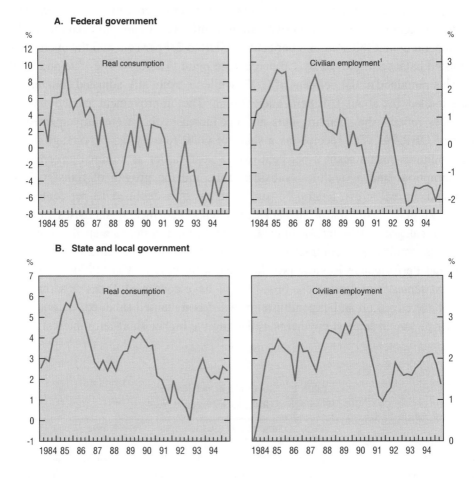

Figure 4. **GOVERNMENT SECTOR INDICATORS**

Per cent change over four quarters

A. **Federal government**

B. **State and local government**

1. Excluding temporary census workers.
Source: Department of Commerce and Bureau of Labor Statistics.

On a unified budget basis, the federal government recorded a $203 billion deficit in fiscal year 1994, over $60 billion (1 per cent of GDP) smaller than had been expected by the Administration when the budget was presented in April 1993 (Table 2). According to Administration calculations, only a small

Table 2. **Unified budget deficit projections**

$ billion

	1992	1993	1994	1995	1996
FY 1994 budget	290[2]	317	264	247	212
Excluding DI[1]	287[2]	314	258	248	225
FY 1995 budget		255[2]	235	165	176
Excluding DI[1]		287[2]	238	176	181
FY 1996 budget			203[2]	193	197
Excluding DI[1]			211[2]	205	203

1. Outlays net of premiums for bank and savings and loan deposit insurance.
2. Actual.
Source: Budget of the US Government.

portion of the difference between the budget proposal and the outcome came from a better-than-expected economic performance or differences between policy proposals and enacted legislation.[6] Over $50 billion came from so-called technical differences, chiefly slower-than-expected growth in Medicare and Medicaid outlays and smaller-than-expected payouts for deposit insurance. With three-quarters of the fiscal year 1995 completed, it appears that the deficit may be close to that proposed in the fiscal year 1995 budget which would be the smallest deficit as a share of GDP since 1979.

The state and local sector finances remain somewhat troubled, especially so for this stage of the recovery.[7] While their social insurance funds (used primarily to finance employee pension plans) continue to record healthy surpluses, operating accounts have not materially improved since the recession. Real purchases have been rising, reflecting increased resources for education and civilian safety (police, fire and corrections), but the bulk of the increase appears in health care transfers, principally Medicaid. In 1994 their real consumption rose just 1 per cent, while transfers rose over 9 per cent.

Both real exports and imports of goods and non-factor services rose briskly in 1994. Export growth was aided by a rebound in activity of trading partners as well as increased market access from implementation of NAFTA. The role of the exchange rate is more problematic; the lagged effects of the dollar's appreciation in 1993 probably restrained export growth somewhat in 1994, while the slight depreciation of the dollar in 1994 probably had little effect. Improved export market performance (Figure 5) may reflect increased US competitiveness stemming from relatively smaller increases in unit labour costs after accounting for

13

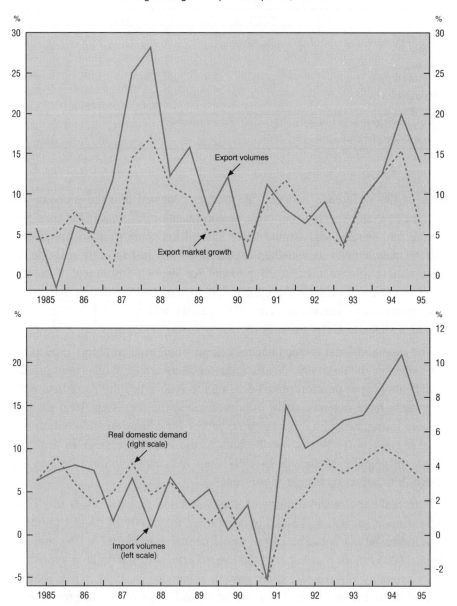

Figure 5. **MERCHANDISE EXPORTS AND IMPORTS**

Percentage change from previous period, annual rates

Export volumes

Export market growth

Real domestic demand
(right scale)

Import volumes
(left scale)

Source: Department of Commerce and OECD.

14

exchange rate movements. All in all, real exports of goods rose 11 per cent in 1994 compared with only 4 per cent in 1993, while real services exports edged up 2 per cent, about the same as a year earlier. Real goods and services imports rose at a 14 per cent pace, more rapid than what would be expected based on aggregate demand growth. This may reflect, in part, the acceleration of domestic demand for computers, peripherals and parts (for which import penetration is high), owing to rising real investment as well as the fact that the mesurement biases imported by using fixed-weights has grown more rapidly for imports than for aggregate demand. The widening of the real external deficit subtracted 0.7 percentage point from GDP growth.

At the beginning of 1995, the Mexican peso crisis – the sharp depreciation of the peso and subsequent contraction of Mexican domestic demand – led to a 20 per cent decline (at an actual rate) in US goods exports to Mexico (which had accounted for 10 per cent of exports in 1994) from the fourth quarter to the first quarter. Imports from Mexico also rose markedly, but the extent to which Mexican products were squeezing out domestic suppliers or displacing other importers is unclear; as the rise in imports was not exceptional, the latter effect was probably the dominant one overall. Monthly data suggest that most of the external shock to final demand was felt in the first quarter as exports to Mexico and imports from Mexico appear to have stabilised in the second quarter. The impact on GDP probably spilled over into the second quarter, with some of the shock initially absorbed by rising inventories. If all of the shift in imports reflected increased market share at the expense of US producers, then the first-round impact on first quarter demand would have been 1.3 percentage points (at annual rates) and on the year 0.3 percentage point. However, if increased Mexican imports came entirely at the expense of other foreign producers, then the first quarter effect would have been only 0.6 percentage point of US GDP and the annual effect may be 0.1 percentage point.

A still tight labour market but moderate inflation

The rapid advance in output led employment (household basis) to increase by about 2¼ per cent during 1994, driving the unemployment rate from 6.7 per cent in January 1994, the first month of the new survey,[8] to 5.4 per cent in December (Figure 6). Lower unemployment rates were recorded across all demographic

Figure 6. **LABOUR MARKET CONDITIONS**

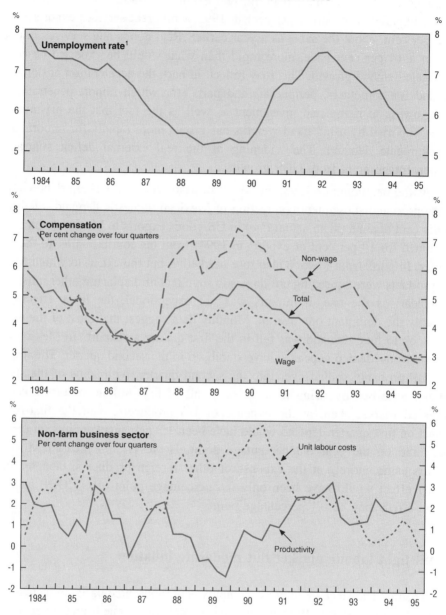

1. Data redefinition in January 1994.
Source: Bureau of Labor Statistics.

16

groups and geographical regions, with the largest improvements generally among those groups and areas that had the highest unemployment rates. The labour force participation rate rose 0.4 percentage point in 1994, but this was probably due to the redesign of the survey. Labour force participation did not advance further over the first half of 1995 and the lack of a material advance despite improving labour market conditions during this expansion remains a puzzle. The unemployment rate began to edge up in the second quarter of 1995 when hiring came to an abrupt halt; the goods-producing industries shed labour in response to the inventory overhang in both manufacturing and construction and hiring slackened in retail trade due to the weakness in goods consumption.

Labour compensation gains continued to slow in 1994 and the first half of 1995 despite the relatively tight labour markets. This is in contrast to the late 1980s, when worker compensation pressures began to build after the unemployment rate fell below 6 per cent. Some of the restraint on compensation undoubtedly comes from the successful efforts by businesses to staunch the growth of benefits, particularly insurance premia for health care, which had greatly exceeded wage growth for many years. Although over time the reduced growth in benefits will tend to result in higher wage growth, because both workers and employers bargain over total compensation, the tradeoff between benefits and wages may not be instantaneous.

Productivity at non-farm businesses advanced 2¼ per cent in 1994, its second largest gain in the past ten years, a particularly strong rise considering that productivity growth often slows as the expansion matures. With compensation rising only 3 per cent, unit labour costs in the business sector increased just ¾ per cent, the best showing in a decade. The productivity gains in recent years appear at first blush not to have been passed on to workers as real wages have stagnated. This is largely the result of two forces, the shift in compensation from wages to benefits and the loss in terms of trade between what labour produces and what it consumes – that is, the wedge between consumer prices and the GDP deflator.[9]

Most indicators of final prices showed further deceleration of inflation in 1994 and posted their lowest rates of increase since the mid-1960s, but improvement in the inflation rate appears to have ended. For example, recent readings of the so-called core consumer price index, which excludes volatile food and energy prices, indicate that prices have risen about 3 per cent over the past year com-

Figure 7. **PRICE PERFORMANCE**

Per cent change over four quarters

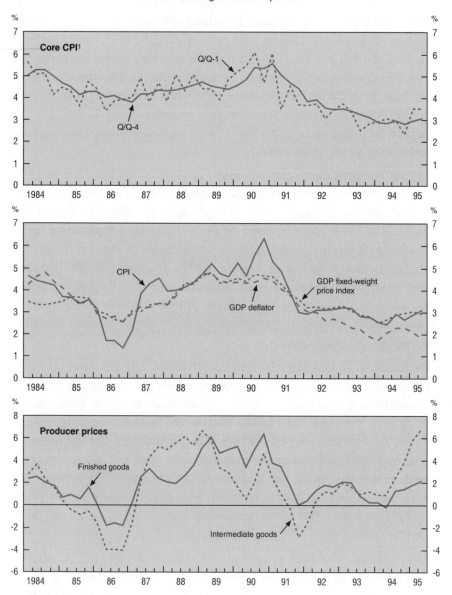

1.   CPI excluding food and energy.
Source: Bureau of Labor Statistics and Department of Commerce.

18

pared with the 2¾ per cent figure for 1994 (Figure 7). The fixed-weight GDP price index, which incorporates a broader range of markets, also rose by 2¾ per cent in 1994 and accelerated to 3 per cent in the first half of 1995. The degree to which recent acceleration reflects a higher underlying inflation rate rather than transitory factors is difficult to discern at this juncture. But some acceleration should be expected given the tightness of labour and product markets; the Secretariat estimates that the level of output was about ¾ percentage point above potential in 1994 and early 1995. Moreover, the performance of producer prices, particularly at the intermediate goods level, indicates upward pressures on downstream prices. Intermediate goods prices began to accelerate in the middle of 1994 as delivery lags lengthened and capacity became strained. An acceleration in final goods prices appeared subsequently, but the extent of pass-through into consumer prices may have been moderated over the first half of 1995 by the sudden slowing in demand; indeed, price increases at the producer level slowed in the spring and summer.

A widening external deficit

The current account deficit widened to $151 billion or 2¼ per cent of GDP in 1994 (Table 3) as the merchandise trade account worsened and the investment

Table 3. **Current account**

$ billion, seasonally adjusted annual rates

	1993	1994	1994				1995	
			Q1	Q2	Q3	Q4	Q1	Q2
Current account balance	−100	−151	−121	−152	−159	−173	−156	−174
Exports of goods, services and income	764	839	789	817	857	893	930	958
Imports of goods, services and income	830	954	880	933	983	1 021	1 055	1 103
Balances								
Goods	−133	−166	−146	−166	−179	−174	−180	−196
Non-factor services	58	60	54	58	63	64	62	63
Investment income	9	−9	0	−9	−10	−18	−8	−11
Private transfers	−14	−16	−16	−16	−15	−16	−16	−16
Official transfers	−20	−20	−14	−19	−18	−29	−15	−13

Source: US Department of Commerce, *Survey of Current Business.*

Figure 8. **FOREIGN INVESTMENT: POSITION AND INCOME**

A. Direct investment
Current cost basis

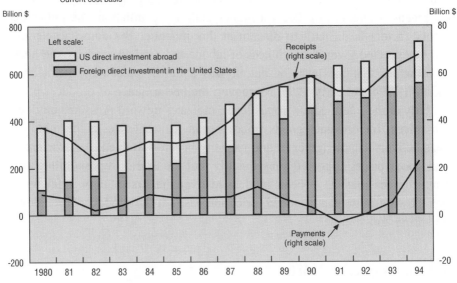

B. Net portfoiio investment

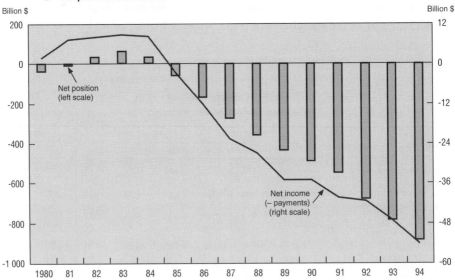

Source: Department of Commerce.

20

Table 4. **Rates of return on direct investment**[1]

Per cent

	1981-85	1986-90	1991	1992	1993	1994
US investment abroad	7.5	9.3	8.3	8.0	9.0	9.2
Foreign investment in United States	3.2	2.2	–0.7	0.1	1.0	4.1

1. Rate of return in US dollars. Numerator is direct investment receipt or payment (balance of payments accounts) and denominator is the average of year end figures for the value of direct investment for the current and previous year, evaluated at current cost.
Source: Bureau of Economic Analysis.

income position deteriorated (Figure 8). The widening of the trade deficit reflected a cyclical deterioration, as the US economy grew twice as rapidly as the rest of the OECD. Indeed, the current account deficit has returned to the levels of the late 1980s when the economy was operating at a similar degree of excess demand (at that time many of its trading partners had a similar degree of excess demand, but in 1994 most had significant output gaps). There was little change in the terms of trade in 1994 as export and import deflators each declined slightly. Investment income turned negative for the first time, reflecting both the continuing deterioration in the US net investment position and as an improvement in rates of return on foreign investment in the United States. While the net international investment position of the United States had turned negative in the late 1980s, net investment income had remained positive because of the higher rates of return on US direct foreign investment abroad relative to that on foreign holdings in the United States.[10] The profitability levels shown in Table 4, are in US dollars; thus, actual returns in home currency vary according to changes in exchange rates. That said, some of the exchange exposure may have been reduced to the extent that foreign direct investment assets were financed by dollar-denominated liabilities.

21

II. The current cycle in perspective and the outlook for 1995-96

Now that the current expansion has passed its fourth anniversary and has, in fact, nearly reached the average duration of all six previous cycles since 1958,[11] it may be instructive to examine it in relation to its preceding counterparts. Many claims have been made in recent years with respect to a variety of economic developments that "this time things are different", but such claims are naturally difficult to judge. This chapter will first juxtapose the performance of a wide range of economic variables across business cycles in order to evaluate the merit of some of these claims and draw the appropriate inferences for the period ahead. It will then present the Secretariat's current (September) projections for 1995-96 which will be updated in the forthcoming OECD *Economic Outlook 58* to be published in December.

The relative strength of aggregate demand and its components

Much has been made that this has been a subpar expansion. Indeed, it is true that real GDP growth has averaged only about 3 per cent since the 1991 trough, down from an average of about 4 per cent in all periods of business-cycle expansion back to the late 1950s (Figure 9).[12] What is often forgotten by those advancing this argument, however, is that the preceding recession was relatively mild – according to Secretariat estimates, economic slack increased only about half as much as it has done on average during previous cyclical downturns – and the growth of economic potential is widely acknowledged to be lower in the 1990s than it was through most of the post-war period.[13] Thus, it is inappropriate simply to compare real output growth across business cycles without taking this into account. If one looks at the rate at which economic slack has been used up since the trough, this expansion, although it was initially quite slow, has for

Figure 9. **REAL GROWTH PERFORMANCE IN PERSPECTIVE**

- - - - · Average of previous cycles[1]　　　　——— Current cycle[2]　　　Q0 = Trough

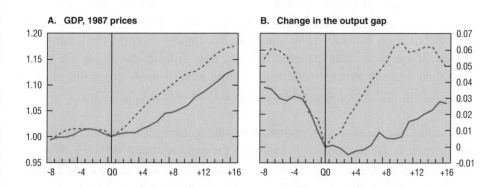

A. GDP, 1987 prices

B. Change in the output gap

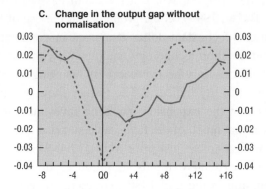

C. Change in the output gap without normalisation

Note: The methodology used for this and the following thirteen graphs is as follows:
　　For variables expressed in levels, with the exception of price indices, the diagrams show accumulated changes from the trough set as 1.0.
　　For price indices, the diagrams represent each quarter's growth over the previous four quarters minus the trough quarter's year-on-year growth rate.
　　Interest rates and ratios are the current quarter figure minus the trough quarter outcome.
　　The number of previous cycles used in the average varies according to the availability of data.
1.　Trough quarters for the five previous cycles are: Q1 1958, Q4 1960, Q4 1970, Q1 1975, and Q3 1982.
2.　Trough quarter for the current cycle is Q1 1991.
Source: OECD.

nearly two years compared reasonably favourably: the rapid rebound usually apparent in capacity utilisation in the first six quarters of the recovery was absent this cycle because there had not been the corresponding increase in slack in the preceding recession. Prior to the recent slowdown, capacity utilisation was approaching the peak range for such a mature phase of the cycle. However, it was still well below the levels reached in early 1973 and late 1978, even if only moderately below the early 1989 outcome. The implications for the longevity of the current cycle are that the economy has now entered the phase where it is susceptible to exogenous shocks which could push it away from full capacity output, but in any case capacity pressures are not severe.

Among the statements most often heard regarding the strength of demand components, surely the most popular is that the recovery has been led by business fixed investment, especially in the form of computers and related equipment,[14] and that the cycle is therefore healthier and more sustainable. Constant-price data provide support for this view, although only as of the past two years; prior to that differences were minor (Figure 10). But the claim has been forcefully attacked (see, for example, Baker, 1994) on the grounds that the use of base-year weights for the determination of constant-dollar outcomes in conjunction with hedonic price indices for information technology equipment (with sharply falling prices) leads to biases which can only be overcome by resorting to either current-price data or chain-linked quantity indices.[15] The former show that it is only since the beginning of 1994 that the expansion has been investment-led to any unusual extent and moreover that much of the favourable surprise is merely compensation for particularly low investment just prior to the 1990-91 recession. Most of this story is driven by the relative trends in producer durable equipment; given substantial overbuilding in the mid-1980s, structures investment has been weak throughout this expansion. In any case, it is clear that the investment boom was financed to an extraordinary extent through sources other than debt: in contrast with the household sector, business-sector indebtedness has fallen in real terms over the past few years (Figure 11, Panel A). Credit market borrowing has averaged a mere 10 per cent of capital expenditures in the nonfarm nonfinancial corporate business sector since 1991, compared with an average of 45 per cent from 1983 to 1990, for example (Panel B). This very marked change is due in part to the end of the leveraged buyouts of the 1980s,[16] as well as a much more limited rate of net acquisition of financial assets, especially liquid assets.[17] But it

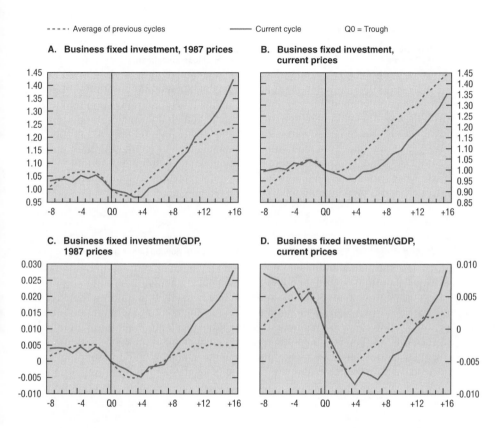

Figure 10. **AN INVESTMENT-LED EXPANSION?**

- - - - Average of previous cycles ——— Current cycle Q0 = Trough

A. Business fixed investment, 1987 prices

B. Business fixed investment, current prices

C. Business fixed investment/GDP, 1987 prices

D. Business fixed investment/GDP, current prices

Explanatory notes given on Figure 9.
Source: OECD.

is not the case that business-sector borrowing has been avoided by relying to a greater extent on internal funds: net cash flow has lagged behind its normal cyclical increase (Panels C and D), although that was, at least until recently, only because net cash flow had not fallen much during the 1990-91 recession. Rather, financing has been assured by greater net new equity issues, greater recourse to borrowing from own pension funds and faster accumulation of trade debt.

25

Figure 11. **DEBT RATIOS: FALLING FOR BUSINESS BUT NOT FOR HOUSEHOLDS**

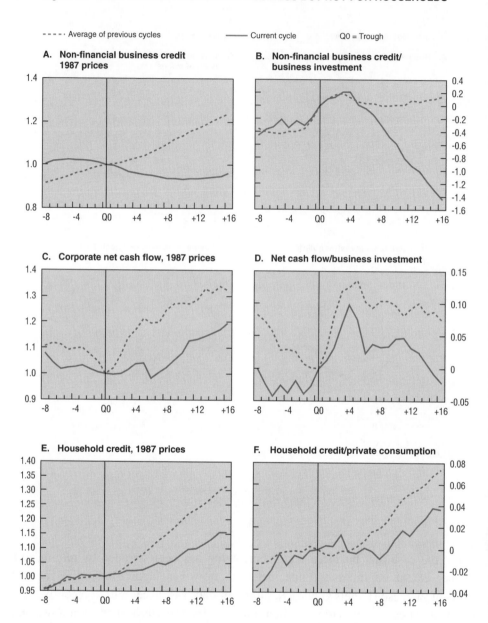

----- Average of previous cycles   ——— Current cycle   Q0 = Trough

A. Non-financial business credit
1987 prices

B. Non-financial business credit/
business investment

C. Corporate net cash flow, 1987 prices

D. Net cash flow/business investment

E. Household credit, 1987 prices

F. Household credit/private consumption

Explanatory notes given on Figure 9.
Source: OECD.

26

Whether or not the expansion is properly characterised as having been "investment-led", it is worthwhile to look at other components of demand which may have behaved differently during this cycle as compared with previous ones. There seems little to remark upon with regard to private consumption in the aggregate, other than the sluggishness of the initial take-off and a slightly slower average pace thereafter (Figure 12). But, as a share of real GDP, household consumption has displayed somewhat less counter-cyclicality than in the past, at

Figure 12. **COMPARISONS OF HOUSEHOLD INCOME, OUTLAYS AND SAVING**

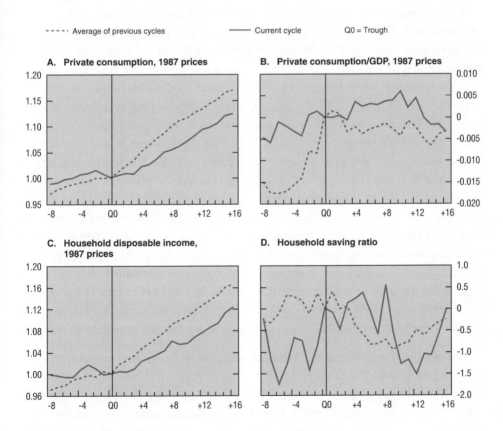

Explanatory notes given on Figure 9.
Source: OECD.

27

least until the end of 1993. Since then, its moderation has been the arithmetic counterpart of the persistent strength in investment described above. Consumer outlays for durable goods have been as procyclical as ever and in fact were unusually strong in 1994, given the maturity of the expansion.

The normal pattern for the household saving ratio is for it to rise slightly prior to the trough and then decline for two years, beginning one quarter after the expansion gets underway. It then recovers about half that decline over the subsequent two years. During this cycle, however, the saving ratio continued to rise during the recovery, and then, with a paucity of real income gains in the middle stages of the expansion, there was an aberrant fall over the four quarters to 1994 Q1. But even though delayed, the subsequent rebound in the household saving rate was sufficiently marked to make up all the lost ground. The initially moderate increases in consumption and housing (see below) slowed the growth of household debt relative to previous recoveries for a time, though it has nonetheless followed the characteristic uptrend in relation to consumer outlays over the past two years (Figure 11, Panels E and F). Led by robust increases in consumer credit since 1993,[18] reminiscent of 1983-84, the weight of debt in household balance sheets has risen somewhat, with the ratio of liabilities to total financial assets moving up from the 25 per cent level, where it had stabilised in recent years, to 27 per cent at end-1994 (Table 5). This has led to concerns in some quarters that overindebtedness might become a problem, especially as assets and liabilities might play separate, asymmetric roles in determining consumer demand (Mishkin, 1976). But declining margins of household borrowing costs over interest rates on riskless securities, forced by increased competition in a deregulated financial environment, have helped keep debt servicing from becoming too onerous: for example, interest paid on consumer debt was still around $2\frac{1}{2}$ per cent of measured disposable income in 1994, virtually exactly the same level as in 1970, 1973 or 1978.[19] Nevertheless, consumer spending would appear to be more vulnerable to any increase in borrowing rates than in the past.

Residential investment has been the most procyclical component of expenditure, not only over the past six years but more generally; indeed, the cycle-on-cycle similarities are strong (Figure 13). Despite unusually low long-term interest rates during this cyclical upturn (see below), the housing construction sector lagged somewhat, and it was not until the tenth quarter of expansion that it began to outpace its average historical performance in relation to real GDP. As well, in

Table 5. **Indicators of households'[1] financial health**

Per cent

	1950	1960	1970	1980	1989	1990	1993	1994
Liabilities/Assets	6.8	10.8	12.4	13.0	15.5	16.4	16.2	16.9
Liabilities/Financial assets	10.3	16.8	19.2	22.5	25.3	26.7	25.5	26.8
Net increase in liabilities/Gross investment	..	..	..	..	31.7	24.2	31.9	33.5
Net increase in liabilities/Net acquisition of financial assets	..	..	..	..	55.6	48.7	63.6	67.8
Home mortgages/Stock of owner-occupied real estate	17.4	27.4	31.5	27.5	37.1	40.8	42.4	43.5
Net increase in home mortgages/Gross residential construction expenditures	..	..	..	..	105.2	93.5	77.4	71.3
Net increase in home mortgages/Net investment in residential construction	..	..	..	..	189.9	182.1	144.8	125.9
Consumer credit outstanding/Stock of consumer durable goods	22.1	31.6	35.9	35.0	41.3	39.7	37.1	39.9
Net increase in consumer credit/Consumer durable goods expenditures	..	..	..	..	10.0	3.4	11.6	19.9
Net increase in consumer credit/Overall consumer expenditures	..	..	..	..	1.3	0.4	1.4	2.5
Net increase in consumer credit/Net investment in consumer durables	..	..	..	..	42.0	17.8	70.1	117.3
Interest paid on consumer debt/Disposible personal income	..	2.0	2.4	2.6	2.8	2.8	2.4	2.4

1. Including non-profit organisations.
Source: Board of Governors of the Federal Reserve System, Balance Sheets for the US Economy 1945-94.

29

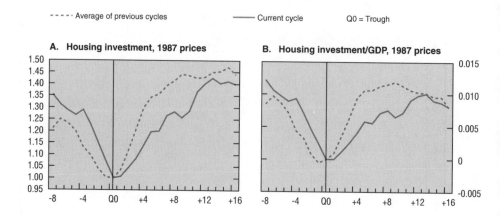

Figure 13. **A LOOK AT HOUSING INVESTMENT**

- - - - · Average of previous cycles ——— Current cycle Q0 = Trough

A. Housing investment, 1987 prices

B. Housing investment/GDP, 1987 prices

Explanatory notes given on Figure 9.
Source: OECD.

the past housing downturns have averaged seven quarters; the current episode began in the summer quarter of 1994 and has therefore now reached the four-quarter mark. With less overbuilding than has sometimes been the case in the past, it seems reasonable to expect a turnaround in the not-too-distant future.

The last component of private domestic demand left to be considered is the contribution from stockbuilding. This residual item is assumed to be pro-cyclical in all but the most classical economic models. The typical inventory cycle is generated by purchasing managers who wish to ensure the availability of raw materials and intermediate inputs as delivery times lengthen as the expansion matures. Yet it has been much pointed out in recent years that "just-in-time" methods of production and inventory control have been increasingly adopted in United States and other economies. It was therefore not surprising that through much of the present cycle inventories rose more moderately than historical averages (about 0.4 percentage point of GDP per year during the first eight quarters or so) (Figure 14). But since the beginning of 1994 that gap has been

30

Figure 14. **THE ROLE OF STOCKBUILDING**

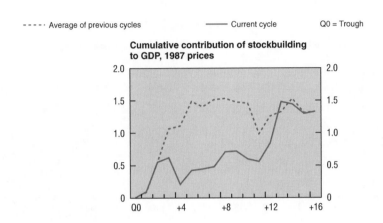

Explanatory notes given on Figure 9.
Source: OECD.

totally made up, as both farm and nonfarm stocks have accumulated rapidly and the stock-to-sales ratio has, at least temporarily, ended its trend decline.

Government purchases and budgetary policy more generally are of course intended to provide counter-cyclical ballast by stabilising overall demand. It can be seen from Figure 15 that this has indeed been the case: in both real and nominal terms purchases rise relative to GDP before the trough and fall thereafter. But in most cycles the decline peters out about eight quarters after the trough and then its GDP share flattens out; this time however, the downtrend has been maintained, thanks largely to the 1990 and 1993 federal legislation (OBRA90 and OBRA93; see Chapter IV below) to reduce the budget deficit. Real purchases have fallen at an average of nearly 1 per cent per year for four years now – about 4 per cent annually at the federal level. Taxes have evolved in relation to GDP in a fairly typical way, with some additional increases in 1993-94 in evidence. Transfers, on the other hand, rose unusually strongly relative to GDP in the first five quarters of the cycle when growth was still weak, and stabilised thereafter, as is typically the case. In the three years after the

Figure 15. **GOVERNMENT CONSUMPTION IN DECLINE**

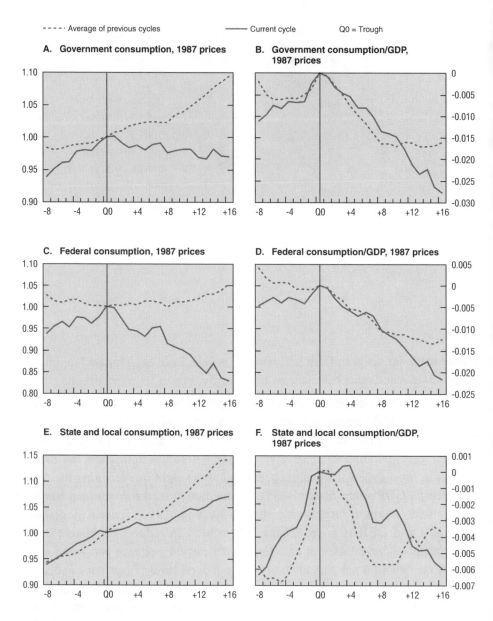

- - - - - Average of previous cycles ———— Current cycle Q0 = Trough

A. Government consumption, 1987 prices

B. Government consumption/GDP, 1987 prices

C. Federal consumption, 1987 prices

D. Federal consumption/GDP, 1987 prices

E. State and local consumption, 1987 prices

F. State and local consumption/GDP, 1987 prices

Explanatory notes given on Figure 9.
Source: OECD.

32

Figure 16. **THE BUFFERING ROLE OF THE TRADE BALANCE**

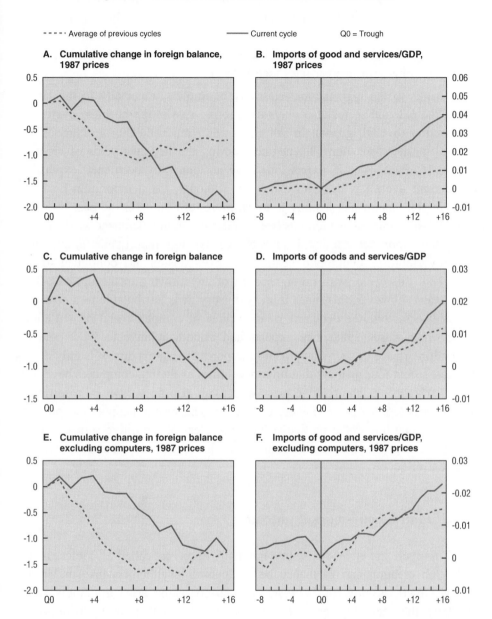

Explanatory notes given on Figure 9.
Source: OECD.

33

trough the general government structural deficit has improved by an average 0.6 percentage point of GDP; this time the reduction has been about double that.[20] This has no doubt been an important factor in preventing the economy from overheating, thereby extending the life of the recovery, and in holding down short- and long-term interest rates (see below).

Thanks to the high income elasticity of imports, especially in the United States, the external sector also plays a buffering role in the business cycle. The contribution to GDP growth in volume terms from net exports of goods and services is, therefore, normally negative during the first two years of recovery (Figure 16, Panel A): US expansions have not generally been (net) export-led. The current cycle has been no exception, although the deterioration has been more durable than usual, leading to much more restraint over the past couple of years. Most of this innovation has been registered on the merchandise trade side. It is in the import column that this has been occurring: import penetration, which normally stabilises about two years into an expansion has continued to rise throughout this cycle, with no signs even of any slowing in the uptrend. To a large extent, however, this innovation is illusory. It is attributable to a combination of two factors: the declining relative price of computers and related equipment, which raises 1987-price exports and imports relative to GDP, and the greater importance of such equipment in imports than in exports. It is only during the most recent four quarters that import volumes excluding computers have been particularly strong. The relative price effect can also be purged by resorting to current price comparisons (Panels C and D). The results support the previous contention that imports in particular have been less of a positive surprise during this cycle, and what surprise there has been has become evident only over the past year or so.

Novelties in labour-market outcomes

This cycle got underway with what many observers called a ''jobless recovery''. Job creation can in theory be disappointing either because underlying output growth is slow or because productivity gains are surprisingly rapid. Similarly, the unemployment rate can stay ''high'' if either employment growth is sluggish or labour force increases are robust. The salient features of this recovery are several. First, the unemployment rate rose a full percentage point over a period of more than a year after the trough was reached; in other recoveries, the upward momentum has been much more limited, and labour market slack has been on a clear downtrend much sooner (Figure 17). However, nine quarters after the trough the average cycle has seen virtually all its reduction in the unemployment rate, whereas this expansion yielded ten quarters of falling jobnessness prior to the recent slowdown in growth. Once the effects of the major methodological changes in the unemployment series in January 1994 are taken into account, the effect of the slow start in reducing unemployment has been virtually completely eliminated, with a maximum decline in the unemployment rate thus far of some 1¼ percentage points.

Second, employment growth has indeed been weaker than average, but the shortfall has been practically non-existent for the past two years or so. And once the slower GDP growth is controlled for, productivity seems to have followed the usual path to an amazing degree: indeed, gains have been slightly smaller than is typical, although as large as any but the most distant cycles (those beginning in 1958 and 1961).

Third, Figure 17 demonstrates that labour force growth in the United States exhibits a very strong trend element with only relatively limited cyclical influences. In the five previous cycles the labour force expanded by an average of just under 2 per cent per year both in the two years prior to the peak in the unemployment rate and in the four years thereafter. This time slow labour supply growth – even given underlying demographics – was already in evidence before the peak in joblessness, with the average growth down to less than 1 per cent per year. Similarly sluggish growth has been recorded for most of the recent past. Otherwise, the behaviour of the labour market seems to have been an appropriate reflection of what has transpired in the goods market over the past four years, with little radically new to report in the main aggregates.

However, there are some features of this labour market cycle that are novel. First, at least until the end of 1993,[21] an atypically small part of the overall decline in unemployment was accounted for by job losers, and a corresponding unusual lack of increase in unemployment resulting from voluntary separations (Figure 18, Panels A and B). The residual share accounted for by entrants and re-entrants was also unusually stagnant until the end of 1993, but has risen appreciably since then. The persistence of layoff announcements due to "downsizing" and "restructuring" during the upswing has been much remarked upon. Simi-

Figure 17. **FAIRLY TYPICAL OVERALL LABOUR MARKET OUTCOMES**

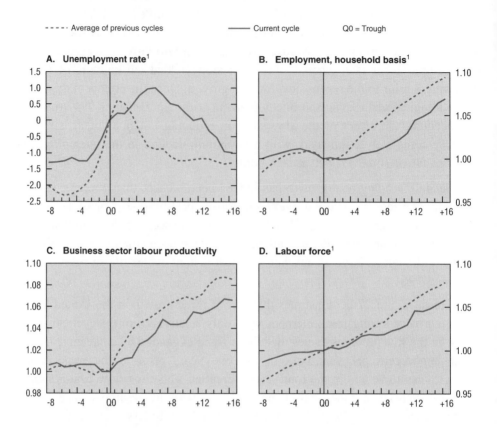

Explanatory notes given on Figure 9.
1.   Break in series in Q1 1994.
Source: OECD.

larly, some observers have speculated that the abnormally low job leavers' share might indicate a labour market which is weaker than experts believe: a lack of confidence in the availability of ''good'' jobs might be dissuading employees from quitting existing jobs and from pressing employers for wage increases. But adding this term to the econometric wage equation which is embodied in the Secretariat's INTERLINK model for the United States provides no support whatsoever for the hypothesis that the job leavers' share provides additional informa-

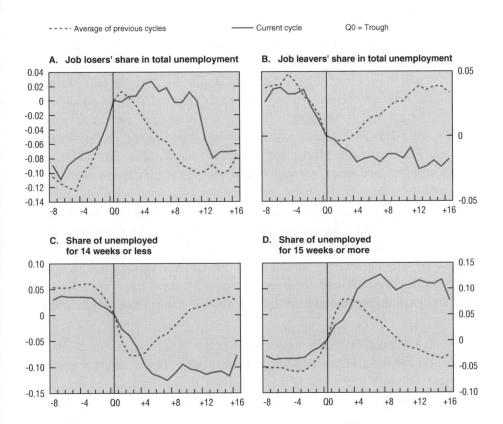

Figure 18. **SOME NOVEL LABOUR MARKET FEATURES**[1]

- - - - Average of previous cycles ———— Current cycle Q0 = Trough

A. **Job losers' share in total unemployment**

B. **Job leavers' share in total unemployment**

C. **Share of unemployed for 14 weeks or less**

D. **Share of unemployed for 15 weeks or more**

Explanatory notes given on Figure 9.
1.   Break in series in Q1 1994.
Source: OECD.

tion beyond what is included in the prime-age male unemployment rate as a proxy for labour-market slack. Regression analysis (reported in detail in Annex I) shows that while the job leavers' share is procyclical, it is less so than the entrants' share and that it is subject to a slight negative trend, so long as the unemployment rate is above about 5.8 per cent. But there does not seem to have been any structural instability in the share; indeed, there is also a negative trend in the entrants' share, and both these are offset by a positive trend in the losers' share. Yet all these trends are of a long-standing nature.

Another labour market characteristic which has evolved differently during this expansion is the mean duration of unemployment spells. Normally, duration is procyclical: the share of the short-term unemployed normally falls during and immediately after a recession and rises during the remainder of the expansion; the share of long-duration unemployed exhibits the reverse pattern (Figure 18, Panels C and D). This time the shift in shares during the recession was as expected, but the usual subsequent shortening in duration has been almost entirely absent. Once again, regression analysis (see Annex I) shows the role of the overall unemployment rate (a proxy for the cycle in the labour market) in determining these duration shares, as well as the strong trends in evidence: it is not just in recent years that a shift has occurred; rather since around 1980 the share of those unemployed for over 14 weeks has risen exogenously at an accelerating rate. The reasons for this trend remain to be explained.[22] So does the relationship between it and some other trends in the labour market such as widening wage dispersion and the aforementioned rising share of job losers.

A final feature of recent labour market outcomes which has been much discussed is the lengthening workweek (Schor, 1992). One claim that is made is that those in work are working harder, while those unemployed are further distanced from the labour market. Another is that the lengthening workweek has resulted in a utility-reducing loss of leisure. For the total private sector the first half of the expansion followed the usual cyclical pattern, but over the past two years or so the lengthening has persisted, while in previous expansions it would have begun to reverse at this stage (Figure 19). Regression results confirm that the average workweek is procyclical (see Annex I): at a quarterly frequency, changing the workweek and changing the size of the workforce are seen to be complementary, rather than substitutes. But the claim that workweek lengthening is novel is seen to be exaggerated: in the goods-producing sector there has been a positive exogenous trend in evidence since around 1977; it is only in the services-producing sector that it has taken until the 1990s to become manifest. Furthermore, some significant part (possibly around half) of the additional time spent working in the market-place has been offset by a reduction in home production (thereby limiting the impact on leisure), as child-care opportunities

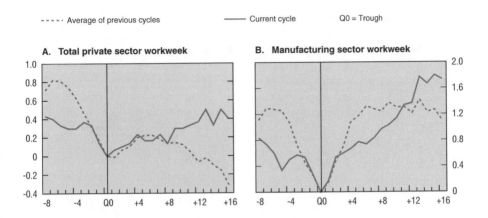

Figure 19. **A STEADILY LENGTHENING WORKWEEK**

----- Average of previous cycles ——— Current cycle Q0 = Trough

A. **Total private sector workweek**

B. **Manufacturing sector workweek**

Explanatory notes given on Figure 9.
Source: OECD.

have expanded, average family size has declined and technological improvements in home production have spread (Roberts and Rupert, 1995).

An expansion purged of a cyclical upturn in inflation

The usual US business cycle expansion brings with it a reacceleration in wage and price increases some time after the cyclical trough. Real hourly wages are normally highly procyclical, but while they followed the usual pattern in falling in this cycle prior to the 1991 trough, they continued to decline in the subsequent two years, followed merely by approximate stabilisation (Figure 20, Panel A). Adding nonwage labour costs and average weekly hours makes the gap between this cycle and the historical norm much smaller, but nonetheless there has been a remarkable stagnation for more than two years (Panel B). In fact, if year-on-year compensation developments are compared with corresponding rates of change at the trough, that is, if one examines acceleration/deceleration in compensation, the cross-cycle similarities are striking. Thus, the novelty of this

39

Figure 20. **REAL WAGE MODERATION**

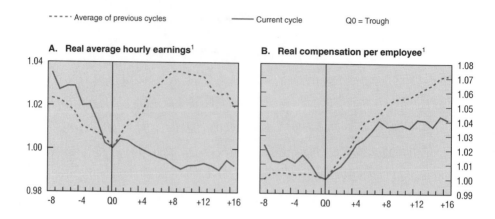

- - - - - Average of previous cycles ——— Current cycle Q0 = Trough

Explanatory notes given on Figure 9.
1.   Deflated using the CPI.
Source: OECD.

cycle was the extent of the decline in real wages and compensation during the 1990-91 recession and that this downshift has persisted.

With productivity growth strong by post-1970 standards, cost-push factors emanating from the labour market have been entirely absent. The disinflation in consumer and GDP prices achieved during and immediately after the downturn has therefore been fully maintained and even extended, in contrast with the usual dissipation of gains beginning in the second or third year of the recovery (Figure 21, Panels A and D). Food and energy prices made proportionately greater contributions to disinflation this time around than on average, but other (core) prices continued to decelerate in the middle years of the upswing (Panel B). A fairly similar pattern of maintained disinflation was manifest in the previous cycle in the 1980s, with the result that that cycle proved to be one of the longest in modern history, whereas the 1970s cycles were cut short by the upsurge in inflation around 1974 and 1979 (OECD, 1988).

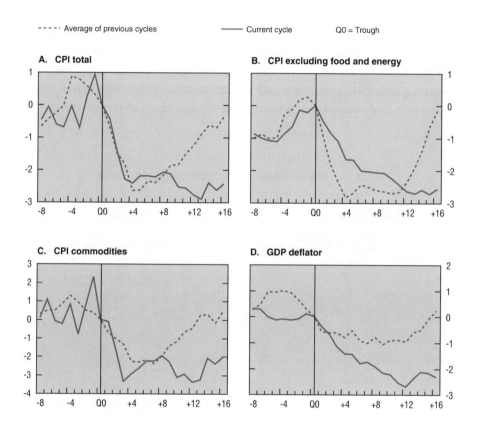

Figure 21. **NO DISSIPATION OF DISINFLATION GAINS**

- - - - · Average of previous cycles ——— Current cycle Q0 = Trough

A. CPI total

B. CPI excluding food and energy

C. CPI commodities

D. GDP deflator

Explanatory notes given on Figure 9.
Source: OECD.

A belated interest-rate cycle

Under no pressure from tightening labour and product markets until 1994, this cycle has seen important differences in interest rate developments. Short-term rates usually reach their trough in the quarter following the trough in activity and then rise by nearly 2 percentage points over the following 14 quarters, bringing them within 1½ percentage points of their previous cyclical peaks (Figure 22, Panel A). This time, with an initially weak recovery, rates fell for a full two years after the trough and only began to rise a year after that; but even with the late-cycle increases they remain below the level recorded at the business cycle trough and some 3 percentage points below previous peak levels observed in early 1989. However, in real terms the uniqueness of the current cycle is more limited (Panel B): while real short-term rates were unusually low in the mid-life of the expansion, persistent disinflation has helped eliminate the differential with the average cycle over the past two years. Indeed, real short-term rates of late have

Figure 22.   **THE INTEREST RATE CYCLE IN PERSPECTIVE**

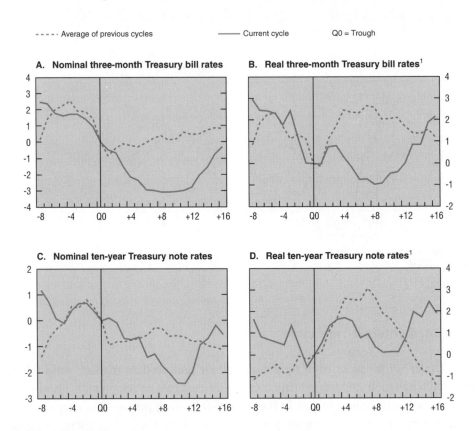

Explanatory notes given on Figure 9.
1.   Deflated by the CPI.
Source: OECD.

been a full percentage point above where they usually are 16 quarters after a cyclical trough, mainly because product markets are tighter and disinflation has been better maintained. The monetary tightening needed to slow the economy to avoid overheating got underway only slightly before inflation began to pick up. But it was more pre-emptive than in the past to the extent that higher real rates have been sustained.

The story is fairly similar with respect to long-term rates. Normally they fall sharply in the two quarters surrounding the cyclical trough in activity, with only limited changes later in the expansion (Figure 22, Panel C). This time ten-year Treasury note yields fell almost continuously for ten quarters after the trough. A sharp four-quarter-long rebound has since been followed by an equally marked two-quarter reversal.[23] Despite the latter bond market rally, real long-term rates (deflated using only the current inflation rate) remain much higher than they were at the cyclical trough in activity, in contrast with previous late-cycle outcomes. The yield gap (the excess of long-term over short-term rates) widened considerably over the first five quarters of this cycle, whereas it has normally remained fairly stable over this period. Even though it has since fallen back, it remains well above historical precedents.

Wrapping up

Real output growth during the current cycle has therefore been below average, but this is in part attributable to a relatively mild recession at the outset, with the rest explained by slower growth in potential output. While output is probably above potential levels (capacity utilisation is high), the gap is smaller than it typically has been at business cycle peaks, enhancing the promise of a soft landing. The cycle has also been marked by a clear maintenance of disinflation gains and of moderate increases in real compensation to this point. The probability of overheating is further lessened by the trend improvement in the fiscal deficit and by the surprisingly rapid rise in import penetration which may indicate that there is some merit to the argument that the US market is increasingly global in nature. The promise of a favourable outcome is also supported by the balance of spending in the economy: even if the expansion only became clearly led by investment in 1994, the likelihood of that trend continuing is high, given the healthy condition of business balance sheets and income statements.

While the other component of investment, residential construction, has been weak of late, it has followed a fairly normal cyclical pattern; this implies a probable rebound beginning by the end of the year, especially given the lack of apparent overbuilding. Households have been heavy borrowers in this cycle, but they have been largely protected from the interest burden of higher indebtedness by the lower average interest rates they have faced. The implication for the future is that rate changes may well have larger effects on consumer spending than in the past. Finally, the inventory situation, which had been advantageous, has deteriorated over the past year, but the build-up is no worse than average at this point in the cycle.

Of possibly greater concern is the pattern of labour market outcomes. While some observers claim that faster labour productivity growth has boosted potential growth rates, whatever acceleration there may have been – and to this point it is merely against poor outcomes in the 1970s – has clearly been at least offset by a noticeable slowdown in labour force growth. Furthermore, the high proportion of new entrants and job losers among the unemployed, along with the increased share of long-term unemployed, may indicate concentrated labour market difficulties for certain low-skilled groups, a topic that is revisited in Chapter VI.

Short-term economic prospects

The US economy is projected to experience moderate growth for the remainder of 1995 and in 1996 (Table 6). After the slowdown over the first two quarters of this year the economy should bounce back in the second half, and real growth should move back towards its long-run average. The return of moderate growth is expected because the effects of the peso crisis and stock adjustments of inventories of goods and housing are largely complete and the impetus provided by lower long-term interest rates will begin to take hold. Overall demand growth should be supported by continued strength in investment and exports but be held back by further retrenchment in stockbuilding in 1995 and government consumption in both 1995 and 1996; private consumption is expected to rise with income and neither propel nor hinder growth prospects. In this context, monetary policy is assumed to maintain the current level of short-term interest rates over the projection horizon and long-term rates are projected to be roughly unchanged. All

Table 6. **Near-term outlook**

Percentage change from previous period, seasonally adjusted at annual rates, volume (1987 prices)

	1994	1995	1996	1994 I	1994 II	1995 I	1995 II	1996 I	1996 II
Private consumption	3.5	3.0	2.6	3.6	3.1	2.9	3.2	2.3	2.4
Government consumption	−0.7	−0.5	−0.6	−2.8	1.9	−1.6	−0.5	−0.6	−0.6
Gross fixed investment	12.3	9.8	5.4	13.0	9.8	12.2	5.4	5.7	5.0
of which:									
Residential	8.6	−2.0	3.5	13.4	−0.9	−4.6	2.0	4.5	3.0
Non-residential	13.7	13.9	6.0	12.9	13.8	18.1	6.4	6.1	5.5
Final domestic demand	4.1	3.6	2.6	3.9	4.0	3.7	3.0	2.5	2.4
Stockbuilding[1]	0.6	−0.3	−0.3	1.2	0.4	−0.4	−0.8	−0.1	0.0
Total domestic demand	4.7	3.2	2.3	5.1	4.4	3.2	2.2	2.3	2.4
Exports of goods and services	9.0	10.3	9.7	7.2	16.6	8.8	7.5	10.5	10.4
Imports of goods and services	13.4	10.7	7.1	13.4	15.3	10.3	7.4	7.0	7.1
Foreign balance[1]	−0.7	−0.3	0.2	−0.9	−0.2	−0.4	−0.2	0.3	0.3
GDP at constant prices	4.1	3.0	2.5	4.3	4.3	2.9	2.1	2.7	2.7
Memorandum items:									
GDP price deflator	2.1	1.9	2.1	2.4	2.1	1.7	2.0	2.2	2.0
Private consumption deflator	2.1	2.3	2.5	2.0	2.8	2.2	2.2	2.5	2.5
Unemployment rate	6.1	5.7	5.8	6.4	5.8	5.6	5.7	5.8	5.9
Three-month Treasury bill rate	4.2	5.5	5.4	3.6	4.9	5.7	5.4	5.4	5.4
Ten-year Treasury note rate	7.1	6.7	6.3	6.6	7.6	7.1	6.4	6.4	6.3
Net lending of general government									
$ billion	−133	−114	−126						
Per cent of GDP	−2.0	−1.6	−1.7						
Current account balance									
$ billion	−151	−171	−164						
Per cent of GDP	−2.2	−2.4	−2.2						

1. The yearly and half-yearly rates of change refer to changes expressed as a percentage of GDP in the previous period.
Source: OECD estimates.

told, real GDP growth for 1995 is projected to be 3 per cent, but only 2¼ per cent over the four quarters of 1995, and 2½ per cent in 1996.

The drop in interest rates during the spring and summer, the rise in stock and bond market wealth and satisfactory labour market prospects should buttress consumption. These same factors and a decline in the stock of unsold homes are projected to reverse the sharp declines in residential construction. Although capacity constraints have eased somewhat since their winter peaks, the still high level of utilisation and cost-reducing modernisation efforts will support continued expansion of plant capacity and robust business fixed investment, albeit at a much slower pace than was recorded in 1994. Export growth is projected to rebound owing to the renewed strength in export markets, with the dissipation of the Mexican crisis and the recovery in Japan. Import demand should weaken, reflecting the easing in domestic demand. Thus, while private final demand will support continued moderate growth, stockbuilding and fiscal consolidation are projected to slow the growth of GDP below potential over the projection horizon. Stockbuilding is expected to be scaled back over the second half of 1995 as firms adjust to the lower demand profile, reversing the recent rise in the stock-to-sales ratio. Deficit reduction at the federal level is projected to lead to real reductions in federal consumption of some 5 per cent at an annual rate. The projections incorporate another round of fiscal consolidation by the federal government amounting to about 0.2 percentage point of GDP in 1996, reflecting the discretionary spending cuts included in the Budget Resolution and FY 1996 appropriations bills. The proposed reductions in transfers to individuals and other levels of government and tax cuts were not incorporated in the projections.

Consumer price inflation is expected to pick up a bit, reflecting the still relatively tight product markets and rising import prices, but the easing of the economy back towards its potential level of output should limit the acceleration. The rise in inflation is projected to lead to a pickup in wage costs;[24] however, advances in real wages should be moderated somewhat by the rise in the unemployment rate which by the end of the projection horizon may be 6 per cent, slightly above the Secretariat's estimate of full employment.[25]

The external accounts are expected to weaken further in 1995 before improving marginally in 1996. The merchandise trade account deficit is projected to widen to around $190 billion in 1995, or 2¾ per cent of GDP, because of continuing growth differentials between the United States and its major trading partners, particularly Japan and Mexico. America's comparative advantage in services should help maintain a healthy surplus in non-factor services, but the increasing debt position is likely to lead to a larger deficit on factor income. Taken together, the current account deficit is expected to amount to some $171 billion in 1995 (2½ per cent of GDP), but to edge down in 1996 as import demand grows relatively more slowly.

As always, a variety of risks are attached to the projection. If consumers become more cautious because of the rise in the unemployment rate and caution then spreads to businesses, then growth in economic activity could stall due to a lack of demand, especially in conjunction with further fiscal consolidation. Indeed, fiscal consolidation may prove to be larger than projected if the government enacts sharp reductions in transfers which are not offset by tax cuts over the near-term. Yet incoming data indicate that there are few of the imbalances that have precipitated other recessions; stock-to-sales ratios, while rising, are still lean outside of the motor vehicle sector, and household and especially corporate balance sheets are in good shape. Indeed, it is the prompt correction of emerging strains that has led to the slowdown and will probably prevent the conditions from developing that would lead to a contraction. Moreover, the rally in bond markets beginning in late 1994 has effectively undone much of the Federal Reserve's earlier tightening. This leads to an upside risk that the lagged effects of lower long-term interest rates and expanding export markets may lead to a stronger rebound in demand than projected which would put renewed pressure on both labour and product markets.

III. Monetary and exchange rate policy and developments

The Federal Reserve is charged with promoting "the goals of maximum employment, stable prices, and moderate long-term interest rates" under the terms of the Federal Reserve Reform Act of 1977. Since the early 1980s it has increasingly made it clear that price stability should be its overriding long-term objective, since that is a necessary precondition for maximising output and employment as well as achieving the lowest possible array of interest rates.[26] The monetary environment over the past year can most usefully be separated into two sub-periods. In the first, which ended during the early months of 1995, the primary concern of many observers was that interest rates might not have risen sufficiently to slow the economy to a sustainable rate of growth in good time to head off a widely predicted, albeit moderate, pickup in inflation.[27] Since then, concerns shifted rather quickly to when the process of unwinding the earlier increases in interest rates should get underway and to what extent they should be unwound, as first demand and then economic activity weakened abruptly, and the leading indicators for inflation began to look more favourable.

The culminating increases in short-term interest rates

A rather modest expansion finally gave way to more robust growth in activity in late 1993 in response to the lengthy period of easy monetary conditions that had been underway since the 1990 business cycle peak. Expectations for real GDP growth in 1994 were continuously being revised upward as from late 1993,[28] and in February 1994 the monetary authorities began to rein in the stimulus provided in the form of short-term interest rates around zero in real terms.[29] The importance of the forward-looking monetary response to the dwindling amount of spare capacity is underlined by some recent evidence that the short-run output/inflation trade-off is non-linear, that is that excess demand gaps may have larger effects on inflation than excess supply gaps (Turner, 1995; Clark *et al.*, 1995). After a series of three ¼ percentage point increases in the target federal funds rate in the late winter and early spring, the Federal Reserve engaged upon a more aggressive path of tightening monetary conditions beginning in May 1994. At that point it also chose to raise the discount rate by ½ percentage point. But while it was widely recognised that the impact of these moves would take some time to be perceptible in terms of slowing demand and output, the economy appeared to be still picking up steam, and full employment was generally thought either to have been already achieved or to be imminent. Accordingly, with price pressures still building in commodity and intermediates markets, a further ½ percentage point increase in both the funds rate and the discount rate was implemented in August.

However, the momentum of activity was still accelerating, with the unemployment rate falling by an average of 0.1 percentage point per month and real GDP growth flirting with a pace of 4½ per cent year-on-year, far above its potential rate. Demand for interest-sensitive capital goods was particularly strong. Furthermore, market estimations of current output growth were rising.[30] The risks of higher inflation continued to mount, especially as all the tightening to that point had failed to generate any flattening of the yield curve – a normal sign of expected slowdown and reduced inflation expectations (see below). In this context, the Federal Open Market Committee (FOMC) decided on an unusually large increase in both the funds and discount rates of ¾ percentage point effective 15 November. For the first time in this episode of interest-rate increases bond markets reacted favourably and did not shortly thereafter reverse the initial gains. But while it was again appreciated that the cumulative increase in the funds rate of 2½ percentage points would have its primary impact only later in 1995, the combination of further upward revisions to expected output growth,[31] a continuing increase in evidence that early-stage price pressures were building, a recognition that banks were persistently making credit available more easily to their customers and strong downward pressure on the dollar (see below), especially against other major currencies, led to a seventh and final increase in the funds and discount rates of ½ percentage point effective 1 February 1995. This brought the cumulative increase to a full 3 percentage points and left the funds rate adjusted for consumer price inflation in the 2½ to 3 per cent range. Such a real rate is in line with points in most previous business cycles when a similar output gap was recorded (Figure 23). According to rules-based analysis which has gained in popularity in recent years, the restraint implied is also at least in line with previous efforts to curb inflation.[32]

Many observers continued to believe that a funds rate of 6 per cent was inadequate to bring about a desired "soft landing" and called for further rises without delay. But, as described in earlier sections, incoming data showed that interest-sensitive spending components were finally beginning to slow apprecia-bly; job creation dwindled, and unemployment stabilised and then even began to rise; there was no sign of demand pressures in labour markets showing up in faster rates of compensation growth; and the bond markets were signalling a sharp decline in the demand for long-term funds, in line with an unexpectedly abrupt economic slowdown and a resulting easing in inflation fears. The Chair-man of the Federal Reserve had already signalled earlier in the year that, in theory at least, he could envisage a situation where it would be appropriate to lower interest rates even though actual inflation was rising, so long as the

Figure 23. **REAL SHORT-TERM INTEREST RATES**

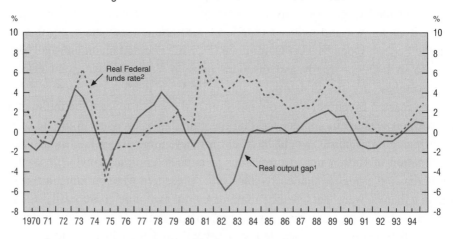

1. Defined as the deviation of actual GDP from potential as a per cent of potential.
2. Deflated using the percentage change in the CPI excluding food and energy over the preceding four quarters.
Source: OECD.

prospects for the eventual reversal of the acceleration were favourable: the mirror image of the so-called "pre-emptive strike" against inflation undertaken in 1994. Accordingly, in July the FOMC decided that inflationary pressures had receded sufficiently[33] to justify a ¼ percentage point reduction in the funds rate, a cut described as a "modest adjustment in monetary conditions". It was immediately matched by an equivalent fall in the prime rate and by a further rally in bond markets. The latter proved short-lived, however, as signs of a revival in job creation and spending curbed hopes of further imminent funds rate declines; indeed, the FOMC left reserve settings unchanged at both its August and September meetings. Renewed downward pressure on long-term rates from late August to early October might be ascribable to prospects for deficit reduction and the rebound in the dollar.

The reaction in the bond markets

Like the sharp distinction in sub-periods for the policy environment, there was also a sea change in the bond markets late in 1994 (Figure 24). Up to that point, 1994 had been known as the year of the "great bond market massacre" or the "great world-wide margin call" (reflecting an assessment that much of the 1993 rally was a speculative bubble built on heavy leverage). In the period of rising long-term rates which lasted about 13 months, the trough-to-peak change in yields on ten-year Treasury notes was some 2¾ percentage points; on 30-year bond yields it was nearly 2½ points. Over much of the year the rise in long-term rates matched that in short-term rates, something which had previously occurred only in the 1983-84 tightening episode.

The reversal occurred around the time in early-to-mid November that: *i)* the extremely strong October labour market report was released, only to be followed by the first signs of easing momentum; *ii)* the magnitude of the Republican victory in the Congressional elections became known, with the consequent increased likelihood of deficit reduction and/or capital gains tax cuts; *iii)* renewed intervention in currency markets after a lapse of several months showed the authorities' determination to resist further depreciation of the dollar; and *iv)* the market view of the Federal Reserve's intentions clarified, once the size of the November rise in short-term interest rates was revealed. In the following seven or eight months the strength and persistence of the bond market rally was also

Figure 24. **INTEREST RATES, SPREADS AND YIELD CURVES**

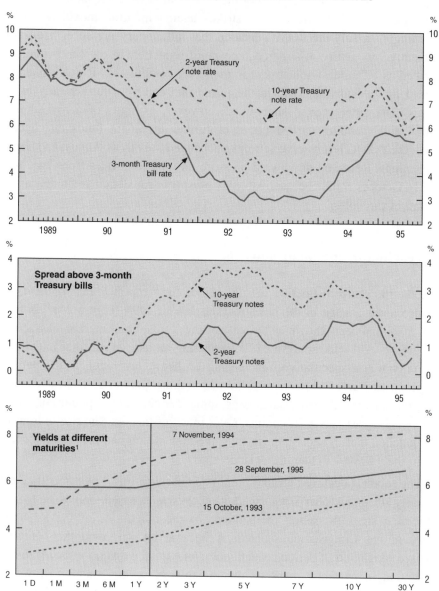

1. One-day to one-year rates are Euro-currency rates; two-year to 30-year rates are redemption yields for benchmark bonds.
Source: Datastream, Federal Reserve Board.

somewhat unusual, even if it was widespread across OECD Member countries.[34] The yield on the ten-year note fell by about 2 percentage points, as the economy slowed much more and much earlier than had been expected, led by interest-sensitive expenditure components, and longer-term budget deficit prospects improved. High-quality corporate bond rates did not rise so much in 1994 and have not fallen as far this year; the differential has long been acknowledged to be counter-cyclical.

The reasons why the yield curve remained so steep for so long in 1994 are by no means entirely clear. On average, the impact effect of changes in the funds rate on the ten-year note rate has been about 0.16 since 1960, but thus far in the 1990s it has risen to 0.36.[35] One explanation is that the traditional term-structure relationship between rates across the maturity spectrum, which had already shown signs of structural instability in the early 1980s, broke down completely, as it was no longer able to capture the role of expectations regarding current and prospective monetary policy (Lee and Prasad, 1994). An alternative, suggested by Campbell (1995), is that required returns on bonds rose because of an increase in perceived risk as manifest in higher volatility but ultimately attributable to uncertainty regarding short-term interest rates[36] or to the well-publicised losses of some highly leveraged bond traders. In any case, the slope of the yield curve has gone from very steeply positive during much of 1994 to quite flat of late. Indeed, at certain times and over limited ranges it has been inverted. This is potentially significant, as all recessions in recent decades have been led by inverted yield curves, with lead times averaging just over a year. The pattern of the yield curve since late in 1994 is more consistent, however, with a severe growth slowdown than with a recession. The speed of the flattening has also been somewhat of a quandary: it has possibly been assisted by purchases of longer-dated Treasuries by holders of mortgage-backed securities, fearful of their early repayment as a result of a resurgence in mortgage refinancing[37] and by reported placement of intervention-related dollars by foreign central banks in medium-term Treasury securities.

Developments in money and credit

For some time now the money and credit aggregates have been downgraded as indicators of economic activity. As a result they have lost their pre-eminent role in discussions of monetary policy. However, developments over the past year have been somewhat more consistent with their determinants than had been the case in prior years. Narrow money (M1) growth had been at a double-digit pace in 1993 and began to slow even before the first hike in the federal funds rate owing primarily to the earlier drop-off in mortgage refinancings.[38] Consistent with its rising opportunity cost, the stock of M1 reached a peak in July 1994 and has stagnated for the most part since then. Other components of M2, on the other hand, were largely unchanged until the bond market reached its trough in late 1994, so that total M2 growth was very weak until that point. However, since March 1995 there has been a reacceleration in M2 which has moved well off the bottom of the target band for the first time in several years. The degree of this pickup has been somewhat of a surprise, but the main factors are likely to have been declining short-term market interest rates as well as a shift in the share of new investment flows away from bond mutual funds and toward money-market funds associated with the flatness of the yield curve. Overall bank credit growth has been robust, with an accelerating trend in loans to business and in consumer instalment credit. Syndicated loan growth has been aided by loan spreads which have declined to levels not seen since the late 1980s. And non-bank credit, especially in the form of new issues of bonds and equities, has also been very strong. Credit growth has been boosted by a surge in merger activity which began in late 1994. Unlike the preceding merger wage in the 1980s, however, little recourse has been made to "junk" bonds in financing these deals; rather acquisitions have involved the use of higher-grade debt, reductions in financial assets and stock swaps (Board of Governors of the Federal Reserve System, 1995).

Differing pressures on the dollar

With rising short- and long-term interest rates in 1994, the normal expectation would have been for the dollar to appreciate in effective terms.[39] However, during most of 1994 the dollar actually declined (Figure 25). It was only late in the year, when bond yields actually began to fall and the peso crisis got underway, that the effective exchange rate of the dollar temporarily recovered. However, the peso crisis was generally perceived by investors as reflecting negatively on the dollar as against G10 currencies. Indeed, the respite was brief, and the persistent declines in the dollar's rate against the yen and most European curren-

Figure 25. **EXCHANGE VALUE OF THE DOLLAR**

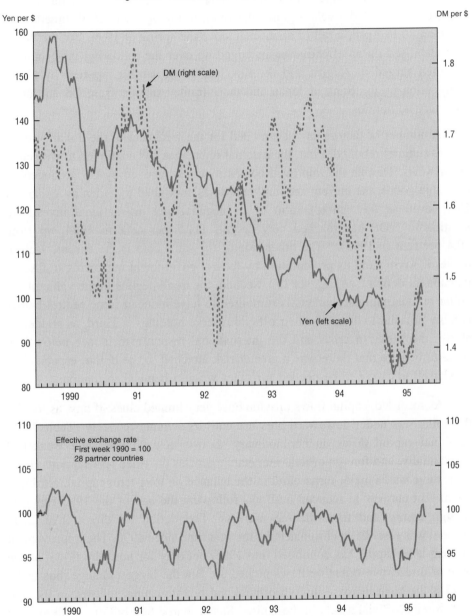

Yen per $

DM per $

DM (right scale)

Yen (left scale)

Effective exchange rate
First week 1990 = 100
28 partner countries

Source: OECD.

55

cies pulled its overall value to the lowest point since late 1992, down about 7 per cent from early 1994 levels. Against the yen it fell to a very brief all-time low of less than 80 in April, a fall of about half since the spring of 1990. But the dollar then stabilised on an effective basis, edged up over the following three months and then surged in August and the first half of September, spurred by heavy intervention by the Bank of Japan and more limited support from US and other monetary authorities.

A number of factors have been cited for the weakness of the dollar prior to its late-summer rebound. First, the external imbalance has continued to worsen in recent years. Despite the improved competitiveness enjoyed by US producers of tradeable goods, the current account deficit has continued to widen as a share of GDP, even as the nation's ratio of its negative net international investment position to GDP has reached new heights (11.7 per cent in 1994, up from 10.4 per cent in 1993).[40] The other side of the same coin is the chronic lack of domestic saving and its pre-emption by federal government borrowing to finance its habitual deficit (see Chapter IV). Second, the trend decline in the value of the dollar on international markets is rumoured to have induced some central banks, notably in Asia, to diversify their official reserve holdings.[41] Third, as alluded to above, the Mexican crisis and the international response to it (see below) led some to believe that there was a greater risk attached to the dollar, especially if similar efforts were to be needed for other western hemisphere nations.

As recorded, capital flows provide only very limited clues, if any, as to why the dollar was under downward pressure until its summer recovery (Table 7). In 1994 net capital flows on nonmonetary short-term capital account weakened substantially, and foreign official monetary agencies provided less support. However, there was a major turnaround in the balance on long-term capital, attributable almost entirely to reduced outflows following the end of the 1993 runup in foreign equity and fixed-income markets. The deficit on direct investment account was essentially eliminated for the first time since 1990. The improvement on long-term capital has continued into 1995, but only for portfolio flows, as the pace of direct investment outflows picked up. But the biggest change thus far in 1995 is the huge increase in both official and private capital inflows: in the first half, foreign official assets in the United States soared $60 billion, while private assets rose by nearly $150 billion, of which $95 billion went to buy US Treasury and other securities. Reserves fell in 1994 but rose during the first half of 1995,

Table 7. **Balance of payments**

$ million, seasonally adjusted

	1993	1994	1995 S1 [1]
Current balance	–99 925	–151 245	–82 647
Long-term capital	–70 589	46 988	49 222
of which:			
Direct investment	–31 494	78	–10 091
Inward	41 107	49 448	28 510
Outward	–72 601	–49 370	–38 601
Portfolio	–40 471	45 021	59 263
Inward	101 336	94 820	86 427
Outward	–141 807	–49 799	–27 164
Official	1 376	1 889	50
Basic balance	–170 514	–104 257	–33 425
Non-monetary short-term capital	50 646	–53 608	32 100
of which:			
Private, net	14 661	–39 339	8 062
Errors and omissions	35 985	–14 269	24 038
Monetary short-term capital	50 806	115 311	–50 343
Liabilities to foreign official monetary agencies	70 440	37 198	59 708
Change in reserves (+ = decrease)	–1 379	5 346	–8 040

1. Preliminary.
Source: OECD.

and there was a large increase in liabilities to foreign central banks. Part of this is ascribable to the swap arrangements contained in the Mexican rescue package announced on 31 January 1995 and signed on 21 February. By means of an Executive Order the Administration offered $20 billion worth of US aid consisting of short-term swaps from the Federal Reserve System and three- to five-year swaps and five- to ten-year loan guarantees from the Treasury's Exchange Stabilisation Fund.[42] By the end of August a total of $13.5 billion had been disbursed by the US monetary authorities as the Mexican authorities drew on both the short- and medium-term facilities; a total of $12.5 billion remained outstanding. Finally, exchange market intervention by the US authorities has occurred with somewhat increasing frequency over the past year. After an absence of intervention from June until November 1994, there had been US sales of yen and Deutschemarks, often in conjuncture with foreign central banks, on seven different days by end-June 1995. The total value of such sales reached $7.6 billion. All of these interventions were undertaken to defend the dollar in a declining market. But in August 1995, the US authorities joined with others and intervened as the dollar was strengthening, thereby changing market expectations and helping to push the currency up substantially over the following month.

IV.   The longer-term outlook for federal finances

The average size of the federal budget deficit as a share of GDP doubled every decade from the 1950s through the 1980s. By the mid-1980s, deficit reduction had come to dominate budget discussions, and the United States government began to struggle to reduce its size. In 1985 and 1987 laws ("Gramm-Rudman-Hollings") were passed requiring a balanced budget by 1991 and 1993, respectively. Then in 1990 a package of spending cuts and tax increases (OBRA90) was legislated that was originally projected to bring the budget into balance by 1995. And most recently, in 1993, another set of tax increases and spending cuts (OBRA93) was implemented with the goal of halving the deficit over the following four years. Although OBRA93 has made an important contribution to deficit reduction, both the actual and structural deficit outcomes have remained stubbornly high. Accordingly, questions of sustainability have come to the fore, especially as the spending burdens of the demographic bulge enter the relevant planning horizon.

Also during the 1980s, private saving declined and thus national saving plummeted, leaving few domestic resources available for investment. With the key role played by investment in productivity and real income growth, the large budget deficits relative to private saving and the implications for the external accounts have troubled many observers, including the Administration and Congress. Against this backdrop, this chapter examines the budget outlook if present policies are continued, reviews the rationale for deficit reduction and analyses the proposals that have been offered this spring to bring the budget into balance. Finally, it examines rules governing the budget process that have received considerable attention.

Baseline deficit projections

The unified budget deficit[43] for 1995 is projected to be 2¼ per cent of GDP, only a bit below the 3 per cent figure registered near the previous business-cycle peak in 1989 (Table 8). The cuts in spending programmes and increases in taxes that have been implemented over this period have been sufficient to reduce the deficit only marginally because, in the aggregate, taxes and spending programmes are currently structured in such a way that the budget deficit rises unless specific deficit-reducing actions are implemented. Looking forward, the baseline deficit projected by the Congressional Budget Office (CBO) remains relatively constant through 1998 because the spending cuts required under current law (the Omnibus Budget Reconciliation Act of 1993 – OBRA93) are just adequate to offset endogenous growth in entitlement spending. After 1998, however, the deficit outlook worsens continuously, owing to the expected rapid growth in health care spending and, as the horizon moves further into the first half of the next century, the ageing of the population.[44]

Budget deficit projections under current policies show deficits that rise exponentially after the turn of the century if current trends are not halted either by significant policy actions or by unforeseen endogenous changes which restrain demand growth in the health-care sector. A key feature of the deficit profile is mounting debt-service costs which reflect an exponentially increasing debt-to-GDP ratio once the primary balance moves into deficit around 2005. The amount of deficit reduction necessary to bring the fiscal situation under control depends on how quickly actions are taken to stem the rise in indebtedness (see Box 2). Long-term budget scenarios are fraught with uncertainties about future trends. Indeed, the Administration's projections of the deficit under unchanged policies show only a marginal deterioration over the next ten years because of small differences in macroeconomic assumptions and projections of the growth in medical care costs that become magnified over time. The basic assumption used for the Secretariat estimates is that current laws are essentially maintained for taxes and mandatory spending. In addition, special assumptions are made for discretionary spending for which current laws are not suitable for long-term projections. These assumptions are made to highlight the magnitude of policy changes and shifts in real resources that are necessary to put fiscal policy on a

Table 8. Baseline budget projections
Unified basis, per cent of GDP

	1965	1970	1975	1980	1985	1990	1995	2000	2005	2010	2015	2020	2025	2030
Revenues														
Total	17.4	19.6	18.5	19.6	18.5	18.8	19.4	18.8	18.8	18.8	18.8	18.7	18.7	18.6
Personal income taxes	7.3	9.2	8.1	9.2	8.4	8.5	8.5	8.6	8.6	8.6	8.6	8.6	8.6	8.6
Corporate income taxes	3.8	3.3	2.7	2.4	1.5	1.7	2.2	2.0	1.9	1.9	1.9	1.9	1.9	1.9
Social security contributions	3.3	4.5	5.6	6.0	6.7	6.9	6.9	6.8	6.8	6.8	6.7	6.7	6.6	6.6
Excise taxes	2.2	1.6	1.1	0.9	0.9	0.6	0.8	0.7	0.7	0.7	0.7	0.7	0.7	0.7
Estate and gift taxes	0.4	0.4	0.3	0.2	0.2	0.2	0.2	0.2	0.2	0.2	0.2	0.2	0.2	0.2
Customs receipts	0.2	0.2	0.2	0.3	0.3	0.3	0.3	0.3	0.3	0.3	0.3	0.3	0.3	0.3
Miscellaneous	0.2	0.4	0.4	0.5	0.5	0.5	0.4	0.3	0.3	0.3	0.3	0.3	0.3	0.3
Spending														
Total	17.6	19.8	22.0	22.3	23.8	23.9	21.7	22.0	22.5	24.1	26.4	29.3	32.8	36.5
Discretionary	12.2	12.6	10.8	10.5	10.5	9.2	7.8	6.5	6.0	6.0	6.0	6.0	6.0	6.0
Defense	7.6	8.3	5.8	5.1	6.4	5.5	3.8	3.0	2.7	2.7	2.7	2.7	2.7	2.7
Other	4.6	4.3	5.0	5.4	4.1	3.7	4.0	3.5	3.2	3.2	3.2	3.2	3.2	3.2
Mandatory	5.0	6.6	10.6	10.7	10.9	11.0	11.3	12.5	13.4	14.4	15.8	17.1	18.3	19.3
OASDI	2.5	3.0	4.2	4.4	4.7	4.5	4.7	4.8	4.9	5.0	5.4	6.0	6.4	6.7
Medicare	0.0	0.6	0.8	1.2	1.6	1.7	2.2	2.9	3.6	4.3	5.0	5.7	6.4	7.0
Medicaid	0.0	0.3	0.5	0.5	0.6	0.7	1.3	1.7	2.0	2.3	2.5	2.6	2.6	2.7
Other	2.4	2.8	5.1	4.5	4.0	4.0	3.2	3.2	2.9	2.9	2.9	2.9	2.9	2.9
Offsetting receipts[1]	-0.8	-0.9	-0.9	-0.8	-0.8	-0.7	-0.6	-0.4	-0.3	-0.3	-0.3	-0.3	-0.3	-0.3
Deposit insurance	-0.1	-0.1	0.0	0.0	-0.1	1.1	-0.2	0.0	0.0	0.0	0.0	0.0	0.0	0.0
Net interest	1.3	1.5	1.5	2.0	3.3	3.4	3.3	3.4	3.6	4.1	5.1	6.6	8.8	11.6
Surplus/deficit (−)	-0.2	-0.2	-3.6	-2.8	-5.3	-5.1	-2.3	-3.2	-3.6	-5.2	-7.7	-10.6	-14.1	-18.0
Primary balance	+1.1	+1.2	-2.0	-0.8	-2.0	-1.7	+1.0	+0.3	0.0	-1.2	-2.6	-3.9	-5.3	-6.4
Debt	38.9	28.7	26.1	26.8	37.8	44.0	51.7	54.1	58.2	66.3	82.8	108.8	144.9	190.1

1. Primarily consists of federal employer contributions for employee retirement and a small amount for rents and royalties for oil and gas exploration on the Outer Continental Shelf.

Source: OECD calculations based on projections by Congressional Budget Office and the Social Security Administration.

Box 2. **Deficit and debt dynamics**

The evolution of the debt-to-GDP ratio depends upon the evolution of the deficit-to-GDP ratio and the growth rate of nominal GDP. A rise in the deficit-to-GDP ratio implies a proportional rise in the debt-to-GDP ratio over time. With a constant growth rate of nominal GDP, the eventual debt-to-GDP ratio is approximately equal to the deficit-to-GDP ratio divided by the nominal growth rate of GDP. Thus, higher GDP growth, for a given deficit-to-GDP level, results in lower debt-to-GDP ratios by eroding the importance of past deficits. Deficits, through the nominal interest payments required to finance the debt, are correlated with debt levels and inflation rates and thus nominal GDP growth rates. For this reason the primary budget balance (the total budget balance less interest payments) is often used for analysis. The debt-to-GDP ratio cannot be stabilised unless there is a primary surplus when real interest rates exceed real GDP growth rates, a condition that has prevailed, on average, since 1980. The reason is simple: if the primary balance is zero, then debt grows at the rate of interest which, if it exceeds the growth rate, would cause the debt-to-GDP ratio to rise without limit. The size of the primary surplus that is needed to stabilise the debt-to-GDP ratio is approximately equal to the product of the debt-to-GDP ratio and the difference between the interest rate and the growth rate. For the United States the debt-to-GDP ratio is about 50 per cent, and the difference between interest rates on Treasury debt and nominal GDP growth may be around 1.5 percentage points;* thus, the necessary primary balance is a surplus of ¾ per cent of GDP, and maintenance of the current debt-to-GDP would require baseline spending or taxes to be adjusted by over 7 percentage points of GDP over the next 30 years. If the adjustment is delayed until the debt-to-GDP ratio is higher, then the total amount of adjustment would become greater in order to generate the necessarily larger primary surplus.

---

* Over the past fifteen years, the difference between the nominal GDP growth and the three-year Treasury note (used because much of Treasury borrowing is in the medium-term market) has been 1.2 percentage points. However, during the 1950s, 1960s and 1970s the three-year rate was consistently below the nominal growth rate of GDP; under such conditions a primary balance surplus is unnecessary. The historical data on growth and interest rates have led Ball, Elmendorf and Mankiw (1995) to conclude that governments need not run a primary surplus to prevent the debt-to-GDP ratio from exploding and that running deficits may be intergenerationally Pareto optimal. They note that their analysis assumes no relation between debt and interest rates and state that the variables have had little apparent correlation empirically. Yet, the more recent experience, during a period with largely unregulated financial markets and higher deficits, may provide a better basis for projections than the earlier outcomes.

solid long-term footing. To maintain the current primary surplus and debt-to-GDP ratio will require reductions averaging 0.2 percentage point of GDP annually over the next 35 years; by comparison, OBRA93 and the proposals to balance the budget by 2002 each improve the primary balance by about 0.35 percentage point annually.[45] Thus, the baseline projections indicate that persistent, moderate deficit-reduction actions, approximately half as large as those recently adopted, are necessary to stabilise the current debt-to-GDP ratio.

As a starting point for these projections, the Secretariat adopted the economic and technical assumptions used by the CBO for its ten-year projections and the long-run population and real GDP projections of the Social Security and Medicare trust funds.[46] It is assumed that over the next 10 years real GDP growth averages 2.3 per cent and then slows sharply to $1^{3}/_{4}$ per cent owing to less rapid increases in the labour force. Inflation, as measured by the consumer price index (CPI), is projected to run at an average rate of $3^{1}/_{4}$ per cent, with the average rise in the GDP deflator of $2^{3}/_{4}$ per cent and an effective average interest rate on government debt of 6.1 per cent. The wedge between the two measures of inflation is important because many spending programmes are indexed to the CPI, while tax bases tend to rise with overall inflation.[47]

Under current law receipts are projected to remain virtually constant as a share of GDP at around $18^{3}/_{4}$ per cent. This is also near the levels recorded over the past several decades, although there has been a sizeable shift away from taxes on corporate income and goods towards those based on labour income. Social Security contributions have grown markedly as a share of GDP over the past 25 years, reflecting provisions that boosted tax rates and increased the share of wages subject to tax. These increases were partially offset by the erosion of the tax base, as labour compensation has shifted from taxable wages towards untaxed non-wage labour costs. Looking forward, there are no more scheduled changes in Social Security tax rates, and these taxes as a share of GDP should edge down following the projected trend in the share of taxable wages in total compensation. Taxes on goods from excise taxes and customs duties have fallen over time, reflecting the removal of some excise taxes, reductions in import duties to liberalise trade, the failure of specific taxes to keep up with inflation and the shrinking share of GDP devoted to the taxed goods; however, the rate increases enacted in 1990 and 1993 have slowed the decline.[48] These taxes are projected to decline owing to the same forces; nevertheless, the baseline projections assume that after 2005 taxes from these sources will remain constant, implicitly assuming modest future changes in current laws. Corporate income taxes have also declined markedly, mainly reflecting the smaller share of corporate profits in GDP as corporations have shifted from equity to debt finance and more business income is taxed at personal rates.[49] However, effective rates were raised by base-broadening changes in 1986, 1990 and 1993. Personal income and estate taxes declined over the 1980s because provisions were enacted to lower effective tax rates; rates were then raised in 1990 and 1993. Also, since 1984 most provisions of the personal income tax code have been indexed for inflation; thus, in the future effective tax rates will rise only from real bracket creep rather than from inflation as well, as was the case in the 1970s. Again, beginning in 2005, it is assumed that these taxes stay constant as a share of GDP, thereby removing any bracket creep.

The baseline projections assume that discretionary spending conforms to OBRA93 until its provisions end in 1998; this will require annual programme cuts of about 3 per cent in real terms, roughly 0.2 percentage point of GDP. From 1998 to 2005 discretionary spending is constant in real terms, and it rises at the rate of growth of real GDP thereafter. Over longer periods of time, it seems prudent to have the baseline projection allow for increases in real spending in order to provide for the same level of real services to the same portion of the population – similar to the definition used for baseline mandatory spending. Even when spending is on pure public goods, such as defence, real spending would probably have to rise to maintain constant real services.[50]

Mandatory spending, excluding debt service, is comprised of a wide variety of programmes including retirement benefits, medical care for the elderly and the poor, transfers and grants to aid the poor, financial assistance for post-secondary education and training, deposit insurance outlays and agricultural subsidies. Among the hundreds of mandatory spending programmes, just three, Social Security, Medicare and Medicaid, account for nearly all of the rise in spending in recent decades and are projected to be the source of long-term spending pressures. Indeed, while spending on all other mandatory programmes combined rose dramatically during the first half of the 1970s (from 2¾ per cent of GDP in 1970 to over 5 per cent in 1975), it has since been declining gradually. In 1995 this assortment of programmes is expected to absorb 3¼ per cent of GDP, before declining to below 3 per cent by 2005.[51] It is assumed that, on balance, these spending programmes remain constant as a share of GDP thereafter.

The Social Security retirement system grew rapidly as a share of GDP from its inception until around 1980 as the number of beneficiaries grew more rapidly than workers and increases in real benefits per beneficiary outstripped real wage growth. In general, legislation was regularly passed over the period to boost both benefits and taxes. After financial imbalances developed, there were important reform efforts in 1977 and 1983 that largely resorted to phased-in reductions in benefits and increased taxes to improve the solvency of the system. There are no further changes in benefit structure scheduled under current law except the raising of the normal retirement age from 65 to 67.[52] The driving force behind the growth in benefit payments as a share of GDP is the projected rise in the ratio of beneficiaries relative to the working-age population (Figure 26). The benefit structure is based on the recipient's wage history relative to the evolution of average wages.[53] Workers who retire at the normal retirement age with a history of average wages will receive benefits equal to about 40 per cent of final wages, indexed thereafter to the CPI (Figure 27, top panel). Special provisions for spouses of single-earner couples and other dependents may significantly increase these benefits. Largely because of the evolution in Social Security tax rates, the internal rate of return for beneficiaries has fallen and will continue to fall over time to below market interest rates (bottom panel).[54] Nevertheless the system as a whole is expected to run a deficit owing to past largesse as well as provisions

Figure 26. **SOCIAL SECURITY BENEFITS AND DEPENDENCY RATIO**

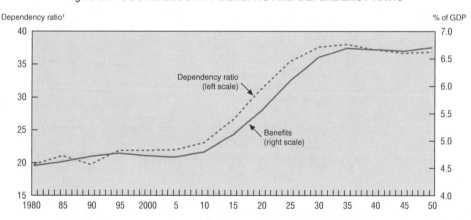

1.   Dependency ratio is the ratio of population aged 65 and over to population aged 20-64.
Source: Annual Report of the Board of Trustees of the Federal Old-Age and Survivors Insurance and Disability Insurance Trust Funds, 1994.

Figure 27. **SOCIAL SECURITY BENEFITS RELATIVE TO WAGES AND TAXES**

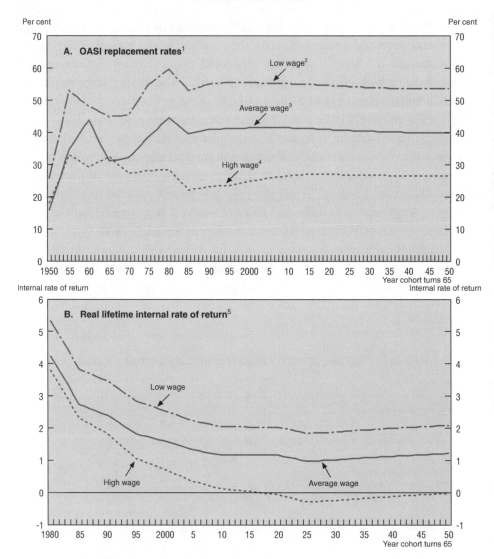

1. OASI benefit as a per cent of final salary for a single worker.
2. Assumes worker earns 45% of average every year (10 500 in 1993).
3. Assumes worker earns average wage every year (23 400 in 1993).
4. Assumes worker earns maximum taxable wage every year (57 600 in 1993).
5. Single male worker.
Source: Steuerle and Bakija (1994).

giving large net transfers to some single-earner couples. Importantly, the system's long-run balance does not change much with different economic assumptions because the system is close to being actuarially fair for future beneficiaries and because of the types of indexing schemes that are used for benefits and taxes.

Medicare is the health care system for the aged and long-term disabled. Its spending is therefore driven by the same demographic forces as the Social Security system (Figure 28). In addition, its expenditures have been, and are expected to continue to be, under extreme pressure by rising real medical expenses. Real health care costs – per capita health expenditures deflated by the overall CPI – have grown by 4 per cent per year over the last several decades reflecting, in part, the fact that the long-run income elasticity of health care is greater than unity.[55] This is also true for the two Medicare programmes, Hospital Insurance (HI) and the Supplemental Medical Insurance (SMI).[56] The split between actual volume increases and higher relative inflation is open to debate. The Medicare Trust Fund's spending estimates for the HI programme provides an indication of the sources of growth for the programme (Table 9). The baseline

Figure 28. **MEDICARE SPENDING**

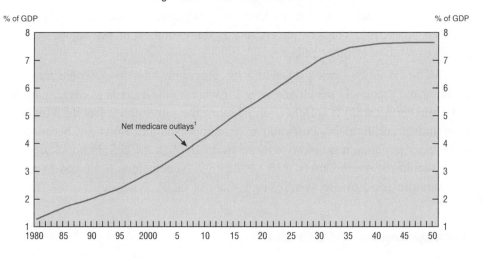

1. Medicare spending less premiums.
Source: Annual Report of the Board of Trustees of the Federal Old-Age and Survivors Insurance and Disability Insurance Trust Funds, 1994.

Table 9. **Sources of growth in Medicare spending**[1]

Per cent change from previous period

	Input prices	Enrolment	Admissions per enrollee	Other	Total payments
1983	5.1	1.7	0.8	3.7	11.3
1984	4.9	1.8	−3.8	9.1	12.0
1985	3.8	1.6	−7.4	8.1	6.1
1986	2.6	2.3	−5.6	4.5	3.8
1987	3.6	1.7	−3.1	−1.0	1.2
1988	5.0	2.5	−2.2	−1.1	4.2
1989	5.4	2.0	−3.1	8.8	13.1
1990	4.9	2.1	−0.2	1.1	7.9
1991	3.7	2.2	0.4	3.7	10.0
1992	3.1	1.9	2.3	3.1	10.4
1993	3.0	2.9	0.7	1.9	8.5
1994	3.6	1.9	1.4	2.3	9.2
1995	4.6	1.8	1.3	0.2	7.9
2000	4.8	1.3	1.1	2.7	9.9
2005	5.1	1.5	0.5	1.8	8.9
2010	5.1	1.8	0.1	1.2	8.2
2015	5.1	2.5	−0.1	1.3	8.8
2020	5.1	2.7	−0.1	1.2	8.9

1. For the Hospital Insurance programme, actual data through 1992.
Source: Board of Trustees, Federal Hospital Insurance Trust Fund.

projections use the Trust Fund's estimates, adjusted for the baseline's lower inflation projection. The key uncertainty is the evolution of per capita medical expenses relative to other prices.

Medicaid is the principal health care programme for low-income families, disabled and especially the elderly poor for what Medicare fails to cover, particularly long-term care.[57] It suffers from many of the same stresses as the Medicare programme: rapidly rising costs and an ageing population. However, because the beneficiary population should rise more gradually than the elderly population, its costs should rise more slowly than Medicare's. Nonetheless, Medicaid expenditures are projected to rise steadily as a share of GDP.

The rationale for deficit reduction

It is clearly necessary to prevent the longer-term baseline scenario from coming to pass because of the ruinous run-up in debt that would occur if the primary balance were chronically and increasingly in deficit. However, how much deficit reduction should be carried out and when is not as obvious. The criteria for this decision should be based on the benefits and costs of deficit reduction. One of the key benefits is the higher national saving that would occur which in turn should, over time, generate higher incomes and higher sustainable levels of consumption. In addition, smaller deficits may allow greater scope for government action to counter cyclical downturns.[58] Abstracting from improvements in public-sector efficiency, the cost of deficit reduction stems from the lower level of current welfare induced by the combination of higher taxation, less generous transfers and a lower level of government services provided. The benefits and costs also depend critically upon the types of deficit reduction that are pursued. For example, increasing marginal income tax rates would increase distortions in the market place, whereas broadening tax bases would tend to reduce distortions.

The federal government absorbs, through the deficit, a high share of national saving, leaving little for private domestic investment purposes; this is particularly true on a net investment basis (Figure 29). While most other OECD countries currently have larger deficits, they also have higher private-sector saving rates from which to draw (Figure 30, lower panel). Increasing federal government saving would increase the funds available for investment if other saving sources do not make offsetting changes. However, there are some natural mechanisms for such offsets to occur. If the federal government increases its saving by reducing grants or shifting responsibilities to state and local governments, then their saving may fall. This channel is somewhat constrained by balanced-budget requirements at the state and local level; but history shows there is some scope for them to run operating deficits in any case.[59] Private saving may also respond adversely to efforts to boost government saving by raising tax rates on saving – *via* income taxes or means testing of spending programmes – or reducing transfers to individuals.[60] Thus, national saving should rise in response to lower deficits, but by less than the change in the deficit; econometric models of the US economy examined by the CBO indicate that the offset may be in the range of 20 to 40 per cent.[61]

In the short run, deficit cuts reduce aggregate demand, particularly in the form of government and private consumption, which may reduce output depending upon several factors. The household sector may not cut consumption by as

Figure 29. SOURCES AND USES OF PRIVATE NET SAVING
Per cent of GDP

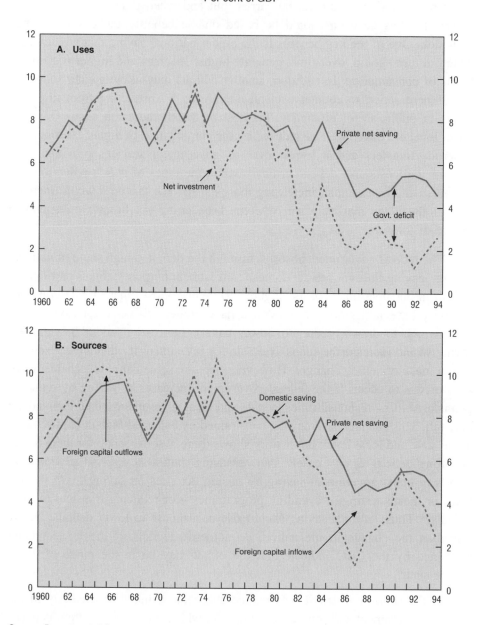

Source: Department of Commerce.

Figure 30. INTERNATIONAL COMPARISON OF NET SAVING AND INVESTMENT

Per cent of GDP, 1984-93

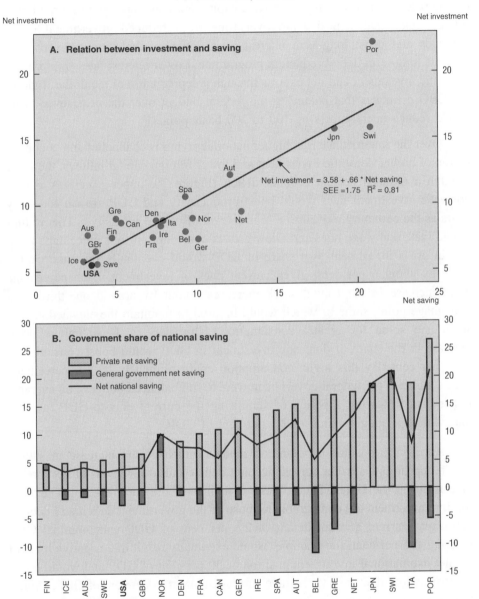

Net investment

A. Relation between investment and saving

Net investment = 3.58 + .66 * Net saving
SEE =1.75 $\bar{R}^2$ = 0.81

Net saving

B. Government share of national saving

Private net saving
General government net saving
Net national saving

Source: OECD, *National Accounts.*

71

much as taxes are raised or transfers are reduced, temporarily damping the demand shock and lowering the household saving rate. The Federal Reserve may cut short-term interest rates, and private capital markets may anticipate the lower interest rates that will develop over time from reduced government credit demands and drive long-term interest rates down on the announcement of a credible long-term deficit reduction programme. Lower interest rates would boost domestic investment and net exports through a depreciation of the dollar. Indeed, the CBO estimates that balancing the federal budget over the next seven years would reduce interest rates by 100 to 200 basis points.

Over the intermediate run, higher national saving is channelled into a combination of higher domestic investment and lower foreign capital inflows, the latter through a reduced current account deficit (Figure 30, upper panel). A rise in domestic investment rates would boost productivity and GDP growth for many years as the economy moved to a higher level of capital intensity.[62] This in turn would raise real wage rates and allow greater consumption. A 1 percentage point rise in gross investment as a share of GDP would eventually raise the capital stock by about 6 per cent, given current rates of investment. Each percentage point increase in the capital stock increases output by around one-third of a percentage point, some of which would be used to maintain the elevated capital stock and some for greater consumption. Ultimately, a 1 percentage point increase in the share of domestic investment in GDP would boost consumption by 1 per cent. By this logic, consumption could ultimately be 1½ percentage points higher if the federal government were to run balanced budgets, on average, rather than following a policy of stabilising the current debt-to-GDP ratio by maintaining a budget deficit of 2½ per cent of GDP.[63]

According to some econometric models, much of the increase in saving would appear as a smaller current account deficit and lower levels of net foreign investment in the United States.[64] The dynamics of the current account and net foreign investment are comparable to those of the government deficit and debt. A permanent current account deficit of 2½ per cent of GDP with nominal GDP growing at 5 per cent, for example, would eventually result in a negative level of the net international investment position of 50 per cent of GDP and would entail a goods and nonfactor services trade surplus of about ¾ per cent of GDP, similar to the primary balance required to stabilise the debt-to-GDP ratio.[65] The reduction in the current account deficit that would accompany budget deficit reduction would not affect GDP, but would boost GNP by reducing the factor service payments and reduce the trade surplus required to stabilise the net international investment position. While, in the short run, a lower budget deficit may result in a depreciation of the exchange rate, over the long haul the exchange rate would need to depreciate less than if the budget and current account deficits were not reduced (see Box 3).

The current policy debate

Deficit proposals under consideration

In February, the President submitted a fiscal year 1996 budget showing little additional progress on the deficit beyond what was required by OBRA93. If implemented, annual deficits would have averaged around $200 billion over the next five years, with the deficit slowly falling as a share of GDP, reaching 2 per cent in 2000. After rejecting a balanced budget amendment to the Constitution, which included a target of 2002 for a balanced budget, the House and Senate passed a Budget Resolution which outlined a plan to balance the budget over the next seven years by sharply constraining spending, with the aim of reducing the scope of government activity and shifting the responsibility for some activities to state and local governments (Table 10). The Budget Resolution also allows for substantial tax cuts that are not included in the deficit estimates, of up to $245 billion over seven years and roughly $50 billion in 2002 (½ percentage point of that year's GDP). Of the total about $170 billion will be offset by the "economic dividend" from balancing the budget, while the remainder will come from either higher deficits or lower spending than is specified in the Budget Resolution. CBO has previously estimated that balancing the budget over seven years would result cumulative budget savings of $170 billion over seven years and $50 billion in 2002 from a decline in interest rates of 160 basis points owing to the smaller deficits and higher real GDP growth of 0.1 percentage point per

Table 10.   **FY 1996 Congressional Budget Resolution**

$ billion

	Fiscal year						
	1996	1997	1998	1999	2000	2001	2002
Deficit, CBO baseline	211	231	233	267	298	312	341
Non-interest spending cuts	–40	–74	–106	–146	–186	–232	–282
Discretionary spending[1]	–18	–29	–39	–59	–75	–99	–121
Mandatory spending	–22	–45	–67	–87	–111	–133	–161
Medicare	–8	–18	–27	–37	–49	–60	–71
Medicaid	–4	–8	–16	–24	–33	–43	–54
Income security	–4	–12	–15	–17	–20	–23	–28
Other[2]	–6	–5	–10	–9	–9	–7	–8
Debt service	–1	–5	–11	–20	–31	–47	–66
Total deficit reduction	–41	–79	–117	–167	–218	–278	–348
Deficit, budget resolution	170	152	116	100	81	33	–6
Memorandum:							
As a share of GDP							
Baseline deficit	2.9	3.0	3.0	3.2	3.4	3.4	3.4
Policy deficit	2.3	1.9	1.4	1.2	0.9	0.3	–0.1

1.   Excludes cuts needed to meet OBRA 1993.
2.   Includes asset sales (spectrum and power).
Source: FY 1996 Budget Resolution and *Congressional Quarterly.*

year from crowding in of investment due to the lower interest rates. Adjusting the deficit projections for the improved economic climate leaves enough room for a $50 billion tax cut in 2002 and a balanced budget.

The Administration has responded to the Budget Resolution by proposing its own plan to balance the budget over nine years with a different policy mix and a different baseline (Table 11). The Administration assumes slightly more favourable economic and technical assumptions which over time become quite significant.[66] In 1997 the baselines differ by an insignificant $14 billion, but by 2002 the difference mounts to $84 billion, and thus the Administration's proposals are more modest than those contained in the Budget Resolution. That said, either plan would put fiscal policy on a firmer footing to confront the mounting expenditure pressures that are projected after the turn of the century and should, even if not fully effective in balancing the budget, do much to boost national savings. Yet, even if budget balance is achieved, other important structural problems

Table 11. **Administration's revised FY 1996 budget**

$ billion

	1996	1997	1998	1999	2000	2001	2002	2003	2004
Baseline deficit	192	217	217	230	245	247	257	264	279
Spending cuts	−23	−20	−31	−48	−67	−90	−118	−144	−170
Discretionary	−7	−5	−11	−24	−34	−46	−59	−74	−89
Mandatory	−16	−15	−20	−24	−33	−44	−59	−70	−81
Medicare	−3	−6	−9	−16	−23	−30	−38	−45	−54
Medicaid	−4	−4	−6	−7	−9	−11	−13	−15	−17
Other	−9	−5	−5	−1	−1	−3	−8	−10	−10
Corporate subsidies[1]	−1	−2	−3	−4	−5	−5	−5	−5	−6
Revenues	−3	−10	−11	−14	−19	−20	−21	−21	−21
Debt service[2]	−2	−6	−11	−18	−29	−41	−55	−71	−88
Deficit, policy basis	163	179	161	146	125	91	58	23	−6
Memorandum item:									
Congressional Budget Office's estimate of deficit under Administration's policies	167	201	196	205	205	192	183	176	172

1. Unspecified reductions to spending and tax breaks that primarily benefit business.
2. Includes effects of lower interest rates owing to moving to a balanced budget.
Source: Office of Management and Budget, and Congressional Budget Office.

would remain largely unattended by these plans; these include the low level of public investment in infrastructure, the uneven access to health care insurance, failures in primary and secondary education and the high rates of social exclusion in urban areas.

The Budget Resolution envisions sharp cuts in discretionary spending over the next two years in virtually every category of spending with smaller cuts in succeeding years (Tables 10 and 12). By 2002, total discretionary spending would have fallen about 20 per cent in real from 1995 levels to its lowest level since the mid-1970s, and domestic discretionary spending would have returned to its level of the mid-1980s; moreover, both categories would reach extremely low levels as a share of GDP (Figure 31).[67] While detailed spending plans have yet to be laid out, it appears that 50 to 60 per cent of the discretionary spending cuts will come from federal government purchases, 30 to 40 per cent from grants to state and local governments and the remaining savings from international aid, asset sales and a small amount of subsidies and transfers. The effect on aggregate demand, government spending and government savings will depend critically on

Table 12. **Discretionary spending cuts**

Percentage change from 1995[1] in volumes

Function	1995 level	1996		2000	
	Billions	Congress[2]	Administration	Congress[2]	Administration
Defence	271	−5	−6	−13	−15
International	22	−9	−7	−40	−21
Domestic	260	−7	0	−24	−13
Science	17	−3	−3	−21	−18
Energy	7	−6	−7	−36	−37
Natural resources	22	−9	−2	−26	−20
Transportation	39	−3	−4	−27	−20
Community development	13	−21	−2	−58	−40
Education, training, social services	40	−4	3	−25	−8
Health	23	−8	1	−21	−17
Income security	39	−1	−1	−3	−8
Veterans	18	2	2	−16	−16
Justice	17	7	11	2	20
Other	33	−20	0	−40	−18

1. Assumes 3 per cent inflation per year.
2. The average of the House and Senate proposals.
Source: OECD calculations based on FY 1996 Budget and Budget Resolution.

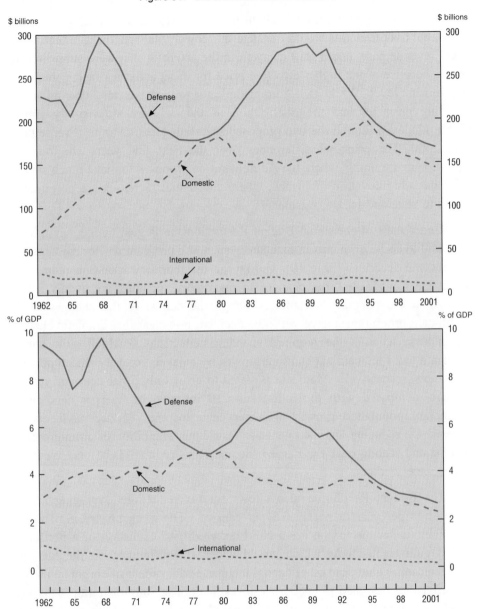

Figure 31. **DISCRETIONARY SPENDING**

Source: Budget of the United States Government (historical data) and Fiscal Year 1996 Budget Resolution (projections).

the reaction of state and local governments to the reduced level of grants. The impact of lower grants may be felt in higher deficits at the lower government levels, but over time this would translate into lower total spending, reflecting the lower revenue base, and a shift away from the activities that were subsidised by grants, because of the higher effective price for these activities facing the lower government level. While the Administration's proposal is less draconian, the spending priorities and the distribution of the cuts are surprisingly similar (Table 12), even though the two proposed spending paths begin to diverge more after 2000. The principal differences over the next few years are found in education and training, where the Administration proposed to make much smaller cuts, and administration of justice, where substantial increases are proposed in grants to state and local governments.

Under the Congressional Budget Resolution the largest budget savings are projected to come from cuts in mandatory spending programmes for medical care and income security (Table 10). Unlike the discretionary spending reductions, which are front-loaded, the changes to mandatory spending are evenly spread throughout the planning horizon. Although the details of the changes to the health-care programmes have yet to be decided, it is clear that dramatic changes are in store to meet the required spending reductions – which slow annual Medicare and Medicaid expenditure growth by an average of $3\frac{1}{2}$ and 6 percentage points, respectively. Medicaid is slated to grow only 5 per cent per year on average, compared with projections of CPI inflation of $3\frac{1}{4}$ per cent and a beneficiary population growth of 3 per cent. Income security payments are lowered by reducing grants to states, restricting eligibility of immigrants to benefits and scaling back the Earned Income Tax Credit (EITC), a tax credit for low-income workers.

The Budget Resolution also allows for tax reductions averaging around $50 billion per year or nearly 0.5 per cent of GDP when phased-in. The key provisions under discussion are a child tax credit, an exclusion of a portion of capital gains realisations which would widen the difference on the tax rates between capital gains and other capital income, and a variety of corporate income tax provisions designed to encourage investment. The Administration's tax proposals are more limited in scope; they include chiefly a child tax credit, a new personal income tax deduction for tuition and fees for postsecondary education and an expansion of Individual Retirement Accounts.

Evaluation of deficit reduction proposals

The key rationale for deficit reduction is to promote greater saving and investment. Therefore, the government should be careful that measures to reduce the deficit do not inhibit private-sector saving and investment or reduce economic efficiency. Some measures may both enhance efficiency and reduce the deficit at the same time, such as reducing agriculture subsidies, shifting from regulation to taxation of activities that have negative externalities, streamlining programmes, and increasing and expanding the use of user fees to approximate the marginal cost of the services provided. But ultimately some increases in distortionary taxation or means-testing of benefits may be necessary, as may be some reduction in government investment activities.

While reductions in discretionary spending can make an important contribution to narrowing the deficit over the next five to ten years, over the longer horizon other sources of deficit reduction must be found owing to the small share of overall spending which is discretionary. That said, by the year 2000, about half of the expenditure cuts proposed by Congress would be from discretionary accounts.[68] While further real cuts are possible, the intended reductions entail a dramatic reduction in the role of the federal government. Some of the scheduled reductions are in areas where perhaps more spending is required rather than less. The federal government's direct and indirect investment activities – construction, research and development and grants-in-aid for state and local infrastructure – are financed by discretionary spending and are scheduled for cuts of roughly 30 per cent in real terms. As the United States already has a low level of public investment, it is unclear whether these further cuts would be optimal, except to the extent that they are offset by other agents.[69] Another area of concern is the proposed reduction in spending, and further devolution of responsibility for elementary and secondary education; if the cuts are made, then grant formulae should be modified to focus funds on the neediest areas.[70]

Payments under the Medicare and Medicaid programmes are the primary source of growing imbalances in the future. Reforms of these systems must be integrated with overall health-care policy because of the possibility that partial reforms may lead to increased cost shifting or the impairment of access. For example, a reduction in Medicare fee schedules to below market rates could result in a loss of access or cause a shift in the cost of the service to other health care users, a potentially inequitable and inefficient form of taxation. Exposing beneficiaries to more of the cost through higher premiums, deductibles and co-payments may improve efficiency but will also lower disposable incomes with important vertical equity considerations. The President's proposed deficit reduction is only 40 per cent of the size of that of the Congress, but his plan also includes insurance market reforms. The Budget Resolution does not spell out the methods to reach the substantial savings that are proposed. One alternative, suggested by the House Budget Committee, is to shift from a government insurance programme to vouchers and private insurance. Such a change would necessitate substantial regulation by the federal government to ensure access by the elderly and perhaps place the greatest burdens on the oldest, frailest and poorest of the Medicare population. The most talked-about solution to achieve the Medicaid savings is to shift from an unlimited matching grant to a block grant – effectively placing all of the marginal burden on state and local governments. Under some proposals states would be allowed to scale back eligibility and benefits which would potentially aggravate the problems of large numbers of uninsured who already have poor access. As a sizeable portion of Medicaid expenditures flow to a relatively small number of aged and disabled, changes which allow benefits to vary even more substantially[71] between states will undoubtedly encourage movement between states and potentially lead to all states offering a lower level of benefits than they would offer if there were no fear of ''benefit shopping''.[72]

The main low-income support programmes are also slated to be cut back (Box 4). Among the proposals are: to reduce sharply Aid to Families with Dependent Children (AFDC) grants to states and fold them into a block grant with some smaller low-income programmes, to tighten eligibility for Supplemental Security Income (SSI) and the EITC, to reduce food stamp payments in real terms, and to eliminate extended unemployment benefits (beyond 26 weeks). While some of the proposed changes will better target the needy population,[73] others appear to single out legal immigrants, and other changes will just reduce aid to the least fortunate. Again, the devolution of AFDC to the state governments may well encourage benefit shopping and a cycle of reduced outlays in response, despite provisions that will allow states to give lower benefits to new residents.

Box 4. **Current welfare reform proposals**

Welfare reform continues to be the focus of much legislative attention at the federal level. After the Administration made its proposals in 1994 and Congressional approval was not forthcoming, the initiative fell to the new Congress to ready a plan. In March 1995, the House of Representatives passed a bill which would reform a myriad of federal programmes, loosely grouped under the heading of "welfare" (cash benefits under the Aid to Families with Dependent Children and other programmes, Food Stamps, school meal subsidies and other nutrition programmes, foster and child care). Most would be consolidated into five block grants for the states, who would acquire programme design responsibilities, while federal control over Food Stamps and Supplementary Security Income (SSI) would be retained. This would end a series of entitlements. Savings are estimated to amount to $102 billion over seven years; average annual outlay growth would be chopped from 7.2 to 3.1 per cent, even less than the assumed inflation rate. Federal regulations would be greatly relaxed in many areas, and the states would not have to spend any of their own money, but they would be required to get at least 10 per cent of their overall case load into a "work activity" by the end of FY 1996 and at least 50 per cent seven years later; an additional hurdle would be to get 50 and 90 per cent, respectively, of two-parent families into such an activity. The CBO has predicted, however, that under these terms no state would meet these requirements, because the cost of doing so would exceed the penalties otherwise imposed. Some other highlights of the bill are: 1) work requirements – benefit recipients would have to work as from two years after getting benefits and a limit of five years of benefits would be instituted, although states could exempt a small proportion of their case load from this limit; and 2) no cash benefits would be available for children of unwed mothers under the age of 18 nor to those in families already on welfare – however, vouchers for basic needs of children would be provided.

The House bill would return the Food Stamp programme (currently provided to about 27 million recipients) to its pre-1990 status as a capped entitlement, but increase the role of the states in the programme and cut its funding by over $20 billion (14 per cent) over five years (included in the $102 billion total above). This would be accomplished by reducing eligibility and average payments: annual cost-of-living increases would be capped at 2 per cent; all able-bodied adults without dependents would be required to work or take job training within six months of first receiving Food Stamps; states could provide Stamps to employers to be used as part of their wage offers; those quitting jobs while receiving Stamps could be sanctioned; welfare benefit losses could not be offset by Stamp increases; and states could take Stamps away from parents not complying with a judicial child-support order. Similarly, for SSI savings would arise from cutting eligibility through the denial of aid to legal immigrants (their sponsors would have to take financial responsibility for them for a longer period of time), drug addicts, alcoholics and certain disabled children.

The Senate passed its version of the bill in September 1995. It differs in several important areas from the House version. First, the total savings amount to only around

(continued on next page)

(continued)

$65 billion over seven years. Also, states would have to spend at least 80 per cent of what they spent in 1994 on cash welfare programmes; and states would not be forbidden from but would have the option to deny cash assistance for children of unwed mothers and for those born to families already on welfare; an additional $3 billion over five years would be provided for child care assistance; and a small contingency fund for states in economic distress would be established. For its part, the Administration also proposed to cut nutrition outlays in its June budget-balancing proposals, but slightly less quickly ($20 billion over seven years). But it has not made clear what features of potential legislation would elicit a Presidential veto.

Fiscal federalism

Many of the aforementioned programmes are implemented as grants-in-aid to state and local governments.[74] Most are matching grants in that states have to put up a share of the money; frequently the share varies with state income. Most grant programmes are closed-ended because funds are matched only up to a limit (this is the case, for instance, for transportation grants), while a few are open-ended, such as Medicaid and AFDC. All have conditions on the uses of the funds which are designed to promote accountability and to ensure that the grant generates additional expenditure on the aided item rather than substituting for own resources. Closed-ended grants will boost expenditures on the aided item (beyond that obtained by unconditional revenue sharing) only if they distort the price faced by the local government by providing a subsidy for the marginal expenditure. The extent to which closed-ended grants actually boost expenditures is unclear, because in many cases states and localities add their own resources, beyond the required match, indicating that the grant is non-distorting. In such cases, unconditional revenue sharing is in fact more efficient owing to the lower administrative costs.[75] Open-ended matching grants generally encourage greater expenditures because they reduce the state's marginal cost of providing the programme. This is desirable when some of the benefits accrue to those outside the jurisdiction (interstate transportation, pollution control) or when competition among jurisdictions yields a low and inefficient level of the good or services provided (low-income support); otherwise open-ended grants generate excessive levels of services. The scaling back and consolidation of the grant programmes may yield some benefits, particularly among the closed-ended grants with high administrative burdens.

The sharp reductions in grants envisioned by the Budget Resolution do much more than create a more efficient grant system: they shift the burden of deficit reduction to lower levels of government, forcing them to cut programmes or raise taxes at a time when state and local government fiscal positions are already under strain. Grant programmes should be carefully examined with a view to determining which elements of government programmes should be national in scope, but are more efficiently delivered locally. Traditionally, experts on fiscal federalism have argued that income redistribution should be the responsibility of the federal government, with allowance for local governments to provide additional aid if they so desire.[76] This has been implemented through a combination of transfers (such as the EITC and SSI programmes) and conditional grants which allow for variation across states (with certain minimum requirements) to account for different conditions as well as different tastes. The proposed conversion of Medicaid and low-income support programmes to closed-ended grants with few conditions may effectively end the federal role, except to the extent that the remaining conditions function as unfunded mandates (see below) or that state funding drops to the point that the federal aid level is binding. Relaxing conditions may improve the quality of expenditures by encouraging experimentation by states (providing an important source of knowledge) and allowing for interstate variation in preferences in the level and mix of government services. But the reduction in federal aid and the likely fall in state funding (because of the higher marginal cost for provision of services) would undoubtedly be greater than the presumed efficiency increases in the provision of the aid, thereby reducing real support and aggravating income inequality. Further, one added advantage of open-ended grants for income support – the regional insurance that is provided when economic conditions vary across the states – would be lost.

Other deficit reduction options

The Social Security system (OASDI) will begin to contribute significantly to rising expenditures beginning in the second decade of the next century and its revenues are projected to fail to keep pace. Although it is not a source for growing deficits currently, that does not imply that it should not be a source of budget savings – yet it has been omitted from deficit reduction plans. There are several compelling reasons to address the system's long-term financing problems now: 1) the earlier the adjustment, the smaller the changes need to be; 2) bringing the system back into long-term solvency will restore confidence in it; 3) announcing changes in advance will allow future beneficiaries more time to adjust their lifetime saving and consumption patterns; and 4) there are currently some inequities that should be addressed.

Proposals to reform the system should be judged according to several criteria: 1) horizontal equity; 2) intergenerational equity; 3) economic efficiency; 4) a fair return on contributions; and 5) progressivity. There are a wide variety of suggestions to cut benefits; reducing the automatic cost-of-living adjustments (COLAs) below the rate of increase in the CPI, raising the retirement age, reducing the generosity of benefit formulae and means-testing benefit payments. Some observers have suggested reducing COLAs below the rise in the CPI because it is argued that the CPI overstates the true rise in the cost of living since it fails to account for the ability to shift to cheaper products when relative prices change and that the CPI fails to capture quality of life improvements from the introduction of new products. However, reducing COLAs below the rise in the cost of living would fail the horizontal equity and progressivity tests because it would reduce real benefits for the oldest of the elderly, typically those with the fewest other resources in terms of other income or labour supply possibilities. Raising the "normal" retirement age (while keeping 62 as the minimum retirement age) and reducing benefit formulae are fundamentally equivalent and would meet these criteria.[77] Changes to benefit calculations that improve horizontal equity and efficiency would be superior to across-the-board reductions. For example, including more years of work in the benefit calculation would lower benefits for all but particularly those who have contributed less; phasing out the spousal benefit or changing it to a small flat rate would remove a regressivity in the system and improve horizontal equity between two-earner and single-earner couples; and reducing the benefits for early retirees to account for their fewer years of contributions would increase economic efficiency.[78] Of course, not all of the adjustment need come on the benefits side of the ledger. One source of revenue would be to expand the tax base to include a greater portion of total compensation. This would increase horizontal equity and economic efficiency. Ultimately, it would result in higher benefits, but owing to the low internal rate of return scheduled for future retirees, it would help move the system into balance. Some have argued that the Social Security system should receive financing from general revenues in addition to earmarked taxes especially because of its role in income support. However, an important advantage to the current trust fund status is that it appears to have provided a meaningful limit on benefits by tying them to corresponding taxes.

Boosting taxes may well be an important source of deficit reduction when spending pressures increase after the turn of the century. Tax increases should be efficiency increasing where possible. Expanding the range of taxes to include a value added tax might meet this criterion by generating substantial revenues that would allow for reductions in marginal tax rates on labour and capital.[79] While the introduction of a VAT would tend to make the tax system somewhat less progressive, adjustments in other areas would allow the system as a whole to stay progressive.[80] While not under active consideration for political reasons, in the past energy taxation – which is extremely modest by international standards – has been discussed as a source of additional revenues, particularly because

Table 13. **Estimated revenue cost of selected tax expenditures**

$ billion

Provision	Tax revenue foregone in 1995
Deductibility of employer-provided benefits	
Health care	67
Child care	1
Life insurance	3
Deductibility of state and local income and property taxes	44
Exclusion of interest on state and local debt	33
Exclusion of government transfers	
Workers compensation	5
Public assistance	1
Veterans benefits	2
Deductibility of mortgage interest	54
Step-up basis of capital gains at death	29
Exclusion of income earned abroad by US citizens	2

Source: Budget of the US Government.

increased taxation may alleviate externalities. Broadening the base of the corporate and personal income tax schedules to include a wider range of fringe benefits, capital income, and transfers could also meet this criterion. There is a wide menu of base-broadening measures to choose from (Table 13).

Managing the budget process and other rules

Recent years have been marked by important changes to the budget process. In 1985 and 1987 legislation was passed with specific deficit targets with the goal of reaching budget balance over the succeeding six years. Both times insufficient deficit reduction early in the programme led to large requirements for deficit reduction in later years which were ultimately met by legislating easier targets. In 1990 fixed deficit targets were abandoned in favour of setting goals for deficit reduction from a moving baseline (the Omnibus Budget Reconciliation Acts of 1990 and 1993). These were enforced by limits on discretionary spending and legislated changes in taxes and entitlements. This procedure has also been found to be lacking sufficient discipline to lower the deficit decisively because there is no requirement to offset overruns in existing entitlement programmes.[81] Many legislators have proposed the added discipline from a balanced-budget amendment to the Constitution, but this has been narrowly defeated in Congress several times over the past decade.

A balanced-budget amendment, properly crafted, might improve economic outcomes compared with a situation in which persistent sizeable deficits that drain an inordinately large amount of other domestic saving are incurred. Put simply, a continuously balanced budget would probably generate higher incomes on average from increased national saving, but incomes could be more variable as fiscal policy might become procyclical. Income variability could be reduced if the amendment had provisions that could buffer undesired swings in fiscal stance through allowances for "rainy day funds",[82] clauses that limit the changes necessary for the current year,[83] and provisions to suspend the requirement through a "super majority" vote,[84] allowing the automatic stabilisers to work if thought warranted by the government. On the other hand, many have argued forcefully against a balanced-budget amendment for a wide range of reasons: it may create a strongly procyclical policy by turning off the automatic stabilisers and limiting the scope for discretionary fiscal policy;[85] balanced budgets may not be optimal and thus should not be enshrined in the Constitution; the definition of the deficit is arbitrary and could be manipulated;[86] a shift in power to a minority group within Congress could lead to sub-optimal budgeting and other policy mistakes, as they could hold hostage necessary budget actions; and it might create unwanted linkages between monetary and fiscal policy, as changes in monetary policy have budgetary consequences. The most serious difficulty with even a well-crafted balanced-budget amendment that included escape clauses is that if persistent deficits became desired they could be held hostage by a minority of members who could block the annual waiver.

The "line-item veto" has also received much attention as a mechanism to improve the quality of spending and reduce the deficit.[87] A line-item veto would allow the President to veto portions of a bill rather than the whole bill, and Congress would have to find support of two-thirds of the members to override the veto. Such a change would clearly shift power to the President and thus spending and other legislation would tilt towards the President's preferred policies. Whether this would improve the quality of spending decisions is open to question. To the extent that the President's decisions rest on the preferences of the median voter, while the congressman's vote is based on those of narrow special interests, then quality might be improved. But the negotiations could result in a shift of spending towards a narrow constituency of the President's choice and not necessarily improve overall quality nor reduce overall spending levels.[88]

Recently passed legislation placed mild limits on the use of unfunded mandates because of the pressures they may place on state and local budgets.[89] Unfunded mandates are those placed by the federal government on lower levels of government that require expenditures but which are not accompanied by grants. Most unfunded mandates result from environment, health and anti-discrimination laws. For example, the Clean Water Act forces local governments to invest in water treatment plants, the Americans with Disabilities Act forces the private sector and governments to modify buildings to improve access for the handicapped, and the Medicaid laws place minimum conditions for providing health care to the poor. Measures of unfunded mandates likely overestimate their impact as they do not clearly differentiate between total spending on the activity and that which is over and above what would have occurred without a federal mandate. For example, although the federal government has expanded Medicaid coverage in recent years, most states provide substantially more than the minimum level of benefits. Thus, while state governments decry the imposition of additional expenditures, it may be the case that the imposition by the federal government concerns the composition of health spending on the poor, for example, rather than its level in a particular area.

V. Other structural policy changes

Perhaps because of the change in control of the Congress, proposals for structural reform abound. While some legislation was also passed by the previous Congress before the elections, other bills languished in the legislative pipeline; and the nature of some reform proposals has been substantially transformed from what was initially submitted. The preceding chapter already dealt in some detail with proposed reforms to the public health-care programmes and the various federal welfare schemes. In this chapter policy developments in a number of other domains are reviewed: the labour market, external trade, regulation, agriculture, the environment, financial markets and other miscellaneous areas. The following chapter will deal in more detail with the subject of adult education and training, upon which the Administration has placed high priority as a means of meeting the increasing human capital needs of the nation.

Developments in labour market policy

There are a number of areas of difficulty for US labour market policy. The need to enhance labour force skills and competences by raising educational achievement in schools and improving the school-to-work transition is widely accepted. The subject of the possible problems of human capital formation – as demonstrated, for example, by the continuing decline in real median wages even as the business cycle looks to have reached its peak – is the focus of special chapters in both the previous Survey of the United States economy (OECD, 1994e), which covered the education system and recent efforts to improve it, and in this Survey (Chapter VI). Suffice it to say here that over the past year no progress was made at the federal level in terms of new legislation in the educational sphere. Indeed, the majority party in the House of Representatives recently proposed to abolish the federal Department of Education within a year, to reduce substantially the generosity of the student loan system, to repeal the Goals 2000 initiative which supports states in their efforts to set subject-content and performance standards for elementary and secondary schools[90] and to transform what the Department spends in aid for primary and secondary schools, as well as colleges, into a block grant to the states. But the states have made only limited progress in dealing with the major inequities in funding that exist even within their own borders. There are, therefore, grounds for concern that diminishing the already small role played by the federal government in primary and secondary education will exacerbate existing disparities in service quality.

Another long-standing OECD recommendation to its Member countries is to introduce active labour market measures for those most at risk of becoming long-term unemployed. While the average duration of unemployment spells, as measured by both the mean and median, has fallen fairly sharply over the past year, the declines have not been commensurate with the economy's cyclical position, as shown in Chapter II. Because of Congressional opposition, the Administration's proposed Re-employment Act was not enacted. It would have consolidated job training and retraining programmes (but that is proposed under other legislation before Congress), made income support available to all dislocated workers in long-term retraining, reformed the unemployment insurance system and created "one-stop career centres".[91] The Administration has repackaged some of these proposals in its 1996 Budget: for example, the GI Bill for America's Workers would consolidate many programmes, create One-Stop Career Center systems in all states, and create a system of Skill Grants (job-training vouchers) available to low-income or dislocated workers. Also advanced is the idea of tax breaks for education expenditures. Finally, last year's Survey praised the Earned Income Tax Credit for enhancing work incentives, but budget-balancing plans would in fact narrow its application slightly and scale back its size (see Chapter IV). Other budget proposals would cut federal spending on youth training.

There have been a small number of other policy developments pertaining to the labour market. On 8 March 1995, the President issued an Executive Order prohibiting federal contractors from permanently replacing striking workers.[92] This would be expected to boost wages and the frequency and duration of strike activity at the relevant firms (Cramton, Gunderson and Tracy, 1995; Cramton and Tracy, 1995). A number of long-standing labour laws are also being challenged. First, a bill that would abolish requirements under the Davis Bacon Act (for construction jobs) and the Service Contract Act (for services employees) that federal contractors pay the prevailing (union) wage is proceeding through the Congress. Second, the final Report of the Commission on the Future of Worker-Management Relations, published in January 1995, recommended that the 1935 National Labor Relations Act be amended to allow employers to set up workplace groups of workers and managers to discuss quality, safety and productivity so long as this does not lead to company unions and it is not used to frustrate employee efforts to obtain independent representation.[93] Third, while legislation has not as yet been introduced, there are Republican proposals to amend the Fair Labor Standards Act in order to ease the requirement to pay overtime rates beyond the standard 40-hour workweek, and to modify worker safety regulations with a view to reducing bureaucratic requirements and resorting to warnings rather than fines for first-time offenders. Finally, in a matter with labour-market implications, the Senate is beginning work on an immigration bill following the report of the Commission on Immigration Reform in September 1995. It recommended that levels of legal immigration be gradually reduced by as much as one third, that preferences for siblings and adult children of US citizens be abolished and that firms be made to pay up to $10 000 when they recruit and hire skilled foreign workers rather than US workers.

Problems and progress on the external trade front

The most important foreign trade policy development for the United States, as for most other countries, over the past year was the passage of the legislation implementing the Uruguay Round agreements. The United States thereby became an original member of the World Trade Organisation (WTO), and the multilateral trade regime was broadened and strengthened in many of the ways policy-makers had hoped for when the Uruguay Round was launched in 1986. Congressional passage of the legislation required the promise of the establishment of a Commission of five federal appellate judges to review all WTO decisions that find a US statute inconsistent with the WTO. The Commission would determine whether any such decision followed the standard of review prescribed in the WTO or exceeded WTO authority; if it were to so find with respect to three cases in a five-year period, any Member of Congress could introduce a joint resolution calling for withdrawal from the WTO (subject to the usual possibility of a

Presidential veto). However, legislation to set up this Commission, introduced in April, has not thus far been enacted. The US WTO implementing legislation also codified the President's Executive Order of 3 March 1994 reinstituting the "Super 301" procedure for calendar years 1994 and 1995. This requires the Administration to identify foreign country practices which are detrimental to US exports. Though the United States considers that it can administer this clause and Section 301 in a fashion consistent with its WTO obligations, other countries have taken strong issue with the US approach.

One of the most impressive achievements of the Uruguay Round Agreements is the dismantling of the Multi-Fibre Agreement. According to the schedule set out in the WTO Agreement on Textiles and Clothing, products accounting for 16 per cent of US textile and clothing imports were "integrated" at the beginning of this year, a further 17 per cent will be integrated in 1998, 18 per cent in 2002 and the remaining 49 per cent in 2005. However, integration of the most sensitive products will be deferred until the end of the ten-year period.

This year's major international trade negotiations took place in the financial services arena under the auspices of the WTO. This was one of the four services sectors in which the Uruguay Round agreements called for extended negotiations. Shortly before the 30 June deadline the United States announced that it was not satisfied with the offers of other nations, especially those of several emerging markets, and therefore would list MFN exemptions allowing it to differentiate in treatment of countries with respect to new entry, expansion and the conduct of new activities by their financial services suppliers in the United States. The US authorities felt that the offers of too many important countries did not provide for new market access, did not fully protect the current market access of foreign firms or reserved the right to force divestiture of the current holdings of foreign firms. The deadline was extended by about one month. Most parties to the negotiations revised their commitments as accepted at Marrakesh in April 1994. Most parties, but not the United States, made commitments that were subject to ratification. They attached their liberalisation commitments to a protocol that establishes the terms for their entry into force. All parties agreed they could revise their commitments in the event that the protocol was not accepted by ratifying members by 1 July 1996. The United States (and certain other countries) did not attach to the protocol its revised commitments which entered into force on 30 June 1995 without further Congressional approval. All parties agreed that they could modify or withdraw their commitments during a 60-day period beginning on 1 November 1997. The revised commitments of the United States provide full protection of established foreign investments in the US market for financial services but do not guarantee new access or the conduct of new activities. In other WTO negotiations the United States and its trading partners reached agreement on the freer movement of persons and continue to negotiate on basic telecommunications and maritime services.

The United States also made progress toward some of its multilateral trade liberalisation goals in recent regional initiatives. In November 1994 at Bogor, Indonesia, the 18 members of the Asia Pacific Economic Co-operation (APEC) forum agreed to move toward free and open trade and investment among its developed country members by 2010 and for the others by 2020; the following January the United States announced that it hoped to have the pace stepped up for the developed countries. In December 1994, 34 Western Hemisphere nations meeting at Miami agreed to set up a Free Trade Area of the Americas by 2005 by building on existing regional and bilateral trade accords. The US Administration has announced its willingness to admit Chile to the North American Free Trade Area (NAFTA) over the next few years; accession negotiations got underway in May 1995. The difficulty there will be to get the Congress to grant fast-track authority[94] including clauses on environmental and labour standards, as preferred by the Administration. Also in December 1994, the United States announced its intention to seek closer economic ties with the European Union, including stricter international limits on export subsidies. In addition, in February 1995, the United States and China reached a much-heralded agreement in the area of intellectual property rights. Finally, the United States has been a strong supporter of the proposed Multilateral Agreement on Investment, the terms of which are being negotiated within the OECD.

It is the relationship with Japan that has occupied most of the attention of US trade negotiators this past year. Under the Framework Talks for a New Economic Partnership initiated by the two countries in July 1993, consultations continued in a number of sectoral domains.[95] In October 1994 successful conclusions were reached in the areas of telecommunications equipment, medical technology, insurance and flat glass.[96] No numerical targets nor any fixed market shares for foreign goods were included. Rather, recent trends would be used to evaluate the extent of progress made in achieving a significant increase in access and sales opportunities for competitive foreign products and services. In January 1995 the two governments also decided to implement market-opening measures in the financial services sector.

But in the area of autos and auto parts further consultations continued until June 1995.[97] The United States sought increased access for foreign auto manufacturers to existing Japanese auto dealerships, significant deregulation of Japan's auto repairs parts market or ''aftermarket'' and expanded sales opportunities for foreign parts suppliers to Japanese auto manufacturers both in the United States and Japan. The United States initiated a Section 301 investigation in October 1994 which determined in May 1995 that certain acts, policies and practices of Japan were restricting US auto parts suppliers' access to the auto parts replacement and accessories market in Japan, thereby burdening US commerce. As a result of this affirmative finding the United States threatened to impose 100 per cent duties on $5.9 billion worth of imports of Japanese luxury cars as from 20 May 1995, to take effect upon final determination by 28 June.[98] The United States held that it had the right to impose such duties under Section 301 of its trade law. But it also announced its intention to file a complaint with the newly formed WTO, alleging that Japan, through its actions and inactions with respect to the automotive sector, has failed to carry out its obligations under the WTO and nullified and impaired benefits accruing to the United States under the WTO. Japan requested consultations under the WTO concerning the US determination and measures, arguing that they either did or would violate various Articles of the GATT/WTO, including the as yet untested Dispute Settlement Understanding, and would have adversely affected efforts to strengthen the multilateral trading system. The two countries were able to conclude auto and auto parts talks, and further proceedings under the WTO dispute settlement procedures were not pursued. It is therefore unknown whether the scope of its new dispute settlement mechanism is sufficiently broad to have dealt with such a complaint in a satisfactory fashion. Problems of interpretation remain. The United States has established a monitoring mechanism to report publicly on Japanese compliance semi-annually.

Following the US-Japan auto negotiations, the Japanese government announced its intention to take deregulation measures in order to improve market access for competitive foreign spare parts. Outside the Framework Talks, Japan's five largest auto companies also announced voluntary plans (so-called global business plans) to increase their parts purchases in North America, to increase their vehicle production in North America and to purchase more competitive foreign parts for production use in Japan. For its part, the Japanese Automobile Dealers Association announced measures to facilitate contacts and enhance opportunities for foreign vehicle manufacturers in the Japanese market; any pressure from Japanese producers to prevent dealers from exercising their free choice on models would be dealt with under existing anti-monopolies laws.

Many of the other recent trade frictions involving the United States have been related to antidumping decisions, many of them against Japanese producers. The United States remains the country with the most antidumping measures in force of any – 280 as of end-1994 –[99] and their net cost to the nation has recently been shown to be significant.[100] Following an antidumping case against a Japanese photographic paper producer in 1993-94, Kodak made another complaint against that firm and the Japanese government in 1995, alleging a whole range of anti-competitive practices in the consumer colour film and photographic paper sectors in Japan. The case was then accepted by the US government as a Section 301 case in July. And there were bilateral civil aviation tensions as well, although these were subsequently resolved.

Not all the frictions are with Japan. In a large number of cases, antidumping/countervailing duty investigations are initiated, and ultimately provisional duties are withdrawn because of a lack of material injury.[101] Tensions also surface when, occasionally, the United States refuses to heed GATT rulings: for example, it continues to resist adoption of the 1992 GATT ruling against its imposition of antidumping duties of 62 per cent on Mexican cement imports in 1990. It has also refused to allow the adoption of the GATT finding against its embargo on imports of tuna caught with nets which allow excessive amounts of dolphin bycatch. Another important case involving dispute settlement procedures occurred in September 1994 when US lumber producers, having lost a NAFTA countervailing duty investigation against Canadian producers, decided to challenge the NAFTA dispute settlement process before the courts on constitutional grounds, but the case was withdrawn before decision. Frictions with Canada in the area of grains have not yet been resolved, pending the submission of non-binding recommendations from a joint commission in September; in the case of wheat, however, the tariff-rate quota imposed in 1994 was allowed to expire, even though monitoring of imports from Canada will continue. The two countries have also agreed to establish a bilateral consultative process on trade in softwood lumber. With respect to Europe, no agreement has been made regarding compensation for European Union (EU) enlargement; frictions persist in the areas of public procurement (power-generating equipment in Germany , for example) and EU banana imports; and in October 1994 a GATT panel ruled largely against an EU complaint against the US set of special taxes on automobiles – the "gas guzzler" tax, the luxury tax and Corporate Average Fuel Economy regulation (CAFE): only the separate foreign fleet accounting provision of the CAFE was ruled to be in violation of GATT agreements. Thus far the EU has declined to adopt the panel report, and the United States government has given no indication of modifying that provision. Finally, there have also been a series of trade frictions with Korea: 1995 saw agreements for steel, cigarettes and cars.

Some recent regulatory developments

The new majority in the Congress has been anxious to ease the burden of regulation on the private sector, but there is a risk that its proposals may cripple the regulatory function. One initiative attempted was a *moratorium on new regulations*, but this was rejected in the Senate in favour of an approach whereby those with an annual impact of $100 million or more would not take effect for 45 days, during which time Congress would decide whether to approve or block them based on cost-benefit analysis. Besides the moratorium, the House version of the bill would require federal agencies to review all major existing regulations every seven years and all new regulations after three years and again every seven years thereafter. This would put a substantial additional burden on many federal agencies. Furthermore, the proposals in the Congressional Budget Resolution effectively cut off funding for the enforcement of 62 federal mandates.

A draft bill that would reform the regulations pertaining to the *telecommunications* sector is making its way through Congress. The main feature of the version passed by the House of Representatives is to allow the seven regional phone companies to enter the long-distance market, but only once they face competition in their local networks; they would also be permitted to engage in equipment manufacturing. But critics (including the Administration) fear that the competition test is too weak and fails to specify how substantial the competitor must be or the extent of its geographical coverage in the area from which the regional company proposes to offer long-distance service. The bill also includes a clause that would lift current restrictions on foreign investment in US broadcasting (if the home country of the foreign firm offers reciprocal treatment to US firms). The Administration had announced in February its intention to end the foreign-ownership limit on US telecommunications firms for countries which reciprocate. The bill would also lift many price controls for cable television firms and would require regional telephone companies to share their networks with would-be competitors. But the bill is opposed by the Administration and some consumer groups who fear price gouging by cable companies once most price controls are dropped, an excessive concentration of media power and the removal of competition in rural areas (as local telephone and cable firms would be allowed to merge).

Another related area where reform efforts are active is *legal reform*. One federal bill (The Private Securities Litigation Reform Act) to reform the 1933 Securities Act has passed the House and, in less sweeping form, the Senate; it would curb allegedly frivolous class-action lawsuits for securities fraud by shareholders against, for example, firms whose predictions of future profitability turn out to be erroneous. Critics say it would erode investor protection against fraudulent claims made with respect to both new and existing securities. In a similar vein both houses have passed legislation which would rewrite rules governing product liability cases in both federal and state courts. The House version, part of the Republican Contract with America, would also cap punitive damages in all civil cases and limit medical malpractice awards, but even the narrower Senate version is opposed by consumer groups who point out that tort cases involve only 9 per cent of the total civil caseload and product liability only 4 per cent of the civil case load and that, excluding the special case of asbestos, filings of product liability cases have declined by 36 per cent since 1985. Nevertheless, there does seem to have been a number of cases of excessive punitive damages in a few states, notably Alabama and California. As a result, besides federal initiatives, there are 70 tort-reform bills pending in 31 states.

Environmental reform proposals[102]

While a number of pieces of environmental legislation made their way through parts of Congress in 1994, none passed before the session ended. With the change in control of Congress, supporters of these bills have withdrawn some of them, while others have introduced new legislation. Critics of the existing regulatory regime argue that part of the $90 billion or so per year that the United States spends on pollution abatement and control[103] is being poorly spent.[104] Regulation is said to be inefficient, as it fails to consider costs in meeting standards and assumes that the benefits exceed the costs. The burden of compliance is also said to be inequitable, as it may fall on parties who took no part in creating the problem. The environmental cleanup system has been termed "short on flexibility and long on litigation" (Boulton, 1995): a significant fraction of the budget of the Environmental Protection Agency ($7 billion) goes into legal costs to ensure that offenders meet their liabilities, the burden of which would otherwise fall on the government. The Agency has recently launched a number of initiatives (voluntary agreements and use of market-based instruments, for example) and approved a 1994 Strategic Plan which emphasises more flexible and cost-effective policy approaches. The *Common Sense Initiative* is one example, involving all interested parties in six main polluting industries in the design of more flexible strategies to achieve environmental progress.

There are four controversial areas where debate has been and is taking place. Legislation has already passed this year to restrict the right of the federal government to impose unfunded mandates on state and local governments (see Chapter IV) to, for example, spend large amounts of money in order to eliminate insignificant risks. Second, a bill has been proposed that would require the government to undertake cost-benefit analyses for all new and or existing environmental or other regulations. Such analyses were also recommended by an Executive Order signed by President Clinton, but they are not strictly obligatory. These risk assessments could be challenged in the courts and lead to paralysis. Third, there is a bill concerning "takings": compensation to private property owners if government actions lower the value of their property. Such compensation would either be extremely costly or prevent the promulgation of a majority of regulation and decisions concerning the use of land. Last, in August in the first step in the US budget-making process, the House of Representatives passed its appropriation bill for the 1996 fiscal year covering the environment; it cut overall funding for the EPA by one-third and enforcement funding by a half. In response, the President threatened to veto the bill and issued an executive order preserving the requirement on all but very small firms who do business with the US government to publish information on their emission of toxic chemicals.

The bill which got the furthest last year was that which overhauled the so-called *Superfund*. The key issue there is one of retroactivity of financial responsibility for cleaning up hazardous waste sites. If this is repealed, it is unclear who will pay the resulting additional cleanup costs, estimated at $1.3 billion per year.[105] It should be noted that the tax which funds this spending is scheduled to expire at the end of 1995. In May the House of Representatives passed legislation to reform the 1972 *Clean Water Act*. It narrows the definition of what constitutes a wetland (which the Environmental Protection Agency estimates would cut the acreage so classified by 50 to 70 per cent), eases the requirements for industry and lower levels of government to clean contaminated and storm water before discharging and transfers the authority for enforcing water quality standards to the states. The Administration has indicated its strong opposition to this bill. In May legislation was introduced in the Senate to amend the 1973 *Endangered Species Act* in order to make it more difficult to declare species to be endangered; in March a Senate sub-committee had voted to impose a six-month freeze on new listings under the Act. An imminent battle is likely in the specific case of various types of salmon in the Pacific North-west. Another existing law under attack is the so-called *Delaney Clause*: dating back to 1958, it prohibits residues from any known carcinogen at any measurable levels in all processed foods.

Agricultural policy initiatives

While the overall Producer Subsidy Equivalent (PSE) for agriculture in the OECD is estimated to have risen in 1994, the United States was one of several exceptions[106] (OECD, 1995). The US PSE fell back to its 1992 level of about $26 billion, mainly because of a decline in disaster payments following the 1993 floods in the Midwestern states. Also contributing to the reduction was an average decline in domestic producer prices of 3.5 per cent, but this was offset by a rise in deficiency payments of over 20 per cent. In percentage terms the PSE fell two points to 21 per cent, less than half the OECD average. The US Consumer Subsidy Equivalent also reversed its 1993 rise and, in percentage terms, remains less than one-third the OECD average. Overall, while reduced support indicates improved market orientation, trade distortions were aggravated by an increase in export subsidies under the Export Enhancement Program (EEP); however, these are being cut back in the current fiscal year.

There have been only a few policy changes over the past year worthy of note. In October 1994, legislation was passed reorganising the Department of Agriculture and requiring it to undertake *cost-benefit analyses* of any new regulations with an economic impact in excess of $100 million per year. It also reformed the federal *crop insurance* programme by instituting a new requirement that producers purchase catastrophic insurance coverage for each crop that is expected to contribute at least 10 per cent of the total value of production in order to be eligible for price support or production adjustment programmes. The intent is to save on the recent annual average of $1.5 billion per year in *ad hoc* disaster relief costs by strengthening farmers' incentives to develop their own risk-reduction strategies. In other matters, the rate of countervailing duty on imports of pigs from Canada was cut by 86 per cent; voluntary export restraints on beef from Australia and New Zealand continue; beef import quotas were cut for 1994; but the tariff-quota for sugar was raised.

1995 is the scheduled year for a new quinquennial *Farm Bill*. The expiring 1990 Act was expected to bring about cumulative payments of about $41 billion, but actual outlays will have reached about $58 billion, of which about $10.6 billion this fiscal year. Overspending is attributable to unexpectedly high outlays for disaster relief and for deficiency payments, due to lower-than-expected world agricultural prices. Existing legislation would probably already have led to a significant reduction in outlays in the future, but it seems very likely that efforts to balance the budget (discussed in Chapter IV) will lead to additional shrinkage. The Administration proposed further small cuts totalling about $1.5 billion over the next five years in its 1996 Budget. The Congressional Budget Resolution included suggested cumulative programme cuts of about $9 billion (leaving only $3 to $4 billion per year by 2002). Indirect subsidies to sugar producers in the form of low-cost loans and price guarantees enforced through border protection are especially under attack.

The main ideas for reform which have been discussed in the context of the new Farm Bill are: to decouple payments fully from the requirement to grow specific crops in order to respond more fully to market forces; or to move toward a system of revenue assurance whereby the government would guarantee, say, 70 per cent of a moving average of farmers' revenues. The Administration made its detailed proposals in May. They include a generalisation of the decoupling idea over five years, along with a means test excluding from eligibility those with more than $100 000 per year in off-farm income, but not the revenue assurance scheme which might have strong moral hazard risks. Rather the Administration supports the idea of public subsidies toward premiums on private insurance with public catastrophic reinsurance. It also called for an unspecified reduction in the share of land eligible for support and the institution of a competitive tendering procedure for EEP funds to minimise the subsidy per unit of commodity. Among many other proposed changes, the Administration recommended the establishment of individual revenue stabilisation (saving) accounts which would receive matching public funds and would be financed by reduced support payments; this idea was patterned after a similar programme in Canada (the ''Net Income Stabilization Account''). However, at this stage the overall outcome for the 1995 Farm Bill is extremely uncertain.

Improving the functioning of the market for financial services

Once again the *banking sector* has been the subject of several pieces of legislation designed to remove artificial restraints on activity. The *Riegle-Neal Interstate Banking and Branching Efficiency Act* was signed into law on 29 September 1994. It eliminates most restrictions on interstate bank acquisitions by bank holding companies (BHCs) as of one year after enactment, thereby superseding laws of 38 states which currently allow interstate banking only on a reciprocal or a regional basis. It will also allow BHCs to convert their banks in various states into branches of a single interstate bank as of 1 June 1997 (something which has not been possible since 1927), provided that capital and Community Reinvestment Act standards are met and certain state and nation-wide concentration limits are not violated.[107] Finally, it establishes a framework for states to authorise the opening of new branches on an interstate basis. The impact of this reform is difficult to gauge, but the intent is to allow greater diversification of credit risks in order to enhance stability and to reduce costs through consolidation. Some large banks estimate that the reform may lead to their saving up to $50 million per year on administrative costs – not having to operate separate banks in each state. Yet most research suggests that economies of scale in banking are limited: for example, when substantial off-balance-sheet activities are absent, Berger and Humphrey (1992) claim that average costs are minimised when assets are in the range of only $75 to $300 million. In this vein some recent analysis based on BHCs' responses to state-level reforms in recent years (McLaughlin, 1995) found that BHCs have generally opted for incremental regional expansion and concluded that "federal reform will speed industry consolidation by facilitating mergers of banks located in different states but may not lead immediately to the formation of coast-to-coast banking companies through bank acquisitions" (p. 2); only over the longer term might a small number of BHCs seek to establish national banking franchises. The Riegle-Neal Act also delayed until 25 July 1997 the statutory provision that would require the Federal Reserve to impose discriminatory examination fees on foreign banks. During its recent examination of the United States, the OECD Committee on Capital Movements and Invisible Transactions expressed concern over this possible imposition and expressed the hope that the United States would find a permanent solution consistent with its responsibilities under the OECD Codes of liberalisation of capital movements and current invisible operations (OECD, 1995d).

After four unsuccessful reform attempts in the past 14 years, another major effort to repeal parts of the much-criticised[108] 1933 *Glass Steagall Banking Act* is underway. The hope is that allowing a broader range of financial activities within a single organisation will also generate production economies and at the same time reduce risk through intersectoral diversification. The concern has been to avoid any extension of the public "safety net" – including deposit insurance, the discount window and access to Fedwire (one of the two large-scale electronic payments systems) – to other types of activities through bank ownership. Only Japan among G7 countries has such limited integration of banking and securities firms, although only Germany, and to a lesser extent France (and Japan with its *keiretsu* system), allow tighter relations between banks and commerce. Yet some, including the chairman of the Federal Reserve, believe that financial reform would recognise evolving market realities, rather than constituting a major innovation, since it is increasingly difficult to distinguish the core functions of banking (the measurement, acceptance and management of risk) from those of other financial institutions (Greenspan, 1995). In any case, 17 states have already authorised state-chartered non-Fed member banks to engage in securities underwriting and dealing, though few have been able to take advantage of this possibility because of the breadth of the federal legal prohibitions.

There are still several competing proposals for reform. The principal House version (The Financial Services Competitiveness Act) is the narrowest: it lifts only the barriers between banking and securities underwriting and dealing, that is between commercial and investment banking. Since 1988, the relevant regulator for bank holding companies – the Federal Reserve – has allowed banking organisations to engage in such securities operations, but only through separate subsidiaries and only if these non-exempt securities activities constitute no more than 10 per cent of the subsidiary's business. This bill would allow the formation of "financial services holding companies", each part of which would continue to be overseen by existing regulators, with overall supervision remaining with the Federal Reserve. Regulatory "firewalls" would protect the bank from potential losses suffered by its securities affiliate and also prevent banks from using insured deposits to subsidise non-bank activities. Alternative "investment bank holding companies" could own wholesale banks (not accepting deposits under $100 000 and not subject to federal deposit insurance) and securities subsidiaries, and these holding companies could – up to a quantitative limit – also invest in insurance and other companies. The Administration believes the bill would transfer too much regulatory authority from the Office of the Comptroller of the Currency (OCC, part of the Treasury) to the Federal Reserve; its preference is to reform the law more broadly to allow direct subsidiaries of banks in order to avoid the holding company structure. More importantly, it originally preferred to include insurance in the reform (that is to allow these financial firms originally preferred also to underwrite and sell insurance), a feature which has led to the previous legislative failures.[109] At a minimum, it seeks to avoid limits on the OCC's ability to expand insurance activities for national banks, a provision of the House bill. The version introduced in the Senate would in addition allow links between banks and nonfinancial firms, barred under the 1956 Bank Holding Companies Act. The Senate has not yet begun serious consideration of a reform proposal, though it is expected to do so this autumn.

In May 1995 the Administration announced a proposal to revamp the *Federal Home Loan Bank (FHLB)* System, the nation's third largest issuer of debt securities. These 12 regional banks were set up by the Congress in 1932 to provide low-cost, collateralised loans ("advances") to savings and loan institutions ("thrifts") in order to provide liquidity to the housing sector. Under 1989 legislation the system was opened to commercial banks, and today they comprise 62 per cent of System membership of 5 563 institutions. The purpose of the FHLB system has become less clear in recent years because most depository institutions that borrow from it also use market sources of liquidity in addition to securitising many of their home loans. The proposal would also make membership in the system voluntary for federally-chartered thrifts (state-chartered thrifts have enjoyed that freedom since April 1995) and would establish minimum, risk-based capital standards, along the lines of the system for commercial banks. There would also be a new requirement that member institutions maintain 10 per cent of their assets in whole residential mortgages in order to strengthen their commitment to the housing sector. Numerous Congressional hearings have been held in the past two years, and more are expected this fall, in order to determine what legislation is needed to clarify the System's objectives.

The relative competitive situation of the savings and loan industry is poor and looks set to deteriorate further, even though their current profitability is satisfactory. While the Resolution Trust Corporation disposed of its last failed institutions in March 1995, bringing down the curtain on the costly clean-up, its effects linger on: the remaining well-capitalised profitable institutions have been unable to rebuild their deposit insurance fund, mainly because their premium payments have been diverted by Congress to pay for expenses related to the closing of insolvent thrifts in the late 1980s. These premia are at a rate of 0.24 per cent of deposits. The outlook is that this rate will remain fixed until around 2002 when it will drop to 0.11 per cent. In contrast, well-capitalised commercial banks have been paying 0.23 per cent to recapitalise their deposit insurance fund,[110] and, now that the task has been accomplished, it is proposed to reduce that to 0.04 per cent; the saving is estimated to be worth some $4.5 billion per year. With a deposit base that has in any case declined by about one quarter since 1989 and a return on assets less than half that earned by commercial banks in 1994, such a large gap in premium rates will place savings and loans at a competitive disadvantage and may lead many to switch their deposits to the comercial bank insurance fund. This could result in the "extinction of savings associations" (Osterberg and Thomson, 1995). Congress is considering ways to recapitalise the savings and loan insurance fund, and thus avoid the large difference in these insurance rates. The proposal is to levy a one-time 85 basis point charge on the deposits of these institutions and a subsequent bank and thrift sharing of the cost of bonds used in the previous thrift bailout. In addition, Congress may merge the savings and loan charter into the commercial bank charter because the need for a depository institution that is focused, by law and regulation, on housing has diminished in recent years.

On the other hand, the financial health of the commercial banking sector is strong. The number of problem banks and the assets they hold have continued to fall – by the second quarter of 1995 there were 190 problem banks with $23 billion in assets, down from 1016 with $528 billion in assets at the peak at end-1991. Moreover, during the first half of 1995 the banking industry continued its string of record earnings. Nevertheless, the industry faces challenges in accepting and managing risk as the demand for loans has increased and competition among banks has intensified. Evidence suggests that many commercial banks have been aggressively making new loans with terms and conditions that have been eased from the tight standards in the early 1990s. Smaller loan fees, narrower rate spreads, lower debt-service coverage ratios, lengthening of maturities, lower collateral coverage and fewer or more liberal protective covenants are a number of the areas of easing cited. Some bankers have voiced concern that overheated competition may be pushing lending standards beyond prudent bounds. The federal banking supervisors have also expressed some concern over the past year regarding the changing lending standards. In April 1995, the OCC set up a new credit review committee and in June of 1995 the Federal Reserve sent a supervisory letter to alert its examiners to the potential that some banks may be relaxing, or may be inclined to relax, lending terms and conditions excessively, as a result of heightened competitive pressures. While credit risk problems may be on the horizon for banks, managing market risk has been another challenge recently faced by the industry. During 1994 and early 1995, rising market interest rates increased pressure on bank interest margins and on the market value of their trading and investment portfolios, although by mid-year 1995 unrealised losses on investment portfolios had largely disappeared. Rising interest rates and other market uncertainties also sharply reduced the trading revenues of most money centre banks from their exceptionally high levels of 1993. These developments, along with the well publicised failure of a major investment bank, Barings, in 1995, underscored the continuing importance of sound risk management practices at banks and other market participants alike.

Other structural policy changes

In the area of *competition policy* the International Antitrust Enforcement Assistance Act was passed in October 1994; it allows greater international co-operation in antitrust enforcement. In the same month the Administration published its draft Antitrust Enforcement Guidelines for International Operations in which the issue of extraterritoriality once again came to the fore. With respect to *industrial policy* the Technology Reinvestment Project (defence conversion) gave some $202 million toward flat-panel display research and development in October 1994 in exchange for promises by the recipients to build domestic manufacturing capacity for the existing technology. Last year's attempt to extend maritime shipping subsidies was revived in a scaled-down form: the current draft legislation proposes a retainer fee totalling $100 million per year for five years payable to the owners of 35 to 50 vessels ($2.1 to $2.3 million per vessel per year) who would have to make their vessels available to the military in times of emergency. In early 1995 the Galvin report on the current state and future of the Department of Energy's national laboratories concluded that the co-operation agreements signed with the private sector had not yielded much in the way of useful innovations and that the labs should focus on nuclear weapons clean-up, for example: the Department has recently estimated that the cost of cleaning up 10 500 sites will be at least $230 billion spread over a maximum of 75 years, with the bill possibly reaching $350 billion.

In June 1995 the Administration announced a package of proposals to streamline the regulation of *private pension plans*, especially for small business, with a view to encouraging the development of such pensions. But the funding shortfall of the government's Pension Benefits Guaranty Corporation (PBGC) was estimated at $71 billion in present value terms in 1994, up 34 per cent in the previous year.[111] The Uruguay Round implementing legislation contained a reform to reduce potential PBGC liabilities by forcing firms with underfunded plans to reach a minimum funding level of three years worth of benefits and to notify employees if funding falls below 90 per cent. This should have the effect of cutting the shortfall to around $30 billion by fiscal year 1996.

A number of reforms which bear upon the subject of *public-sector efficiency* have been passed or mooted. The first bill passed by the new Congress in January 1995 ended the numerous legal exemptions that Congress had granted itself over the years, forcing it to comply with all laws that apply to the rest of the country. The Paperwork Reduction Act of 1995, which was passed in May and takes effect in October, aims to cut government paperwork by 10 per cent in each of the first two years and a further 5 per cent in the following four years; the Office of Management and Budget is to review all existing paperwork requirements. The Administration's latest initiative in the Reinventing Government programme was published in May: it restructures the National Aeronautics and Space Administration, the Small Business Administration, Federal Emergency Management Agency and the Department of the Interior. A total of 4 805 jobs are to be eliminated with a budgetary saving of $13.1 billion over five years.

VI.   Training and adult education

Introduction

Many have come to doubt that US workers have the skills needed to earn high wages in the competitive world economy. Officials in major American corporations have described the quality of the work-force as "the makings of a national disaster" or as "the American Dream turned into a nightmare".[112] And yet, the proportion of adult Americans completing university education, at 27 per cent, is twice the OECD average. The United States spends a larger percentage of its GDP – 2.5 per cent, compared with an OECD average of 1.7 per cent – on tertiary education than any other reporting country. Likewise, the proportion of adults of all age levels who reported having participated in job-related education in 1991 – at 38 per cent – is high relative to most other reporting countries (Figure 32). Thus, several quite different pictures can be painted of the US work-force's human capital attributes, each accurate for different segments of the workforce.

The debate on adult education and training is motivated in large part by concerns over the distributional impacts of ongoing developments in US labour markets. While it is widely recognised that the current "system"[113] works well for people in high wage segments of the labour market, the adequacy of current arrangements for the middle- and low-wage end of the market is much less clear. Some analysts hold forth the hope that, by increasing skills and knowledge in this segment of the workforce, one might reverse the disturbing wage trends that are documented in this chapter.[114]

This chapter examines this question in some depth. Such an examination needs to be put in the context of the social and economic environment in which the US adult education and training system operates. Schematically described, the principal features of this environment are: unregulated labour markets that have

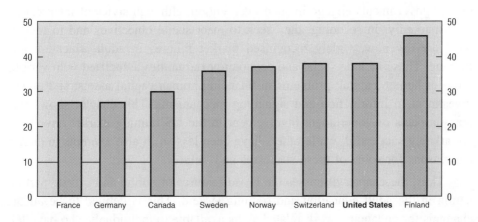

Figure 32. **CONTINUING EDUCATION AND TRAINING FOR ADULTS**
Age 25-64

Note: Participation in job-related continuing education and training as a percentage of the employed population aged 25 to 64.
Source: OECD, *Education at a Glance,* 1995.

generated a wage profile that reflects the prevailing supply and demand for different kinds of skills; strong incentives to work; high regional and inter-firm mobility; and a scarcity (relative to many other OECD countries) of institutions that bring together workers and employers to discuss matters of shared interest. The current chapter argues that the influence of these features on the adult education and training system has been to skew it heavily toward individual acquisition of general skills that are portable in the sense that they can be readily signalled to labour markets. Accordingly, US labour markets assign a rather narrow role to firms in the provision of general skills. This contrasts with the extensive role played by German firms in developing the general skills of their employees (Harhoff and Kane, 1995). Any policy initiatives in this area must take these basic socio-economic features into account.

When examining the scope for further improvements in the adult education and training system, it is also necessary to understand the nature of current government involvement in the system. And, indeed, intervention is pervasive. Governments at the federal, state and local levels are heavily involved in these markets: they subsidise education and training services in various ways; they provide services directly; they set standards in some occupations. Indeed, all OECD governments engage in such intervention, although styles of intervention vary markedly. In so doing, they seek to meet social objectives and to redress what are, by now, widely recognised market failures in adult education and training. These include social and economic externalities associated with various types of human capital; problems in financing human capital assets; and under-investment in information and signalling mechanisms. This chapter shows that many aspects of government involvement in the US training market have been remarkably successful, while others have been less so. It also attempts to clarify the reasons for some of these successes and failures.

Thus, the chapter discusses the broad features of public and private partici-pation in the adult education and training system. This is defined to be all the channels for enhancing work-related skills available to individuals who have left the compulsory system and have entered the work-force. As such the chapter follows up on the analysis of the US primary and secondary education system provided in the 1994 Survey (OECD, 1994e). The first section of the chapter – "Labour market developments" – deals with trends in job creation, earnings, wage disparities and job turnover. The second section, entitled "The institutional framework for adult education and training", discusses the various organisations involved with education and training services, such as private and public univer-sities and colleges, firms and federal and state agencies. Section 3 discusses recent and proposed policy initiatives. Section 4 assesses both the performance of the system as a whole and the suitability of recent initiatives and proposals. It also identifies the scope for future action.

Labour market developments

This section focuses on two features of US labour markets that are related to economic security of working Americans and to the incentives underlying human capital accumulation. First, the evolution of real wages for various categories of worker is described. Second, trends in job turnover are discussed. Earnings and turnover trends are influenced by broader forces such as technological and organisational change, demographic evolution, immigration, globalisation of trade and investment flows, and ongoing change in the structure of demand for goods and services. These forces are so closely interlinked that the economics literature has not yet managed to disentangle the various contributions that each makes to labour market outcomes in any given period or place. Taken together, however, they appear to have generated shifts in wage and employment patterns that have strengthened the labour market positions of some workers, while weakening the positions of others. Much of the US training debate centres precisely on these distributional effects and, more particularly, on the fear that the economic security of many working people is being eroded.

The data discussed below show that this fear appears to be at least partially justified. The wages of workers on the lower half of the distribution have declined substantially over the last two decades, although the data are less conclusive regarding job security. Compensating in part for this somewhat sombre picture has been the accompanying process of rapid job creation. Table 14 presents data on job creation over the 1980s in different occupations for 13 Member countries. The United States experienced a comparatively high average annual growth rate of 1.6 per cent, with robust growth in both high-skill occupations (professional and managerial) and lower-skill occupations (sales and service workers). The only countries showing higher rates of job creation were Australia and Canada.

Although employment has grown dramatically, there is considerable concern about the quality of jobs created and about the possibility that the United States might be caught in a "low skills, bad jobs" trap (Snower, 1994). Some have even suggested that more restrictive labour market regulation and more centralised wage setting would improve labour market outcomes (Freeman, 1994). Looked at another way, though, the creation of so many jobs – not just in high technology and in well paid services, but also for the large population of poorly educated workers with low skills – could be considered a tribute to the flexibility of US markets and to the entrepreneurial skills of its business class. Responding to relative wage signals, they have identified the promising activities, implemented suitable technologies and marshalled the financial resources needed to employ the existing stock of workers and skills. According to this view, then, recent trends in wages and job creation reflect a market system that, in the course of equating labour supply and demand, has merely placed a price tag on the economic dimension of some deeply-rooted problems. Principal among these is an initial education system that is functioning very poorly for many communities.

Table 14. **The composition and growth of employment by occupation**

Annualised percentage change

ISCO-1968 Occupational groups	Australia 1979-90	Austria 1984-91	Belgium 1983-90	Canada 1979-90	France 1982-91	Germany 1980-91	Greece 1983-90	Ireland 1983-90	Japan 1979-90	Portugal 1983-91	Spain 1979-90	United Kingdom 1984-90	United States 1979-90
0/1. Professional, technical, etc.	4.3	2.7	3.0	2.9	2.2	2.8	4.0	1.5	4.5	5.5	5.4	3.7	3.0
2. Administrative and managerial	4.0	3.5	0.5	6.7	2.8	2.0	-0.9	0.3	0.8	10.1	2.4	2.3	3.8
3. Clerical and related workers	2.9	1.4	0.8	1.5	0.3	1.4	3.5	-0.5	2.3	2.8	2.7	1.7	1.3
4. Sales workers	2.6	1.2	0.1	1.0	0.9	1.4	3.0	1.3	1.7	2.9	1.4	1.5	2.6
5. Service workers	4.0	1.5	0.5	2.0	1.0	1.1	2.3	1.9	0.7	4.5	1.9	0.9	1.8
6. Agricultural workers, etc.	1.3	-2.6	0.3	-1.1	-3.4	-2.8	-2.4	-1.7	-2.7	-2.3	-3.8	-1.0	-0.6
7/8/9. Transport and production workers and labourers	0.7	0.5	-0.2	0.2	-0.9	-0.4	0.2	-0.6	0.7	0.6	0.2	-0.6	0.0
Total	2.4	1.1	0.8	1.7	0.3	0.9	0.7	0.0	1.2	1.4	0.7	1.3	1.6

Source: OECD (1994b).

As was shown in the 1994 Survey, the fact that large numbers of people exit from the initial system with substandard educations constitutes a failure of US human capital policy that has few, if any, parallels in the OECD area. This is not a new problem for American society,[115] but it would appear that the general economic forces mentioned above are making it a costlier one.

Wage growth and the distribution of income

Real wages have been stagnant from the early 1970s to the present, according to most measures of hourly and annual compensation for individual workers.[116] Both median and average real hourly wages have been roughly constant or slightly declining from 1973 to the present (Figure 33). Other measures of compensation, however, have followed somewhat different trends: real average annual earnings increased slightly, while average real hourly compensation (including health care benefits and employers' pension contributions) shows rapid growth throughout the seventies and eighties.

Figure 33. **GROWTH IN VARIOUS MEASURES OF REAL PAY**

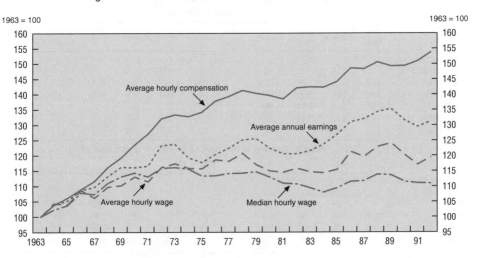

Note: CPI-U-X1 is used as the deflator.
Source: Economic Report of the President, 1995.

113

Growing wage disparities have been an important labour market development in the United States and in much of the OECD area since the 1970s (Table 15). The trend appears, however, to be more pronounced in the United States, where both workers with low educational attainment and younger workers experienced the least favourable relative wage evolution of any of their counterparts in 11 reporting countries. Over the last 20 years, then, the United States has shown a pronounced shift in relative wages against those without a college degree.[117] The bottom of the distribution has experienced the steepest decline in wages. This occurred for male high school drop-outs, whose average real wage fell 27 per cent during the 1973 to 1993 period, from $11.85 to $8.64 in 1993 dollars (Figure 34). Trends for women show a similar but less extreme widening in the college wage premium, and women have fared relatively better in labour markets than men since the 1970s. Another notable development of the 1980s was the widening (after two decades of narrowing) of the wage gap between black and white males (Saunders, 1995).

Table 15. **Earnings differentials by education and by age**

Panel A: Earnings of university-educated men relative to men with lower secondary education or less

Late 1970s = 100[1]

	Aus-tralia	Canada	Den-mark	France	Ger-many	Italy	Japan	Norway	Sweden	United Kingdom	United States
Early 1970s	..	124	..	91	..	..	102	..	..	..	..
Mid-1970s	109	..	..	..	..	109	..	..	123	108	99
Late 1970s	100	100	100	100	100	100	100	100	100	100	100
Mid-1980s	91	..	101	90	..	105	..	..	..	..	..
Late 1980s	96	112	102	..	97	103	105	92	115	111	120
Early 1990s	..	123	..	..	..	101	105	94	113	121	127

Panel B: Earnings of men aged 15-24 relative to men aged 25-54[2]

1980 = 100

	Aus-tralia	Canada	Den-mark	France	Ger-many	Italy	Japan	Norway	Sweden	United Kingdom	United States
1970	..	98	..	107	..	..	103	..	90	97	114
1975	..	95	..	103	..	..	107	..	99	103	105
1980	100	100	100	100	..	100	100	100	100	100	100
1985	96	86	99	95	..	95	98	..	100	92	89
1990	95	82	96	..	..	105	97	84	103	89	90

1. Early 1980s for Germany, Norway and Sweden.
2. Earnings for both sexes for France and Sweden.
Source: OECD (1994b).

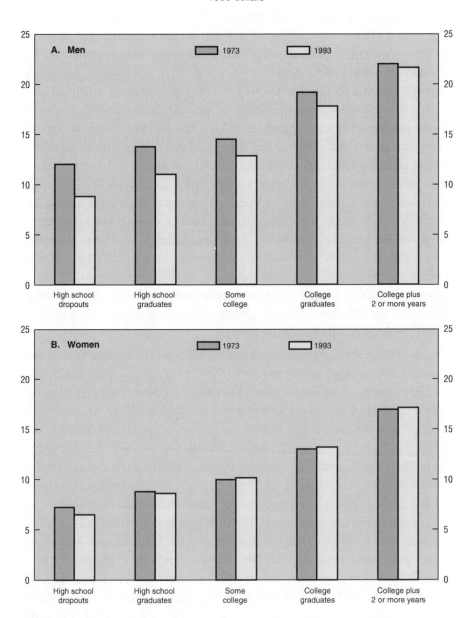

Figure 34. **REAL HOURLY WAGES BY LEVEL OF EDUCATION**

1993 dollars

Source: *Economic Report of the President*, 1995.

115

Training and job turnover

Job turnover is relevant to the training debate in two ways. First, it provides (incomplete) evidence on whether or not job security has, in fact, declined in recent years. Second, it both influences and reflects the training incentives facing various labour market participants; more specifically, low turnover increases the incentives for firms to provide training, while high turnover will tend to shift incentives toward individual acquisition of general skills. Empirical studies of trends in job turnover have produced mixed results. For example, one study estimates retention rates using survey data and finds "approximate stability" in these rates over the 1980s (Diebold *et al.*, 1994). However, there were declines in relative job stability[118] for the same groups that experienced declining relative wages, notably blacks and youth. College graduates experienced slightly higher job stability. Only the deterioration of job stability among black workers was found to be statistically significant, however. Using a different data source, another study (Rose, 1995) comparing job turnover in the 1970s and 1980s finds slight declines in job tenure for most categories of worker during the 1980s. None of these studies show whether observed tenure patterns reflect stable patterns of separation of workers from firms or, alternatively, whether separations are somehow less "voluntary" now than in the past.

Viewed from a comparative perspective, US job turnover appears to be high or, equivalently, average job tenure low. Table 16 shows average job tenure for ten OECD countries. The United States has one of the lowest average tenures – at 6.7 years in 1991. The only country showing faster turnover in some years is Australia.[119] On the whole, the differences between the United States and such countries as Canada, Australia, the United Kingdom and, increasingly, the Netherlands, are quite small. In contrast, the gaps between US average tenure and that of Japan (its average tenure of 10.9 years in 1991), Germany (10.4 years in 1991) and France (10.1 years), were large. While the United States shows lower tenure for all categories of workers, the differences are particularly marked for young adults (15 to 24 years old). Comparison of the United States and Japan, for example, shows that turnover rates for this age group are high relative to older workers in the United States and relative to the same cohort in Japan (Figure 35). These data point to basic differences in the functioning of these countries' industrial relations systems and labour market policies and probably also reflect differences in the sectoral orientation of economic activity.

Table 16. **Workers with tenure under one year and average tenure**

Wage and salary employment

	1979		1985		1989		1991	
	Tenure < 1 year (%)	Average tenure (years)	Tenure < 1 year (%)	Average tenure (years)	Tenure < 1 year (%)	Average tenure (years)	Tenure < 1 year (%)	Average tenure (years)
Australia[1]	22.3	6.5	22.9	6.6	27.9	6.5	21.4	6.8
Canada[1]	26.2	7.3	26.6[5]	7.6[5]	27.3	7.4	23.5	7.8
Finland	17.0	7.8	18.4	8.4	22.2	8.0	11.9	9.0
France	–	–	13.1[5]	10.7[5]	–	–	15.7	10.1
Germany	–	–	8.5[4]	11.1[4]	18.2	10.3	12.8[7]	10.4[7]
Japan	10.6	8.9	9.4	10.3	9.4	10.8	9.8[7]	10.9[7]
Netherlands	–	–	11.7	8.9	–	–	24.0[7]	7.0[7]
Spain[1]	–	–	15.2[6]	11.2[6]	–	–	23.9[8]	9.8[8]
United Kingdom	–	–	18.0[5]	8.3[5]	21.5	7.8	18.6	7.9
United States	29.3[2]	6.4[2]	28.9[3]	6.7[3]	29.7[6]	6.8[6]	28.8	6.7

1. Total employment growth is used because tenure data include self-employment.
2. 1978.
3. 1983.
4. 1984.
5. 1986.
6. 1987.
7. 1990.
8. 1992.
Source: OECD (1993b).

Figure 35. **DURATION OF JOB TENURE BY AGE GROUP**
Japan and the United States
Per cent

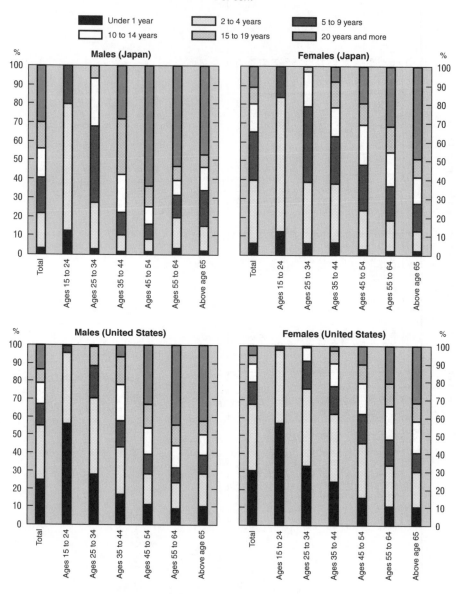

Source: *Economic Survey of Japan*, Economic Planning Agency 1991-92.

Thus, the data on turnover rates and job tenure point to a great deal of movement in the US economy. Less well documented are the microeconomic incentives and constraints underpinning this movement. Comparative data indicate that US workers have a relatively high propensity to move from one region to another (Table 17). Eichengreen (1993) estimates, for example, that the elasticity of internal migration with respect to wage levels is at least five times greater in the United States than in Great Britain or Italy. This openness (or at least lack of resistance) to geographic mobility is probably influenced by cultural and economic characteristics that tend to lower the monetary and psychological costs of such moves.[120] Other features of the US labour market also tend to increase turnover in the United States relative to other Member countries. Unlike some continental European countries, the United States imposes relatively few constraints on employers' ability to dismiss workers. Unlike Japan, whose labour markets are also largely unregulated, there are few socially-enforced constraints on worker mobility or on poaching. Japanese managers reinforce these social constraints with various management techniques in order to retain employees. These include defining clear and attractive career paths, seniority pay and job rotation within industrial groups.[121]

Although US firms are subject to few external constraints on how they manage employee turnover, they can, and often do, replace regulatory and social controls on turnover with private, contractual ones. Keltner (1994) found, for example, that one US bank was able to attain much lower turnover rates (averaging only 8 per cent per year, as compared to 22 per cent average for all banks) by offering employees greater employment security, pay tied to firm performance, more input into corporate decision making and opportunities for ongoing training and learning. Other companies seek to retain their highly skilled employees through stock options that can only be exercised if the person is employed more than a certain period of time. Retirement plans are frequently structured so as to reduce turnover. There are many examples of firms that have been able to reduce turnover for parts or all of their workforces by locating in areas where the potential for poaching is low (Finegold, 1995). Thus, many US firms could reduce turnover if they chose to do so, and many presumably do reduce it for certain employees (those for whom they feel there will be a pay-off to building up intangible relationship-specific capital). But many firms have apparently decided that the costs of investing in such long-term relationships in the US

Table 17. **Internal migration in selected OECD countries**

Persons who changed region of residence in percentage of total population[1]

	Australia	Canada	Finland	France	Germany	Italy	Japan	Norway	Sweden	United Kingdom	United States
1970	1.7	1.9	2.5	..	1.8	1.1	4.1	3.8	..	..	3.6
1971	1.9	1.9	1.7	..	1.8	1.1	4.0	3.1	..	..	3.4
1972	1.8	1.8	2.1	..	1.7	1.1	3.9	3.0	..	..	..
1973	1.9	1.8	2.3	..	1.7	1.0	3.9	3.0	4.8	..	..
1974	1.6	2.0	2.5	..	1.5	0.9	3.6	3.0	4.9	..	..
1975	..	1.8	..	..	1.3	0.8	3.3	2.9	4.8	1.2	..
1976	1.6	1.6	1.8	..	1.3	0.8	3.2	2.7	4.5	..	3.0
1977	1.7	1.7	1.5	..	1.3	0.7	3.1	..	4.0	1.0	..
1978	1.9	1.7	1.4	..	1.3	0.7	3.0	2.7	3.7	..	..
1979	1.7	1.7	1.5	..	1.3	0.7	3.0	2.6	3.9	1.2	..
1980	1.8	1.7	1.6	..	1.3	0.7	2.9	2.7	4.0	..	..
1981	1.8	1.8	1.5	..	1.3	0.7	..	2.6	3.5	1.1	2.8
1982	1.9	1.8	1.5	..	1.2	0.7	2.8	2.5	3.4	..	3.0
1983	1.5	1.5	1.5	..	1.1	0.6	2.7	2.5	3.4	0.9	2.7
1984	1.5	1.6	..	1.4	1.0	0.6	2.6	2.4	3.7	1.1	2.8
1985	1.6	1.5	1.6	1.2	1.0	0.6	2.6	2.4	3.9	1.2	3.0
1986	1.6	1.5	1.5	1.3	1.1	0.6	2.6	2.5	4.0	1.1	3.0
1987	1.6	1.5	1.6	1.3	1.1	0.5	2.6	2.6	3.9	..	2.8

1. Population 15 years old and over for Australia and the United Kingdom. Data exclude persons who changed country of residence.
Source: OECD (1994b).

environment outweigh the benefits. Similarly, workers themselves may be reluctant to invest in firm-specific skills if the employment relationship can be easily broken.

In summary, then, international comparisons of job tenure show that the average length of job tenure is significantly lower in the United States than in many other OECD countries. Attaching any normative significance to this characteristic, however, is not an easy matter. This is because, as noted, job tenure reflects more deeply embedded social and economic characteristics – the propensity toward mobility, for example – whose origins reside only partly in the labour market. Furthermore, while high turnover may be a distinct liability in sectors that require the gradual accumulation of firm- or activity-specific knowledge, it can be an advantage in others. More precisely, some activities – particularly in fast moving sectors producing once-off products – could benefit from the ability to create and then dissolve purpose-built teams of workers. What does seem clear is that higher labour market mobility will tend to shift the training and education mix away from company-sponsored provision of firm-specific skills and toward individual initiatives to acquire training in portable skills. As the following section shows, this is indeed the training pattern that is observed in the United States.

The institutional framework for adult education and training

Numerous institutional channels are available for imparting or upgrading the knowledge needed to engage in various productive activities. The relative importance of these channels differs by sector and by occupation. Agriculture, for example, has traditionally relied on inter-generational transmission of farming knowledge and on extensive learning by doing; formal levels of educational attainment tended to be low relative to other occupations (OECD, 1994d). But, with increased professionalisation of the sector, today's farm operator is twice as likely to have some college education as his predecessors of the mid-1970s (Ilg, 1995). Likewise, the computer industry, with its rapid turnover of technologies, has exhibited shifts in mix between learning-by-doing, informal sharing of information between colleagues, formal company training and university or college courses. IBM, for example, first developed the FORTRAN computer language and then taught it to its employees and customers. Colleges and universities began offering courses in FORTRAN and eventually took over most teaching of this skill (Bishop, 1994). More recently, as special-purpose languages have grown increasingly common, training in these languages has tended to be provided by vendors or to occur through learning-by-doing and self-teaching. Each of these training channels has its own inherent advantages and disadvantages, and the dynamics of the training sector reflect the ongoing competition between them in different market settings.

Over many decades, the formal tertiary sector has consolidated its hold on many types of training in many professions. Often, the long-term movement of training – especially of qualifying training and of retraining[122] – away from the work site and into formal institutions of higher education reflects these institutions' competitive advantage in some areas. The shift of training functions to universities, colleges and specialised institutes can be a natural part of the life cycle of a technology and its associated skills. As a technology matures and its use grows, the technology-related skills become standardised (*i.e.* the skill becomes general rather than firm-specific), the demand for formal training grows and formal tertiary institutions enter the market as training providers (Bishop, 1994). Once skills become standardised, colleges, training institutes and universities have natural advantages as competitors in this market: they offer students flexibility in scheduling and the choice of courses; hourly costs of training are lower because teaching staff are specialised and because economies result from spreading the cost of developing courses over many students. Even very large enterprises often do not have a sufficient flow of trainees requiring instruction in a particular subject to warrant developing in-house the expertise necessary to teach that subject.

School-based training is not, however, a perfect substitute for some kinds of employer-provided training and is generally less effective than employer-provided training in the same skills (Bishop, 1994). There are a number of advantages to locating skill training at firms rather than at schools. Sometimes training in a skill can only be organised by the employer. This is obviously the case when skills are specific to the firm. But even general skills are often easier to learn when they are integrated into a training programme that is specific to the context of a particular firm. Often, employer-provided training is more effective than school-based training because it has a higher probability of actually being used.

For example, only 43 per cent of the employed graduates of vocational training programmes who had been out of school between one and ten years had a training-related job (broadly defined) in the 1985 National Longitudinal Survey of Youth (Bishop, 1994). Other studies of high school vocational education using the same methodology obtain similar results. When, on the other hand, employers are heavily involved in providing occupational training, it is much more likely to be used. Mangum and Ball (1986) found that employer-controlled training institutions have much higher training-related placement rates. When training fields were matched to occupations, they found that the proportion of male graduates who had at least one job in a related field was 85 per cent for company training and 71 per cent for apprenticeship training, but only 52 per cent for vocational-technical institutes and 22 per cent for proprietary business colleges.

Thus, all these training channels – specialised institutions such as universities, in-firm formal training, informal on-the-job training, learning-by-doing, or even self teaching – may be used as substitutes for one another, although they are often highly imperfect substitutes. Responding to market pressures these channels have evolved over the last several decades, and this has led to two main developments. First, formal education has tended to move beyond the traditional youth market and to become more spread out over the life cycle. Thus, part-time involvement in education is quite significant, even for workers who are well past the usual age for school enrolment. This can be seen in Table 18. The age group most likely to have taken at least one course during 1991 was the 35 to 44 year-olds, among whom 44 per cent reported taking at least one course during the year. Most of these reported that they were taking the course for career advancement (66 per cent) or to retrain for a new job (8 per cent) (US Bureau of the Census, 1994). One-third of the young adults (17 to 24 years old) reported having taken one or more classes during 1991. The table also points to a second important trend in adult education. Of the 32 per cent of the total adult population that participated in coursework in 1991, 64 per cent reported some type of employer involvement, but only 32 per cent said that they took a course at the place of work. Thus, employers are relying on formal training institutions to provide large parts of their training. A growing tendency is for employers to contract out for tailor-made training programmes with formal education and training institutions. This has tended to blur the boundaries between firm-provided training and training provided by formal education institutions.[123]

Table 18. **Participation and employer involvement in adult education** [1]

17 years old and older, by selected characteristics of participants: 1991

Characteristics of participants	Adult education participants in the past year		Type of employer involvement (per cent of adult education participants)					
	In thousands	Per cent of population	Any type	Given at place of work	Employer paid some portion	Employer provided course	Employer required course	Employer provided time off
Total	57 391	32	64	32	51	38	30	48
Age								
17 to 24 years	7 125	33	54	28	39	36	26	39
25 to 34 years	17 530	37	68	31	55	40	36	50
35 to 44 years	17 083	44	70	35	56	40	30	53
45 to 54 years	8 107	32	71	39	59	44	32	55
55 to 64 years	4 516	23	64	30	48	36	27	45
65 years and over	3 031	10	18	8	12	9	9	12
Racial/ethnic group								
White, non-Hispanic	47 401	33	65	32	53	39	30	49
Black, non-Hispanic	4 586	23	59	36	48	41	38	44
Hispanic	4 032	29	58	30	39	33	31	43
Other races, non-Hispanic	1 371	29	56	28	36	30	20	40
Highest level of education completed								
Less than high school diploma	3 437	12	35	17	21	19	21	19
High school diploma	31 602	29	62	31	50	36	31	45
Associate degree	2 461	49	76	47	66	51	39	63
Bachelor's degree or higher	19 891	52	71	34	57	44	30	56
Labour force status								
In labour force	49 242	39	72	36	58	43	34	54
Employed	47 143	41	74	37	60	44	35	56
Unemployed	2 099	21	35	12	13	12	19	18
Not in labour force	8 149	14	16	7	11	9	8	10
Current occupation of employed persons								
Total professional	11 067	63	81	42	64	51	34	62
Executive, administrative and managerial	3 479	65	79	34	68	44	34	67

Table 18. **Participation and employer involvement in adult education** [1] *(cont'd)*

17 years old and older, by selected characteristics of participants: 1991

Characteristics of participants	Adult education participants in the past year		Type of employer involvement (per cent of adult education participants)					
	In thousands	Per cent of population	Any type	Given at place of work	Employer paid some portion	Employer provided course	Employer required course	Employer provided time off
Technical and related support	1 566	65	87	58	76	57	46	65
Sales workers	5 242	41	69	31	53	40	33	56
Administrative and clerical support	11 816	44	76	37	68	48	32	58
Service	5 081	28	67	34	49	37	41	48
Agriculture, forestry and fishing	257	10	63	22	29	11	23	56
Precision production, craft and repair	3 001	31	67	33	53	38	35	45
Machine operators, assemblers and inspectors	2 436	30	75	47	62	46	38	55
Transportation and materials moving	949	29	80	25	45	34	55	51
Handlers, equipment cleaners, helpers and labourers	587	22	84	34	57	55	53	66
Nonclassifiable, undetermined	1 662	27	24	17	22	19	15	13
Annual family income								
$10 000 or less	3 843	14	39	18	25	24	23	29
$10 001 to $15 000	3 178	21	52	27	37	24	27	37
$15 001 to $20 000	3 308	21	57	28	42	35	29	39
$20 001 to $25 000	4 063	25	67	34	46	37	34	48
$25 001 to $30 000	5 445	30	58	30	48	38	29	39
$30 001 to $40 000	9 043	35	68	35	57	43	35	50
$40 001 to $50 000	9 313	44	67	34	55	42	33	50
$50 001 to $75 000	11 235	46	72	35	61	43	32	58
More than $75 000	7 963	48	68	30	54	37	24	53

1. Adult education is defined as all non-full-time education activities such as part-time college attendance, classes or seminars given by employers, and classes taken for adult literacy purposes, or for recreation and enjoyment.
Source: US Department of Education (1993).

125

Public universities and non-profit private universities

The US system of formal adult education is a mixed public-private system offering a diverse array of services[124] to a diverse set of customers. Like primary and secondary education, the public adult education system is controlled – under arrangements that vary by state – by state and local governments. Generally, though, these arrangements give significant managerial autonomy to the institutions themselves. Thus, they are rarely, if ever, subject to the centralised control that characterises public universities in some other OECD countries (France, Germany and Italy, for example). The privately-owned part of the tertiary education sector is itself quite diverse. Most major private institutions have non-profit status, but numerous private technical institutes and colleges are run on a for-profit basis. Although the role of private organisations is extremely important, public institutions dominate the tertiary sector (at least numerically). They accounted for about 11 million of the total of 14.3 million fall enrolments in 1991 (US Department of Education, 1992) and for about 65 per cent of the total expenditure on tertiary education in 1992 (OECD, 1995a). This is somewhat below the OECD average of 80 per cent but is higher than the public share in the Netherlands, Japan, Belgium and the United Kingdom (Figure 36). The public share of total funding for the tertiary sector was 77.4 per cent in the United States, which is comparable to the public share in Japan but below the mean of 91.9 per cent calculated for ten reporting countries (OECD, 1995a).

These arrangements have led to lively competition between institutions of higher education. Colleges and universities compete with each other in many areas:[125] enrolling the best or the most students, hiring the most renowned professors, attracting "endowment funds" or other charitable contributions, producing the most prestigious research, entering into the most innovative or most profitable alliances with businesses. Responding to competitive pressures, the institutions have differentiated along lines of relative strengths: some attract students or produce research services with reference to a market that is national or international in scope; others specialise in meeting various local or regional needs; some cater to segments of the education market along ethnic, religious or gender lines; and some (especially public institutions) aim at the more price-sensitive segments of the market, while others offer costlier services.

This diversity shows up in an array of funding patterns of the tertiary sector. For example, private institutions in the 1989-90 academic year received very

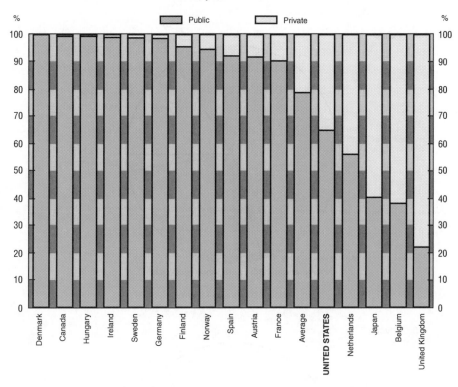

Figure 36. **EXPENDITURE OF PUBLIC AND PRIVATE EDUCATIONAL INSTITUTIONS**

Tertiary education, 1992

Countries are ranked in order of decreasing expenditure share of public educational institutions.
Source: OECD, *Education at a Glance,* 1995.

large portions of their $51 billion of current funding from tuition and student fees and relatively less from the federal government and from state and local governments (Figure 37, Panel B). Public institutions, on the other hand, receive most of their roughly $89 billion dollars of current revenue from state governments (Figure 37, Panel A). Charitable contributions are another important revenue source for some institutions. The tax expenditure associated with the deductibility of charitable contributions was estimated to be worth about $1.6 billion in 1994,

Figure 37. **SOURCES OF CURRENT-FUND REVENUE FOR INSTITUTIONS OF HIGHER EDUCATION: 1990-91**

A. Public

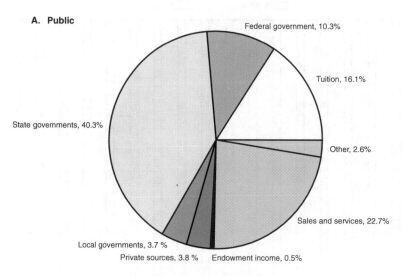

Total revenues = $94.9 billion

B. Private

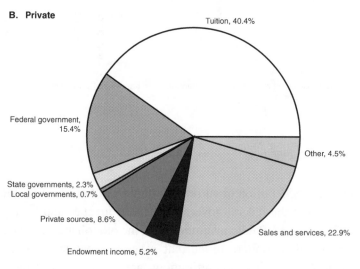

Total revenues = $54.9 billion

Source: *Digest of Educational Statistics,* 1993.

128

which is quite small in relation to the sector's roughly \$150 billion total revenue.[126]

A notable development in the sector over the last three decades is the emergence of community colleges. They have grown from 297 in 1949 to about 1 000 in 1990; their fall enrolment increased from 740 000 in 1963 to 4.9 million in 1990 (Finegold, 1995). Community colleges are public institutions that offer associate (two-year) degrees and shorter certificate programmes and are controlled in most states by local "districts".[127] They are also involved in delivery of federal and state training programmes and in providing specialised training services for local employers. Modelled neither on purely academic lines nor on traditional technical lines, these institutions offer, for example, certificate programmes in auto mechanics or refrigeration alongside courses in philosophy, mathematics and history. Following this strategy, they seem to have discovered an unusually successful niche by responding to the varied educations needs of their local communities. Recent analyses suggest that a full year's credits in community college programmes increases annual earnings by 5 to 15 per cent, which is similar to the earning impact of their four-year counterparts.[128]

Also competing in the "sub-baccalaureate"[129] market are for-profit private training institutes offering only occupational training. Although these institutions are private, some portion of their students' tuition fees are often paid by federal student loans or grant programmes (described below). Indeed, some of these institutions appear to have been created mainly in order to capture these programme benefits. Some offer high-quality training in specialised occupations that are often poorly served by the state sector (Karim and Patton, 1995). Many have been criticised, however, for excessive reliance on federal support, for the fact that many graduates from these schools default on their tuition loans and for the poor quality of services provided. Recent econometric analysis suggests that, despite these problems, the average individual who takes courses in proprietary institutions records significant wage gains[130] (Lynch, 1992).

A major problem in the market served by both community colleges and two-year technical institutes is the lack of reliable information about the quality of their programmes and about associated labour-market outcomes. This is not a problem for four-year colleges and universities, about which plentiful information is publicly available.[131] But in the sub-baccalaureate market potential employers, prospective students and government officials providing grants and loans find it difficult to determine the quality of these institutions' courses and the impact they have on graduates' careers. These information problems have been compounded by the absence of nationally recognised skill standards or qualifications in most industries and occupations. This makes it difficult for outsiders to assess exactly what skills have been mastered by graduates.

The array of colleges, universities and proprietary institutes have evolved in an environment where the wage incentives to acquire skills are apparent to many labour-market participants. The evolution of the system reflects the broader evolution of these incentives[132] (Mincer, 1994). The system seems to have responded effectively to the challenge of meeting the rapidly evolving training needs of the labour market, not only by allowing enrolments to expand and contract in response to shifting human capital premia, but also by offering the specific programmes required by employers and workers at various times and places. Naturally, the production of such services absorbs resources that need to be paid for. Tuition and fees have grown rapidly since the 1970s, and have involved increases in the cost of private education relative to public education and of four-year colleges relative to two-year institutions (Table 19).

Table 19. **Average undergraduate tuition and fees: 1976-77 to 1992-93**

By type and control of institution (in dollars)

Year and control of institution	All institutions	Tuition and required fees (in-state)			2-year
		4-year institutions			
		All 4-year	Universities	Other 4-year	
Public institutions					
1976-77	479	617	689	564	283
1980-81	635	804	915	722	391
1985-86[1]	1 045	1 318	1 536	1 157	641
1990-91	1 454	1 888	2 159	1 707	824
1992-93[2]	1 787	2 352	2 610	2 190	1 018
Private institutions					
1976-77	2 467	2 534	3 051	2 351	1 592
1980-81	3 498	3 617	4 275	3 390	2 413
1985-86[1]	5 789	6 121	7 374	5 641	3 672
1990-91	8 772	9 083	11 379	8 389	5 570
1992-93[2]	10 031	10 393	13 043	9 636	6 101

1. Room and board data are estimated.
2. Preliminary data based on fall 1991 enrolment weights.
Source: US Department of Education (1993).

Although the federal government does not directly control the tertiary education sector, it nevertheless plays an important financial role in it. In addition to purchasing research services from universities, it operates programmes that extend grants and loans to students. Under these programmes, annual awards worth many billions of dollars have been distributed in recent years (Table 20). This is obviously very large in relation to the total revenues from tuition and fees of roughly $37 billion in 1990. Table 20 shows how this is allocated between the various grant and loan programmes. The Pell grants mentioned in Table 20 provide aid to financially-needy undergraduate students to meet the costs of post-secondary education. The Perkins loan programme authorises the federal government to make capital contributions to qualifying institutions, which then make long-term low interest loans to eligible students with demonstrated need. Under the work study programme, federal grants are awarded to qualifying tertiary institutions, which then develop and provide part-time jobs for students with demonstrated need. Stafford loans are government-backed loans made to students by commercial lenders.[133] Defaults on these loans reached almost 13 per cent of the annual outlay for the Stafford loans in 1992. High default rates and the interest rate subsidies mean that the average federal cost per $1 000 of Stafford programme lending was $400 in 1989 (Congressional Budget Office, 1991). In order to reduce such costs, in 1994 the Department of Education initiated a Direct Student Loan Programme that, in effect, eliminates the role of banks in extending student loans. Under the programme, the Department makes the loan directly and contracts out for loan processing services on a competitive basis. The Department of Education is also strengthening its oversight of tertiary institutions and insisting that they meet stringent requirements before being eligible to participate in Federal student aid programmes.

Thus, the amount of subsidy in the system – although difficult to measure precisely – appears to be substantial. The states and the federal government offer various scholarship and student loan programmes as well as tax incentives. Many types of services, especially in the public sector, are priced below the cost of production. Given all of these subsidies, how accessible (from a financial point of view) are colleges and universities to most students? Table 21 shows that, on average, low-income students or their families bear 38 per cent of the cost at the average public institutions, 36 per cent at the average private institutions and about 31 per cent of the cost at a high-cost private institution. This is lower than

Table 20. **Major federal student financial assistance programmes**

	1970	1980	1985	1988	1989	1990	1991 Estimates	1992 Estimates	1993 Estimates
Pell grants									
Number of recipients (1 000)	..	2 708	2 813	3 198	3 322	3 405	3 786	4 171	4 300
Funds utilised ($ million)	..	2 387	3 597	4 476	4 778	4 935	5 793	6 303	6 099
Average grant (dollars)	..	882	1 279	1 399	1 438	1 449	1 530	1 511	1 418
Supplemental educational opportunity grants									
Number of recipients (1 000)	253.4	716.5	686.0	678.8	727.6	761.2	881.3	907.0	908.0
Funds utilised ($ million)	134	368	410	423	466	503	586	648	663
Average grant (dollars)	527	513	598	621	641	661	665	715	730
Perkins loans									
Number of recipients (1 000)	452.0	813.4	700.9	692.1	695.9	660.2	654.2	699.0	571.0
Funds utilised ($ million)	241	694	703	874	903	870	868	873	720
Average grant (dollars)	532	853	1 003	1 262	1 297	1 318	1 326	1 250	1 261
Loans in default ($ million)	n.a.	612.0	690.0	749.8	741.1	727.5	n.a.	n.a.	n.a.
Default rate (per cent)	n.a.	11.6	8.3	7.3	6.8	6.2	n.a.	n.a.	n.a.
College work-study									
Number of recipients (1 000)	425.0	819.1	728.4	672.7	676.7	687.4	697.3	812.0	813.0
Funds utilised ($ million)	200	660	656	625	664	728	760	808	813
Average annual earnings (dollars)	470	806	901	930	980	1 059	1 090	995	1 000
Stafford loans									
Number of recipients (1 000)	1 017	2 905	3 730	4 584	4 558	4 587	4 403	4 677	5 551
Funds utilised ($ million)	1 015	6 200	8 839	11 965	12 166	12 669	12 336	13 427	16 425
Average grant (dollars)	998	2 135	2 369	2 610	2 669	2 762	2 802	2 871	2 959
Loans in default ($ million)	n.a.	1 440	4 256	8 417	10 454	13 134	16 373	19 452	n.a.
Default rate (per cent)	n.a.	10.1	8.9	9.2	9.6	10.4	11.6	12.9	n.a.
Total awards	1 590	10 309	14 205	18 363	18 977	19 705	20 343	22 059	24 720

n.a.: not available.
Source: US Bureau of the Census (1994).

Table 21. **Estimated costs and funding sources for higher education in five countries**[1]

	Annual cost (dollars)	Share of total costs borne (percentage)					
		Low income			Middle income		
		Family	Public	Institution	Family	Public	Institution
Britain	3 280	6	94	0	71	29	0
West Germany	4 398	42	58	0	86	14	0
France	2 016	17	83	0	85	15	0
Sweden	4 217	55	45	0	62	38	0
United States							
Average public	5 314	38	62	0	89	11	0
Average private	9 659	36	47	18	65	19	17
High-cost private	15 000	31	33	36	51	15	33

1. Family share includes contributions by students and parents.
Source: Clotfelter, C.T. *et al.* (1991).

the proportion of costs borne by such students in Sweden and West Germany, but higher than in Britain or France. However, because tuition is higher in the United States than in an any of the European countries shown in the table, the actual outlay by families tends to be quite high. Despite the widespread availability of tuition subsidies, the public institutions continue to play an important role in providing services whose cost is within the reach of large proportions of low- and middle-income families.

In-company training

Although data on in-firm training expenditure are scarce, US companies appear to spend about $40 to $50 billion annually on formal training. Since firms do not generally conduct controlled experiments as to the efficiency of their training programmes, reliable estimates of the returns to in-firm training are not available. Table 22 provides sectoral data on the incidence of formal training by tenure for the United States and for five other OECD member countries. Formal training appears to be relatively low in the United States, especially for employees with low tenure. For longer-tenure employees, the US formal training incidence is comparable with those of the Netherlands and Norway. But Japanese employers provide much more training than any country in the list, and the

Table 22. **Incidence of formal enterprise training by tenure with current employer**

Percentages of employment

Tenure intervals	Australia 1989[1] In-house training courses during previous year	Finland 1989[2] Formal company training courses during previous year	Japan 1991[3] Formal company training since joining the firm	Netherlands 1990 Formal company training course during previous two years	Norway 1989[4] Formal company paid-for training during previous year	United States 1991 Formal company training since joining the firm
0 to 1 year	27.4	24.3	79.3	19.1	21.3	8.4
2 years	25.5	38.6	–	24.1	–	14.8
3 years	36.7	43.6	–	28.6	33.2	15.8
4 years	–	46.6	–	20.7	–	16.5
5 years	37.8	–	–	21.0	–	18.1
0 to 5 years	32.8	–	76.2	22.1	32.1	12.5
6 to 9 years	40.2	49.9	74.1	29.0	37.8	22.4
10 to 14 years	–	49.3	75.2	29.5	33.7	23.4
15 to 19 years	39.4	53.0	–	29.7	37.0	24.8
20 years and over	36.4	51.4	–	23.3	28.6	26.2

1. Tenure categories are less than 1 year, 1 to less than 2 years, 2 to less than 3 years, 3 to less than 5 years, 5 to less than 10 years, 10 to less than 20 years, and 20 years and over.
2. Tenure categories are less than 1 year, 1 year, 2 years, 3 to 4 years, 5 to less than 10 years, 10 to less than 15 years, 15 to less than 20 years, and 20 years and over.
3. Tenure categories are less than 1 year, 1 to less than 3 years, 3 to less than 10 years, and 10 years and over.
4. The two first tenure categories refer to less than 9 months, and from 9 months to less than 5 years.
Source: OECD (1993*b*).

incidence of formal training for new recruits (tenure of less than one year) is almost ten times larger than in the United States.

The incidence of training also depends very much on establishment size. One survey shows that only 45.8 per cent of firms with fewer than 50 employees offer any formal training, compared with 85.8 per cent of mid-sized establishments and 95.9 per cent of large firms (Table 23). The most commonly type of training is managerial (48.6 per cent of establishments provided this), followed by sales and customers relations skills (28.1 per cent) and by computer skills

Table 23. **Formal enterprise training by establishment size, 1993**

Characteristic	Total	Fewer than 50 employees	50 to 249 employees	250 or more employees
All establishments (thousands)	4 501	4 198	257	46
All establishments that provided any formal job skills training:				
Number (thousands)	2 188	1 923	220	44
Per cent	48.6	45.8	85.8	95.9
Per cent of all establishments by type of formal job skills training: [1]				
Management skills	24.4	21.1	66.7	85.6
Professional and technical skills	18.5	17.2	33.8	53.9
Computer skills	25.7	23.1	58.1	82.6
Sales and customer relations skills	28.1	25.8	57.7	71.1
Clerical and administrative support skills	16.9	15.1	38.9	61.1
Food, cleaning, protective, or personal service skills	8.4	7.2	25.2	27.6
Production-related activities	17.4	15.7	38.1	58.4
Other formal job skills	8.0	7.2	17.3	23.3
Per cent, by reason:				
To provide skills specific to establishment	75.0	73.4	86.8	87.2
To help retain valuable employees	52.6	50.1	69.8	75.8
To upgrade employee skills in response to changes in technology, production methods, or both	53.4	51.7	63.5	78.3
Inability to hire employees with adequate skills	13.0	12.9	12.4	18.7
Requirement of law or regulation	24.6	22.7	37.5	43.6
Requirement by collective bargaining agreement	1.4	1.1	3.0	9.6
Other reasons	6.5	6.7	4.5	6.5

1. Respondents could choose more than one category.
Source: Frazis, Herz and Horrigan (1995).

(25.7 per cent). The most frequently-cited reason for offering skills training was "to provide skills specific to the establishment" (75 per cent), followed by the need "to upgrade employee skills in response to changes in technology or production methods" (53.4 per cent). The question of which workers receive formal training has also been thoroughly researched in the United States. As can be seen by referring back to Table 18, the incidence of training varies markedly by worker characteristic. The workers who are most likely to obtain firm-sponsored training have high formal educational attainment, are between the ages of 25 and 54 years, are white and are already earning relatively high salaries. Therefore, firm-sponsored training plays a highly variable role in the human capital development of the US workforce, but it also tends to reinforce initial inequalities.

Thus, firm-sponsored general training is less important in the United States than in some other countries and tends to be focused on workers that already have high skills. It is reasonable to ask whether training practices in other countries with different training outcomes contain any useful lessons for the United States. The German dual system – under which the employer plays a major role in the training process – is particularly interesting in this respect. Naturally, though, since circumstances are so different in the two countries, any lessons must be drawn cautiously. Nevertheless, the German system embodies at least two ideas that may be loosely applicable in the US environment. The first is the recognition of the usefulness of bringing together the relevant parties – businesses, worker representatives, educators and others – to invest in the "infrastructure" of training (although the exact institutional mechanisms by which this accomplished could probably not be duplicated on a large scale in the United States). In Germany, centralised employee representatives and employer associations (notably chambers of commerce and industry, in which membership is compulsory) co-operate to ensure that employee skills are of high quality and nationally standardised. Americans seem to be either less willing or less able to organise themselves into what might be viewed as "clubs" for the purpose of making such decisions jointly.[134] At the present time, there is no national system for standards setting, although work on creation of voluntary national standards is underway (see below). Current standards-setting processes bring together professional societies, state governments, educators, accreditation groups and individual businesses in ways that vary by occupational group and by region. Although the lack of nation-wide occupational training infrastructure is a problem in the United States, its impact is not evenly felt in all sectors.[135] German-style consensual decision making on standards and credentials is of relevance mainly to those occupations where there is a significant economic return to high-quality portable skills and where the skills themselves evolve rather slowly. The slow evolution of skills is necessary to ensure that the standards are not rendered obsolete before they are defined or before the cost of developing them can be recovered.[136]

The second idea that may be applicable to the United States is the special training wage provided for in German wage-setting institutions. This has permitted a rather successful solution to the problem of financing general training. Such problems arise because households, especially those headed by younger workers, may face binding liquidity constraints.[137] Firms generally have better access to capital markets, which means that they are better placed to finance general training than most young people. The training wage arrangement is tantamount to the firm providing a loan to pay for what are often very expensive training services. The loan is then amortised through below-market wages for a given period of time. Obviously the risks for the firm associated with this arrangement tend to increase when, as in the United States, the rate of employee turnover is high. But, the fact that firms are able to offer what amounts to a low-cost financial service to their workers increases firms' ''share'' of the training market in general competences. This may already occur in the United States, especially on the higher-wage end of the market, but could be constrained from below by minimum wage laws. The extent to which such an arrangement could actually be used in the United States is unclear, however. First, the mobility of American workers raises the costs of such an arrangement for firms. Second, as was just discussed, the government has created subsidised channels for financing general training and adult education, which tends to decrease firms' share of this service.

When pointing out the relevance of the German dual system for the United States, it is worth noting that some of the lessons might run in the other direction. In particular, the dominance of firm-provided training in Germany reflects not only the genuine strengths of the dual system, but also certain weaknesses of German universities and colleges in the occupational field. The US university and college system, with its highly decentralised control, strong competition and heavy use of market testing of services in public universities, could be a more suitable model for adult education than the dual system for certain sectors or occupations. In some very dynamic sectors or occupations, the consensual decision-making needed to co-ordinate decisions among many market participants – a key feature of the dual system – is probably too slow to be viable.

Federal government training programmes

The federal government will spend approximately $20 billion in 1995 on work-related education and training (General Accounting Office, 1995). It specialises mainly in programmes that target disadvantaged groups. Most of these initiatives are concentrated in the Departments of Education (61 programmes) and Labor (37 programmes), but overall there are more than 100 separate programmes administered by 15 separate agencies[138] (General Accounting Office, 1995). This multiplicity of training programmes has developed over time in response to the perceived need to tailor services to the diversity of training needs. A partial list of the specific "niches" covered by federal programmes includes disabled people, Native Americans, veterans, minority and women's business development, migrant and seasonal workers, and disadvantaged youth. The major legislative programmes that make up this federal effort are described in Box 5.

Many federal employment training programmes target overlapping populations. One study (General Accounting Office, 1994a) found that the overlap ranged from a low of four programmes, each serving refugees and older people, to a high of 18 programmes serving veterans. When looked at individually, each training programme generally has a well-defined and reasonable purpose (and, indeed, targeting programme services on the needs of specific groups is important for the effective functioning of active labour market policies (OECD, 1994b). However, this multitude of programmes creates the potential for duplication of effort and for raising the programmes' administrative costs.

Services financed by the federal government and delivered by state and local agencies include counselling and assessment; remedial education; vocational skills training; and placement assistance. In recent years, many of the agencies responsible for these services have not collected information on participant outcomes nor do they generally conduct studies of programme effectiveness.[139] As a result they do not know whether their programmes help participants to get jobs or, more generally, to improve their long-term career prospects. The reasons that so little outcome analysis is performed are probably two-fold. First, one of the fundamental precepts of the Job Training Partnership Act (see Box 5) was

Box 5. Major federal training and employment programmes

Many federal departments operate training services. Most federal activities for training and employment are financed through grants to states. The states, in turn, provide such services as training and educating economically disadvantaged youths and adults, helping displaced workers find new employment, sponsoring subsidised jobs and training or remediation for youth in the summer; and operating the Employment Service. In a limited number of cases (*e.g.* Job Corps), the federal government contracts out with individual service centres for the provision of other job training programmes.

Job Training Partnership Act. The main piece of legislation under which federal training takes place is the Job Training Partnership Act (JTPA). Programme expenditure this year is projected to be $5 billion and more than 300 000 people are expected to receive services. Under the Act, states control the use of most of the funds. In each state and locality, the private sector – through the "Private Industry Councils" – is heavily involved in planning and carrying out the programmes. The primary JTPA programme is a block grant that provides states and localities with discretion to design programmes within broad federal guidelines. Activities are designed in conjunction with the Employment Service, educational institutions, and other service providers to prepare individuals for jobs in the local areas. Although few restrictions are placed on the states and localities, JTPA requires that at least 70 per cent of the grant be used for training and 90 per cent of the participants must be economically disadvantaged. At least 40 per cent of the resources must be spent for youth, and welfare recipients must be served on an equitable basis.

Job Corps. The Job Corps is a JTPA programme that provides disadvantaged youth with remedial education and job skills training in residential centres. It also provides meals, lodging, recreation, medical care, and living and readjustment allowances. Funded at nearly $1.1 billion in 1995, it is one of the Federal government's largest programmes for low income youth between the ages of 16 and 24. At an estimated cost of $23 000 per student, the Job Corps is the most costly domestic job training programme financed by the federal government. It serves about 60 000 young people per year. Although it has not yet been subject to rigorous evaluation, the Job Corps is widely believed to be the only federal youth programme to have impacts that approach the effects of high school vocational education in terms of raising participants' earnings and improving their career prospects (Bishop, 1994).

Assistance to Dislocated Workers. Two programmes are available to help displaced workers. The Economic Dislocation and Worker Adjustment Assistance Act (EDWAA) requires each state to designate an agency that can respond rapidly to major layoffs and plant closures. In addition, EDWAA establishes a sub-state service delivery system similar to the other JTPA programmes and authorises funds for rapid response assistance, basic readjustment and support services, retraining services, needs-related payments, and the promotion of labour-management committees to assist in transition activities during a plant or facility closure. The programme is funded at $1.2 billion in 1995. Individuals

(continued on next page)

(continued)

eligible for assistance include those affected by layoffs or plant closings, unemployed persons who have exhausted their eligibility for unemployment compensation, the long-term unemployed, and self-employed persons, including farmers.

The second set of programmes for helping dislocated workers is trade adjustment assistance (TAA), funded at $381 million in 1995. This programme provides unemployment benefit payments for a period beyond that available from regular unemployment insurance. This aid is available only to workers who are determined to have been displaced from their jobs by imports. The programme has been extended recently to workers judged to have been adversely affected by NAFTA. TAA also pays for retraining workers whose skills are obsolete or for job search and relocation costs.

Federal-State Employment Services. Grants (worth $836 million in 1995) are made to state employment service agencies under a formula based on each state's share of the civilian labour force and of unemployed individuals. The employment service is a nation-wide system providing no-fee employment services to individuals who are seeking employment and employers who are seeking workers. Certain employment services designed to meet national needs are financed with grants under specific agreements with the state agencies. These national activities include special services for veterans and collection of general labour market statistics.

Summer Youth Employment. Under JTPA's summer youth employment programme, grants are made to states in the spring of each year to subsidise minimum-wage public sector jobs or so that academic enrichment programmes can be provided during the following summer for disadvantaged youth between the ages of 14 and 21.

devolution of programme control to the states. The devolution of accountability and programme control systems may have been seen as a logical extension of this general philosophy. Second, rigorous assessment of programmes outcomes requires random assignment[140] of thousands of applicants for programme services between a group that receives services and a "control" group that does not. Both groups of people must then be followed. This is costly and yields results only after several years.

Several conclusions can be drawn from the limited number of rigorous studies of this type that have been performed.[141] First, at least some services have been moderately successful (in the sense that they yielded income gains in excess of programme costs) for every population group examined. Some fairly inexpensive services – such as job placement assistance and counselling – seem to have rather large pay-offs for some groups of people, especially for displaced adult workers. Second, programmes are often successful for some population groups and not for others. For example, a random assignment study of a particular JTPA programme indicates that the programme raised the participants' earnings (over 18- and 30-month follow-up periods) of some groups (adults over the age of 22) but that for other groups – essentially youth between the ages of 16 and 21 – the programme produced no gains. For male youth, the programme resulted in statistically significant losses[142] in earnings over the 18-month follow-up and negligible impacts over the 30-month period (Abt Associates, 1994).

In reviewing these results, it appears that disadvantaged youth are the most difficult programme "niche" to serve. Indeed, the statistically significant negative returns found in the Abt study are startling. In youth programmes, however, it may not be advisable to focus exclusively on short-term earnings effects. A random assignment study of Jobstart (a JTPA-funded programme that offers basic education and training to disadvantaged high school drop-outs) shows that – while the programme had very weak impacts on earnings and employment over a four-year follow-up period – it had a strong impact on programme participants' educational attainment, roughly doubling the percentage obtaining the so-called "General Education Development (GED)"[143] certificate relative to the control group. Subsequent evaluation of the results shows that the people who earned the GED then used this degree as a means of forming stronger attachments to the labour market and had significantly higher earnings as a result (Cave and Bos, 1995). In this sense, Jobstart could be viewed as a success inasmuch as it gave significantly greater numbers of disadvantaged young people an entry-point into mainstream labour markets.[144]

In summary, the general impression left by these impact evaluations is that some programmes work for some groups of programme participants and that none (with the possible exception of Job Corps) can be said to have unambiguously strong, positive results. Even more troublesome from a policy design standpoint is the fact that little is understood about why some programmes work while others do not: How important are local economic conditions in determining whether a programme works? How dependent are programme outcomes on the mix of services provided? Despite the problems encountered, there are some grounds for optimism that successful programmes will be developed.[145]

Recent and proposed initiatives

Congress passed two major pieces of legislation related to education and training in 1994: "Goals 2000" and the "School-to-Work Opportunities Act". These were discussed extensively in the 1994 Survey. Goals 2000 seeks to improve the quality of the education system in a variety of ways, including the creation of "voluntary" national standards for initial education and for vocational skills. The "School-to-Work Opportunities Act" provides "seed money" to states and localities to plan and develop improved systems for preparing students for college and careers. The Act provides financial support for developing linkages between high school vocational studies and the vocational programmes offered in the tertiary sector (notably by community colleges). Last year's Survey pointed out that these pieces of legislation attempt to redress problems in the US education system, notably by moving forward on the gradual process of establishing national educational and skill standards and by improving the much-neglected vocational dimension of the secondary education system.

Under Goals 2000, the Departments of Education and Labor have continued to work on 22 pilot projects to develop voluntary skills standards covering some 19 major industrial areas. As of the end of 1994, skills standards had been completed for ten industrial areas ranging from agricultural biotechnology to retail trade. The National Skill Standards Act creates a national skill standards board to encourage the development of such standards. The Department of Labor has also sponsored some projects for "one stop" career shops that would combine all public counselling and placement services (generally run by the state governments) in a single place. The Administration is also promoting development of a new system of labour market information that will be accessible to jobseekers, employers and those considering further education and training.[146] Another recent initiative seeks to improve the functioning of various student loan programmes. A new type of loan is now on offer which allows for variable amortisation as a function of the recipient's income. It is hoped that this will reduce the default rate. A new lending process is now being phased in, which – if carried to completion – will eliminate the role of private financial institutions in providing student loans, assigning it instead to the Department of Education. Thus, the system will continue to assign a screening role to the colleges, universities and technical institutes, but the Department of Education will be responsible for following students after graduation and for collecting payments. In a related initiative, the Administration is strengthening its oversight of schools by insisting that they meet more stringent criteria in order to be eligible to participate in federal student aid programmes. More broadly, the total federal expenditure on training has been largely shielded from budget cuts in recent years. The budget outlook for federal adult education and training programmes in future rounds is difficult to assess, but future cuts are likely.

There is widespread consensus on the need for major reforms of the federal government's training programmes (US Senate Budget Committee, 1995). Among the points of agreement between the Administration and the Congress are the need to:

- consolidate the many separate federal training programmes;
- shift resources from those programmes that have little or no positive effect to those interventions that have demonstrated positive outcomes;
- improve the information available to consumers and employers by continuing to develop industry skill standards and "one-stop shops", where individuals can go to receive advice on their labour market options;
- reform the welfare system to create strong incentives for recipients to find employment;
- encourage states and local areas to build their own comprehensive workforce development systems.

New legislative initiatives in adult education and training have yet to take definitive shape. At the time of the writing of this document, two bills were before the Senate and the House of Representatives. Both bills would involve some budget cuts and further devolution of decision-making powers for training programmes to States relative to that already embodied in the Job Training Partnership Act. The Senate bill, for example, would freeze funding at current levels for most major programmes, but would cut others. Most of this money would be allocated to the states, which would be required to use 25 per cent of it to develop state-wide systems of work-force development (including one-stop career centres that would collect and disseminated information about education and training services and employment opportunities). An additional 25 per cent would have to used for work-force education initiatives such as vocational training and adult literacy programmes. The remaining 50 per cent would be used at the states' discretion for education and training programmes. The bill would also turn the federally-sponsored Job Corps centres over to the States.

The Administration's "GI Bill for American Workers" also proposes to restructure federal training services. Its proposed changes emphasise training grants (or vouchers) and would give the participants themselves increased flexibility and control. Improved information about local labour markets and training services are also emphasised in the proposals. Thus, compared to the Congressional proposals, the Administration would shift the locus of decision making more toward the individual and less toward state governments. The Administration would increase funding for the programmes. Another Administration proposal of (indirect) relevance to training markets would raise the federal minimum wage (see below). At the present time, the federal minimum wage is set at $4.25. Still another proposal focuses on tax incentives for education.

Assessment and scope for further action

The distinctive features of the US system of workforce development reflect the influence of several forces operating on a flexible, largely unregulated labour market in which incentives to work are strong. One of these forces is an apparent preference for (or at least lack of resistance to) geographic or job mobility. Another is the absence of effective mechanisms for bringing together labour representatives, educators and businesses to make decisions on matters of shared interest. These features have historical and cultural origins that extend well beyond labour and training markets, but that nevertheless exercise an important influence on such markets. Taken together, they appear to have fostered a much greater reliance by US training and labour markets on arms-length contracting than is observed in many, if not most, other OECD countries. Indeed, this tendency is apparent not just in employment relationships, but in nearly every other US factor and product market as well.[147] As such, it appears to be a deeply embedded feature of the American economy – one that training policy will have to take largely as given.

What pattern of adult education and training has this fostered? First, many members of the workforce show relatively strong human capital development on the portable end of the skills spectrum and relatively weak development on the firm-specific end. Second, the formal tertiary education sector – responding to labour market signals and to intense competitive pressures within the sector itself – has evolved over many decades into a diverse and, on the whole, successful system with a strong occupational or career development orientation. In effect, most adults with the inclination and the resources needed for taking time off from work or from other activities can avail themselves of a wealth of relatively high-quality training and general education services. An extensive array of subsidies (scholarships, guaranteed loans and state-subsidised institutions) is available to many of them if they so desire. Large portions of the US workforce use the adult education system for life-long learning. Thus, the US system of adult education and training enjoys many strengths.

Many aspects of current and proposed reforms to federal training programmes seek to build on the system's strengths and to improve upon some of its weaknesses. One example is the attempt to establish nation-wide skills standards and certification systems; this represents an appropriate and (for the federal government) relatively inexpensive remedy to a what is widely accepted as a market failure in the training sector. By bringing together businessmen, educators, worker associations and others to develop occupational skills standards, the programme will allow some sectors to take the first, tentative steps toward developing the type of training infrastructure that is taken for granted in many other member countries (but the actual scope for this kind of development in specific sectors and occupations is not yet clear). The proposal to create "one-stop" career counselling centres should streamline public services and increase their transparency to users. Likewise, the Administration's proposal to re-orient federal training and job-assistance programmes so that the eligible individuals would use (for example) training grants to finance the programme of their choice would reinforce existing features of the system, which already relies heavily on individual choice. As the Administration recognises, though, such a shift requires greater dissemination of information to "consumers" about the quality of training services on offer. Indeed, US experience with Pell grants has underscored the problems encountered in offering training grants if they are not accompanied by a supporting system of consumer information and institutional accountability. Recent attempts to improve information about post-secondary institutions and to tighten federal oversight on the quality of their services are therefore reasonable measures Thus, most of the recent initiatives appear to be worthwhile attempts to increase the effectiveness of federal training and adult education programmes (without spending more money on them) and to reduce the associated bureaucracy at all levels of government.

One possible problem area in this otherwise positive assessment is the Administration's proposal to increase the minimum wage, a move that it believes will improve equity outcomes in the US labour markets. But it is unclear whether such a measure would help the working poor, many of whom earn wages that exceed the federal minimum wage.[148] Also, many minimum wage workers belong to family units with aggregate incomes well above poverty levels. The minimum wage – which is set at both federal and state levels – is thought to be relatively low in the United States compared to those prevailing in some other countries.[149] In 1993, 3.5 per cent of all workers were earning the federal minimum wage.[150] The segment of the work force that was most affected by the minimum wage was 16 to 19 year-olds, among whom 26 per cent were earning the minimum wage or less in 1993[151] (US Bureau of the Census, 1994). A significant proportion of these youths are working on a part-time basis and are also enrolled in school. The proposed increase in the minimum wage may cause these youths to allocate more time to minimum wage employment and less time to effort in school. In contrast, some very low-skills youth form their initial attachments to the labour market through their minimum wage jobs. This latter segment of the youth labour market may well be crowded out of the market at the new minimum wage and shift into the informal economy or into inactivity. Unemployment in the youth segment of the market is consistently more than double the rates for older workers, while the unemployment rate for black youth not enrolled in school was 28.2 per cent in 1992 (US Bureau of the Census, 1994). The Administration notes that the number of jobs available at the minimum wage is not likely to be greatly reduced by the proposed increase. The empirical research has not yet produced definitive conclusions on the labour market effects of minimum wage increases in the United States. There is some empirical support for the view that their effect on the number of workers employed at the minimum wage is small – see, for example, Card and Kreuger (1995). But, as just discussed, there may also be undesirable human capital impacts on various segments of the youth market – see, for example, Neumark and Wascher (1994 and 1995).

More broadly, though, the US system of adult education and training is beset by many shortcomings that will require the sustained attention of policy makers. The most serious and least tractable of these problems is that the system, for all its strengths, fails to work for so many people. This, however, appears to be more a symptom of a broader failure of the American social "model" and less a failure of the adult education and training system *per se*. Indeed, the heavily subsidised, but market-oriented adult education system could be viewed as ameliorating what would be, in the absence of such a system, an even worse problem. The current system offers even illiterate adults relatively easy access to remedial services. Thus, for the self-selected group that chooses to participate there are plenty of education and training opportunities.

For those who cannot or will not use the adult system, problems range from mild to severe. This chapter has shown that the typical high school graduate who does not move on to higher education has experienced steady erosion of wages over the past 20 years. Despite the uncertainty surrounding the underlying causes of this erosion, the outlook for a turnaround is not good.[152] Forecasts of skills demands – though notoriously difficult to make – point to continuing increases in the demand for better educated, more skilled workers. To the extent that wage erosion on the low-skills end of the labour market is due to the triple pressures of trade with low-wage countries, immigration of low-skills workers and foreign direct investment in low-wage countries, the outlook is even more grim. Last year's Survey noted the large variations in US educational achievement: international achievement comparisons show that American students on the low end of the US achievement spectrum might not be highly differentiated from their counterparts in many low-income countries.[153] The competitive position of this segment of the American workforce may also be eroded by the fact that many low-income countries have themselves implemented successful mass education programmes (Meyer, Ramirez and Soysal, 1992). Thus, while basic education systems are largely mature in the OECD area, the developing world has seen brisk growth in all types of education (Figure 38). The expansion of public education in low-income countries and concurrent policies of liberalisation and structural adjustment mean that their workforces have become and will continue to be more formidable competitors. Such developments may further undermine the economic security of the sizeable portion of American workers who are not highly differentiated from them in terms of skills and work habits.

Thus, the United States finds itself burdened with a primary and secondary education system of variable, but often poor, quality, at a time when economic penalties for such shortcomings are growing. These shortcomings in basic educa-

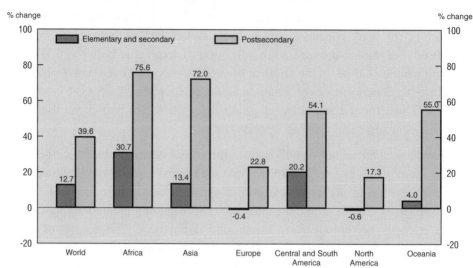

Figure 38. **WORLD ENROLMENT IN EDUCATION: 1980 TO 1990**

Source: UNESCO, *Statistical Yearbook,* various years.

tion translate, quite naturally, into a need for remediation as young people enter the workforce, and the current system responds to this need for those adults who choose to use it. It is clear, though, that any long-term, efficient solution will necessarily involve significant improvements in the performance of the primary and secondary systems. This is because the adult education system – by definition following up on compulsory education – requires that individuals be willing and able to participate. Unlike compulsory education for younger age groups, its mission is not to ensure that the entire student population adheres to some socially-determined minimum performance standard. If the primary and secondary system fails to ensure adherence to such a standard, the adult system can be at best only a partial remedy. Remediation entails other costs as well. It is inherently more expensive than providing adequate services at the primary and secondary levels because remediation means that the direct costs of education services are paid twice and often involves the opportunity costs of removing adults from the workforce or from other activities. Finally, the effectiveness of some remediation programmes for very disadvantaged groups has been shown to be diminished by stigma effects (Bishop, 1994). Thus, it will be important to continue the slow, painstaking process of improving the primary and secondary system along the lines identified in last year's Survey.[154] Indeed, this is the most critical challenge now facing US education and training policy-makers.

Most federally-sponsored training programmes target people who are experiencing severe socio-economic difficulties: many of them are high school drop-outs; many have arrest records;[155] many are single mothers. This is an inherently difficult population to serve effectively. Furthermore, they are often living in failing local economies, which may be sending out only weak signals for active participation in formal, legitimate labour markets. For many disadvantaged youth, law enforcement officers and correctional authorities play a more "formative" role in their youth experiences than does participation in formal education or in-firm training. There has been a rapid increase in the proportion of the youth population that is subject to "criminal supervision",[156] with more than 25 per cent of black males between the age of 18 and 34 years being subject to such supervision in 1993 (Figure 39). Total government expenditure on police services

Figure 39. **SHARE OF POPULATION UNDER CRIMINAL SUPERVISION: MALES AGED 18 TO 34, BY RACE**

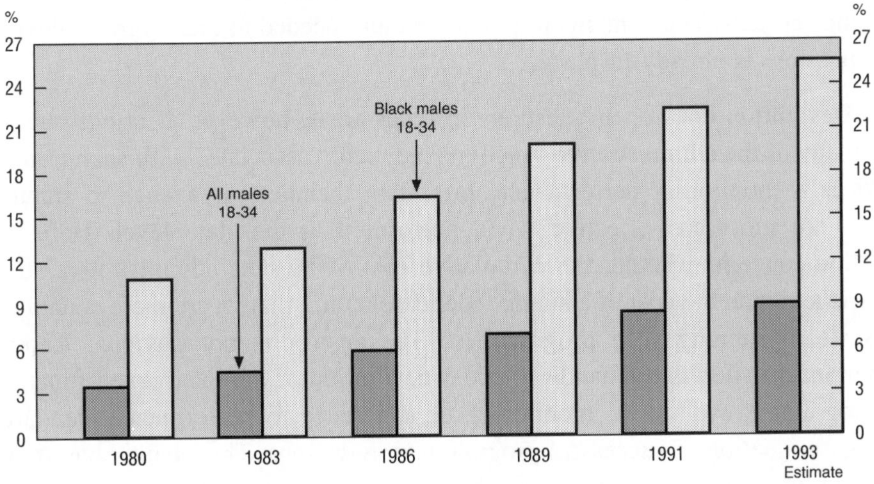

Source: Katz (1995).

and corrections rose by about 10 per cent per year over the 1985 to 1992 period. Thus, the *de facto* strategy for dealing with these communities' problems that appears to be emerging is to increase the investment in law enforcement infrastructure. Aside from the generally deleterious effects such experiences (especially imprisonment) have on the human capital of the people concerned, the direct costs of such services – at an average of $22 600 per year of incarceration in 1990 –[157] are high.

Thus, it would appear to be both good economic policy and good social policy to adjust the mix of services toward more productive investments in members of disadvantaged communities. Unfortunately, as noted, the federal programmes that attempt to provide the members of such communities with training and remedial education tend to produce modest (although often positive) economic returns. Inefficient management of these programmes is part (but not necessarily a major part) of this problem. In particular, the fragmentation of the programmes has resulted in inefficiencies in delivery and confusion among clients. There is a bipartisan consensus about the need to streamline and consolidate programmes, and something is likely to be done in the near future. Some of the proposed streamlining activities involve block funding and devolution of further decision making power to the states or even, under the Administration's plan, to individuals. In either case, this will expand the already significant role that states and individuals play in "contracting out" for federally-sponsored education and training services. Thus, the institutional structure needed to make further devolution possible is already in place.

Devolution does open questions in other areas, however. It is not obvious that many of the administrative functions inevitably associated with such training services – monitoring performance, providing technical assistance to trainers, etc. – are most cost-effective when performed at the state level. Here, the question concerns whether the cumulative cost of 50 state administrative structures is less than the cost of a single federal structure; that is, are there economies of scale in running such programmes? The answer is not obvious. Another important question is the handling under devolution of the interrelated functions of programme evaluation; monitoring of adherence to performance standards; and dissemination of successful programme innovations. This chapter has shown that relatively little is known about why some programmes work for some people and not for others. Federally-sponsored training programmes still need to be honed by a process of trial and error. In such a context of uncertainty about why some programmes work while others do not, rigorous evaluation of the outcomes of various training programmes has public good characteristics: the states will be using each others' experiences to improve programme design. There is, then, reason to believe that states might under-invest in evaluation and information systems relative to the true national value of such systems. This would seem to argue for a strong federal role in providing research and formal evaluation under future devolution scenarios.

VII. Conclusions

The past year has been one of mainly gratifying outcomes for the US economy. Contrary to expectations, demand and output continued to accelerate until near the end of 1994, but activity began to moderate just in time to avoid any significant overheating. Employment growth of about 3 per cent during 1994 was the fastest of any Major Seven country and far in excess of the rise in labour supply, and the unemployment rate fell to around 5½ per cent around the turn of the year, a level which past experience would indicate is sufficiently low to begin to put upward pressure on rates of labour compensation. But, thus far, reduced non-wage labour costs, especially in health insurance, have kept increases in compensation on a downward path, and unit labour costs have been essentially flat. There has been a clear slowdown in the growth of production in 1995. This has taken the edge off capacity tensions in the labour market, keeping current inflation below previously projected rates and reducing inflation expectations and, therefore, long-term interest rates. This has allowed the possibility of achieving the much-sought-after ''soft landing'' and extending the expansion into its fifth year. Real disposable income per capita grew by 2½ per cent last year and, despite the slowdown, appears likely to maintain that rate on average this year.

The expansion has also been marked by a healthy balance in terms of the components of demand and spending. In particular, in 1994 the current cycle finally began to justify the description of investment-led, after particularly weak investment outcomes late in the previous cycle. Further, the boom in business capital formation has been financed with only limited recourse to credit-market borrowing through judicious management of the corporate sector balance sheet. Real exports of goods and services last year turned in their best performance of the 1990s, even if their contribution was no greater than usual at this point in the cycle. The shift away from government as a source of demand has also persisted,

152

with public consumption falling for the third year running, led by a sharp decline at the federal level. While household balance sheets have continued to grow more debt-laden, the burden of that debt has not increased, as lower market interest rates and intermediation margins in the 1990s have held interest payments and servicing costs down to relatively low levels. And saving rates seem to have stopped falling early last year. But firms apparently allowed the leanness of their stocks in earlier years of this cycle to diminish in 1994-95, probably due to the suddenness of the slowdown in demand: the trend decline in the stock-to-sales ratio was interrupted, despite widespread adoption of ''just-in-time'' methods of inventory control.

The key short-term analytical and policy question is: what caused the abrupt slowdown in the first half of 1995 and does it signify an increased sensitivity to a negative shock which might, as in 1990, induce a recession, even if only a mild and short-lived one? Alternatively, could growth soon resume at rates sufficient to once again put downward pressure on unemployment? The primary reason for the moderation in domestic demand was higher interest rates, but the satisfaction of pent-up demand for housing and durables was also important. Interest-sensitive demand components showed the earliest signs of peaking, led by weakness in new home sales as from November 1994, in non-auto consumer durables purchases starting in December and in automobile sales beginning in January 1995. While a deceleration in these outlays had been predicted, it arrived earlier than most observers had expected, probably because of the unusual speed and degree with which long-term interest rates had responded to higher short-term rates. This was attributable to extrapolative expectations regarding monetary policy, a correction from the unusually low rates of 1993 and/or higher risk premia resulting from interest-rate uncertainty. Once compounded with the effects of the shock to exports resulting from the Mexican crisis, which also turned out to be much more front-loaded than many had expected, and persistent declines in federal purchases, the stage was set for a fairly significant moderation in growth.

However, large, temporary variations in growth are by no means unusual. Real GDP even contracted for a quarter in the middle of what turned out to be continuing expansions in 1962, 1977 and 1986. Since the usual excesses which prefigure recession – especially in the form of high inflation rates and speculative inventory behaviour – are conspicuously absent at this juncture, it seems more likely that the recent fall-off in growth is a mid-cycle correction and that the expansion will resume in the second half of this year. Long-term interest rates have fallen sharply since last November and are already beginning to stimulate demand for new housing and automobiles. Credit supply conditions are favourable, as banks continue to ease lending terms and conditions. Inventories do not appear excessive in most sectors, and correction of the problem in the automobile industry is well underway. Private consumption has already picked up somewhat since the spring: household debt growth has slowed noticeably; debt servicing does not represent a particularly high share of income by recent historical standards; delinquency rates are low; and confidence remains fairly solid. And despite the Mexican shock, merchandise export growth in recent months has still been running at an annual rate of over 10 per cent in volume terms and should continue at about that rate. Yet a return to the robust growth prevailing in 1993-94 is also less likely: new orders have fallen sharply, indicating moderating capital formation; interest rates remain well above 1993 levels; pent-up demand has to a large extent been satisfied, and the household saving rate is near recent historical lows; further budget cuts are quite likely; and the dollar has recovered to a level above recent lows.

The risk of either a recession or a renewed boom would therefore appear to be modest over the next year or so. Accordingly, the Secretariat projects that real GDP growth in terms of 1987 prices (up to now the habitual measure) will average 3 per cent this year (which implies $2^{1}/_{4}$ per cent on a fourth-quarter to fourth-quarter basis). However, probably about $^{3}/_{4}$ of a percentage point should be subtracted from these figures in order to put them on a chain-weighted basis (the officially preferred measure as of the end of 1995). For next year private consumption should maintain a modest growth rate, and housing investment could well revive somewhat. But the growth of business fixed investment will probably slow sharply in line with moderating capacity pressures, though it should remain positive owing to the unending need to modernise plant and equipment to remain competitive, and the financial ability to do so: both unit profits and rates of return are likely to remain at or near record levels. The principal imponderable at the moment is how much of a cut in spending is likely to emerge from the budget negotiations ongoing at the federal level. With the assumption that outlays will be cut somewhat more slowly than currently implied by the Congressional

Budget Resolution, the Secretariat's projection embodies overall real GDP growth of about 2½ per cent in 1996 (1¾ per cent on a chain-weighted basis).

Under that sort of scenario the probability of more than a slight further rise in underlying inflation is rather low, but so is the likelihood of a decline. The unemployment rate may edge back up to 6 per cent next year, perhaps slightly above estimated full-employment levels. Even with a cyclical slowing in labour productivity gains, unit labour costs should provide little impetus toward a pickup in inflation, and global markets will probably be sufficiently slack to prevent any further widening in markups. But the cost of imports has picked up appreciably in recent months due to the fall in the value of the dollar earlier in the year, and any renewed decline in the effective exchange rate might be sufficient to convince foreign exporters to pass on some of the cumulative effects of previously absorbed cost increases when calculated in dollars.

In this context monetary policy should be consistent with moving toward the long-run objective of price stability. The Federal Reserve has engineered the slowdown it rightly believed was required to sustain the longer-term disinflation trend, even if it, too, was surprised by the promptness with which the slowing arrived (as it had been by the sustained strength of activity in 1994). It has now made a modest move to ease monetary conditions in order to avoid the risk of an unnecessary rise in unemployment, pointing out that such a move is justified even when current inflation is rising, so long as prospects are favourable that the increase will eventually be reversed – as has begun to occur in recent months. However, the likelihood of joblessness going much above what most experts believe to be its minimum structural level (5½ to 6 per cent) is fairly low, even if the slowdown lasts longer than foreseen, given the substantial decline in long-term rates seen since November 1994 and the likelihood of continued slow growth in labour supply. But even at its trough in 1994 the inflation rate had not dropped to a level low enough that households and businesses would have neglected it in their economic plans: inflation, even at recent and prospective rates, is still costly. The danger is that further reductions in short-term rates, as have been expected by the market in view of previous experience that successive rate changes go in the same direction, might ultimately prove inappropriate and could need to be quickly reversed. Indeed, in the case of an economy producing at close to its potential level, there is no *a priori* reason for rate movements to be persistently in one direction. Overall, a cautious stance seems desirable, one that demonstrates vigilance against any return to inflationary tendencies and sustains the medium-term trend towards price stability. Standing firm in the face of a brief period of slow growth should lock in most of the recent decline in long-term bond yields by reinforcing a durable lowering of inflation expectations and allow investors greater confidence that dollar-denominated instruments will perform well over the long haul, so crucial for the maintenance of the dollar as the foremost international currency.

The dollar's poor performance in the first half of 1995, especially against the yen and the Deutschemark, was of concern, but its intervention-assisted third-quarter rebound probably reduced its divergence from its underlying value. Dollar weakness is to some extent a reflection of the United States' longer-term inflation record and the fear that it is no longer a good store of value on the international scene, at least for yen-based and European investors. But over the long term, dollar depreciation is more fundamentally attributable to the chronic scarcity of domestic saving in the economy and the resulting persistent saving-investment imbalance. This may have restrained the trend rate of capital formation – with important negative consequences for long-term living standards – and also led to a build-up in the nation's negative net international investment position (to some 12 per cent of GDP) as a result of the perennial deficit on current account. The projected slower growth in domestic demand over the next 18 months as well as the continued strength of export markets and the still-competitive level of the dollar should help to stabilise the current external deficit and to reduce it somewhat in relation to GDP. However, a sizeable structural imbalance will remain, especially in view of the cost of servicing the net foreign liabilities. And, as the record of the dollar's trajectory in the first half of 1995 showed, attracting sufficient net capital inflows to match the current account deficit can be costly.

Since there is a consensus that no simple policy actions can do much to stimulate private saving – although a deliberate overhaul of the tax system designed with a view to increasing the weight on consumption rather than income as the basis for taxation might provide a helpful contribution – it remains crucial to keep downward pressure on the federal budget deficit, especially in view of the demographic pressures on entitlement spending which are known to come into play in little more than a decade. Merely to head off further deterioration in the ratio of federal debt to GDP will require cutting the deficit by some 7 percentage points of GDP over the next 35 years from a reasonable baseline scenario. By keeping up the declining trend in the deficit since 1992, the interim results for fiscal 1995 are a notable achievement, both by historical US standards and in comparison with many other OECD Member countries. In part, recent progress is attributable to the buoyancy of the real economy, but structural improvement has also been substantial, thanks to the effects of the 1993 budget package. Even though yet another attempt to force budget balancing by means of a constitutional amendment was narrowly defeated earlier this year, the likelihood of such an outcome has risen appreciably in recent months with a determined effort by the Congress to describe a path to the elimination of the deficit in seven years. The Administration has also recognised the value of deficit elimination by proposing what has become a nine-year passage to a balanced budget. The difficult task will be to agree on where, how and how fast to trim the deficit, especially since all sides have agreed to pass tax cuts as well and to rule out changes to Social Security (which will be needed in any case in the fairly near future) and additional defence cuts. Front-loading the fiscal consolidation would enhance the credibility of the policy change and thereby boost the chances of an offsetting reduction in market interest rates, with beneficial impacts on the build-up of government debt and private investment over time. However, it might also make the adjustment costs more severe in the short run.

The result of these political commitments is that the final outcome, whatever the details, will most likely weaken the social safety net. Responsibility for some existing social programmes will be devolved to lower levels of government. Initially, adequate financing may be provided, but, over time, it seems quite likely that state and local governments will have to cut public services, even if substantial efficiency gains are realised, since in aggregate their existing fiscal positions and/or state constitutions do not permit them to increase their deficits materially. The pressures for states to cut back on the generosity of social programmes will be strengthened by the risk of interstate "benefit shopping"; they will face clear incentives to trim the benefits they offer, thereby aggravating worsening income inequality trends. Further reducing the federal government's economic role will also curtail its ability to buffer regional shocks.

In addition, it seems likely that the federal government itself will reduce its presence in a wide variety of areas, with important ramifications. Cutbacks in agricultural subsidies and some tax and spending programmes primarily benefiting individual business sectors are welcome for their probable efficiency gains. However, paring the income security function, reducing taxes for the middle and upper income groups and slashing health-care spending from reasonable baseline levels (thereby risking restricting access to satisfactory care by the growing numbers of uninsured) would add up to a substantial diminution of the role of the federal government in income redistribution. And pruning the government's already limited investment activities might also have foreseeable longer-term costs.

An extremely wide range of structural policy reforms are currently under consideration or have recently been implemented. Some have had long-standing recommendations from the Committee such as last year's elimination of restrictions on interstate banking and branching or the current attempt to remove barriers to intersectoral competition within financial services, both of which should yield efficiency gains at little cost. Others too should prove helpful: allowing greater competition in the burgeoning telecommunications sector; reducing the potential unfunded liabilities of the government's Pension Benefits Guaranty Corporation; boosting public-sector efficiency by continuing with the Reinventing Government programme and further reducing paperwork requirements; establishing free trade areas in the Pacific and in the Western Hemisphere; requiring cost-benefit analysis for major new regulations; and means testing of support payments to farmers and reforming crop insurance so as to encourage to develop their own risk-reduction strategies. On others, such as various changes which would ultimately restrict the influence of unions in the labour market, opinions may vary.

But in some other areas recent and prospective developments are clearly troublesome to the Committee. Foremost among these domains is that of trade policy. While the successful conclusion to the Uruguay Round was gratifying, portending, as it does, the lifting of burdensome trade barriers, the recent heightening of trade frictions with Japan is regrettable, because such tensions could threaten the stability of the international trading system. The strategies chosen by the US authorities to deal with trade issues with Japan are predicated in part on arguments that the closed nature of Japanese markets contributes to the US trade deficit *vis-a-vis* Japan and that it is to the advantage of the world economy generally to pry open closed markets, even under the threat of unilateral sanctions. But the US external deficit is a macroeconomic phenomenon, not caused by

Japanese trade policies or business practices. Rather it is the direct result of a structural lack of saving in the US economy, and hence exogenously imposing higher imports by Japan will not resolve the deficit problem. It will merely displace it. Further, the Committee feels that threatening unilateral sanctions prior to adjudicating cases by the new dispute settlement mechanism of the World Trade Organisation runs counter to the spirit of multilateralism. In this regard, the recent decision not to offer ''most-favoured nation'' treatment on new foreign investment into the US financial services market has been interpreted in some quarters as a move by the United States away from its traditional commitment to multilateralism; but the decision is only interim, and full protection for established foreign investments has been guaranteed.

Rapid job creation in US labour markets has been accompanied by trends in wage formation over the last twenty years that are also a source of disquiet. Many measures of real wages have stagnated, while the lower-skilled segments of the market have experienced steeply declining real wages. Evidence regarding trends in job security is more ambiguous but seems to indicate deterioration for some segments of the labour market. In this context, it is reasonable to question the proposal to reduce the generosity of the Earned Income Tax Credit. The potential role of the system of adult education and training in reversing wage trends is also a subject of debate.

The adult system – with its heavy subsidies for those who are prepared to take advantage of them and its vast array of coursework addressing a wide range of adult educational needs – already does a good job of providing valuable opportunities for people from diverse social and economic backgrounds. Although it is exceedingly difficult to determine an optimal level of education and training subsidy for adults, the current system – involving significant, but not total subsidisation for most coursework – seems to strike a reasonable balance. It provides reasonable access while making sure that training and education services are subject to market testing by customers. Federal education and training programmes have been largely shielded from past budget cuts and any future cuts should be made with care. Substantial reductions in some of the spending items mentioned above (agriculture, for example) should take place before education and training expenditure is reduced.

The system of higher education is a source of strength for the US economy. For the considerable segment of the US workforce that does not participate in higher education, however, there are serious problems of human capital accumulation. But the sources of these problems seem to lie largely outside the adult education and training system, and there are limits to how much the system can do to alleviate inequalities in living conditions in American society. Ultimately, some progress must be made in addressing the deeper sources of these inequalities. One essential front for policy action is improving the initial education system and the transition from school to work for the non-college bound along the lines laid out in last year's Survey and included in the "Goals 2000" and School-to-Work Transition legislation of 1994: working on improved vocational secondary studies and on other ways of keeping people in school longer and defining basic standards more clearly so that all those involved in education understand clearly what is expected of them. This would not only improve the overall functioning of the adult system by enhancing the general quality of incoming students, but it would put a larger proportion of the adult population in a better position to use the system. For the very disadvantaged, another major impediment to economic progress is that the local economies in which they live – basically the inner cities and certain rural areas – may not be providing strong signals for active participation in formal labour markets and for investing in human capital. Again, though, the solution to the problem of poorly functioning local economies must extend well beyond adult education and training.

There are nevertheless some improvements that could usefully be made to the adult system, and some of these are in progress. Work on creating nationwide voluntary occupational skill standards is under way, for example. This should redress some of the information problems inherent in training markets by allowing more reliable signalling of skills by workers and by making it easier for training institutions to design programmes that have broad recognition among employers. However, such initiatives will be more relevant for some occupations (for example, those where skills do not become obsolete quickly) than for others. The federal government is also trying to improve the efficiency of the training programmes that it sponsors; the principal thrust of these initiatives involves consolidating programmes in order to reduce overlap, increasing information on occupational training institutions that receive federal funding, and further devolution of decision making to the states or even to individuals. On the whole, these seem like worthwhile initiatives that seek to build on the system's current strengths and to attenuate its weaknesses.

The devolution question and, more specifically, the issue of how programme accountability is to be handled under devolution are currently important policy matters. In many respects, further devolution will reinforce features of the current system (in which individuals and state and local governments already play very large roles). For this reason, the institutional structures needed to make devolution feasible as a near-term policy option are already in place. What should be kept in mind, however, is that not enough is known about whether or not specific government-sponsored training programmes work and, more importantly, about the reasons for these successes and failures. For this reason, devolution should be accompanied by a significant effort toward maintaining rigorous programme accountability. Since investment in such accountability can be expensive and has public-good characteristics (that is, states will be using each others' information to improve programme design), it would seem reasonable that the federal government play a significant role in keeping track of programme results.

Once again it seems appropriate to summarise by pointing to the contrasts in the past and likely future performance of the USy economy. Macroeconomic outcomes have continued to be favourable, with strong growth easing up just in time to avoid overheating, low inflation maintained, full employment reached and average real incomes still rising. But even though the elusive ''soft landing'' seems likely to have been managed, the dollar has been intermittently weak, external debt is growing in relation to GDP, and there has been a sudden and unanticipated slowdown in growth. However, in all likelihood the slowdown will prove temporary, calling for caution in the exercise of monetary policy in order to safeguard and build on the hard-won gains of the past decade in reducing inflation expectations. In finally reaching a consensus to balance the budget, the nation's policy makers have recognised the longer-term gains in terms of higher standards of living that are likely to result. But the impact on the nation's social cohesion of the even heavier reliance on individual incentives and responsibilities and the further dismantling of the already limited social safety net entailed by the favoured means of deficit reduction can be known only with time. The outcome will be watched attentively both at home and abroad.

Notes

1. The time period when increased taxes should have slowed consumption is open to debate. Forward-looking consumers may have begun to scale back consumption in 1993 when the plan was announced, while myopic consumers may have waited until payments were due, and because they were unlikely to be liquidity constrained, may have phased in their response.

2. Some of the rise in consumer debt may reflect increased transactions use of credit cards. The average monthly balance, even when paid in full at the end of the month, appears as consumer debt. The increased use of promotional tie-ins as well as a wider range of products covered – from university tuition to groceries – has probably accelerated the shift in payments from cheques to credit cards. On the other hand, consumer debt is understated to a moderate degree because of the shift from purchase to leasing of automobiles.

3. Required debt service payments are also biased by the same factors that affect consumer debt: leasing of automobiles and convenience use of credit cards. These aggregate measures also do not show the distribution of debt across households. Over the 1983 to 1992 period, when overall debt burdens rose rapidly, the share of consumer debt owed by households with high debt payments to income (greater than 30 per cent) fell sharply, particularly over the 1989 to 1992 period when consumer debt delinquency rates tumbled – perhaps reflecting tighter credit standards. While the share of total debt owed by households with high ratios of total debt payments to income (greater than 40 per cent) rose, their share of assets also rose.

4. The trend need for housing is approximately $1\frac{1}{2}$ million units a year, composed of trend household formation, second homes and replacement of existing structures, net of conversions of non-residential structures. Of course, these variables are affected by demographic and economic factors. Of the $1\frac{1}{2}$ million units, a quarter million are supplied by mobile homes, not included in housing starts, and a small amount from reduction in the vacancy rate in multi-family housing, leaving roughly $1\frac{1}{4}$ million units to be supplied by new housing starts. See Hirsch (1994).

5. In the US national accounts, government purchases of investment goods and consumption goods and services are aggregated together.

6. Faster economic growth boosted receipts by $6 billion, lower interest rates cut debt servicing by $8 billion and lower inflation and unemployment cut other spending by $3 billion; thus, the better economic performance reduced the deficit by $17 billion. Failure to pass the 1993 stimulus package was more than offset by additional spending for emergencies such as

162

the flooding in the Mid-west; on net, policy actions were about $7 billion less restrictive than originally planned.

7. These data must be interpreted with caution as they are subject to large revisions later in the year when much of the Census data will be incorporated for the first time.

8. Last year's Survey, OECD (1994e), describes the changes made in the labour market survey design which are estimated to have boosted the unemployment rate by about 0.1 percentage point. Other indicators, such as labour force participation, were estimated to have experienced much larger changes. In addition, incorporation of the decennial Census was thought to boost unemployment rates by 0.1 percentage point compared to 1993.

9. Bosworth and Perry (1994) calculate that productivity rose 0.9 per cent annually from 1973 to 1993. Over the same period, hourly compensation when deflated by the CPI rose only 0.4 per cent per year, but when deflated by the non-farm business deflator the increase was 0.8 per cent. The difference primarily represents terms-of-trade changes.

10. Many reasons have been put forward for the gap. Foreign investment in the United States is more recent, and frequently investments do not return a profit for several years. In addition, profits from foreign investment is subject to manipulation from transfer pricing. For example, tax reasons may encourage firms to price trade flows within the firm so as to boost the cost of imports and shift profits offshore. This would leave the current account unchanged but would redistribute the flows from payments on investment income account to imports.

11. The current expansion is dated from the trough in 1991 Q1. To this point it has, therefore, lasted 18 quarters. The mean duration of the six previous expansions dating back to 1958 is 18 quarters. However, in the remainder of this chapter the brief cycle whose trough was the second quarter of 1980 and whose peak was the first quarter of 1981 will be omitted. Excluding this cycle, the average historical duration of expansions is 22 quarters. Furthermore, only the first 16 quarters of this and previous expansions are considered herein, as data for the 17th and 18th quarter (Q2 and Q3 1995) were not available when the anaylsis was undertaken. The other cycles considered are those with troughs in the following periods: 1958 Q1, 1960 Q4, 1970 Q4, 1975 Q1 and 1982 Q3. It should be noted that by the ninth and eleventh quarters, respectively, of the cycles beginning in 1958 and 1971, the expansions had ended and recessions were underway, making for predictable patterns when making the cross-cycle comparisons which follow.

12. These figures as well as all others cited in this analysis are based on the official 1987-price data. Using the chain-linked data which will become the officially preferred measure at the end of the year, the gap is even larger: the average historical expansion recorded output growth of some $4\frac{1}{2}$ per cent, while real GDP has risen only $2\frac{1}{2}$ per cent since the 1991 trough.

13. This was argued at length in the previous Survey of the United States economy (OECD, 1994e) and was also the conclusion of the Council of Economic Advisers in its 1995 Economic Report of the President (Chapter 3).

14. This question has been examined for the OECD overall in the most recent issue of the OECD Economic Outlook (Number 57, June 1995, pp. 26-32).

15. Possibly in part for this reason the US government is planning to switch its main focus for estimating real GDP to one based on chain-linked indices later this year (see Box 1, in Chapter I).

16. However, net new equity issues did turn negative again in 1994 for the first time since 1990.

17. This shows up mainly in the category of "checkable deposits and currency" and is presumably the manifestation of the spread of cash management accounts.

18. In 1994, for the first time ever, the increase in consumer credit exceeded household net investment in durable goods (expenditures less capital consumption) and comprised nearly half the growth in aggregate consumer expenditure – see Table 5).

19. Nevertheless, it has been argued that official measures of disposable income do not reflect economic realities, as a substantial share in the form of interest and dividends earned on tax-assisted savings plans such as Individual Retirement Accounts (IRAs) and so-called 401k accounts may not be readily available to finance current consumption. But the counter-argument is that these household assets have in turn largely replaced others, principally defined-benefit pension plans, to which accessibility is in effect nil.

20. All of this is attributable to the federal government, for which the decline in the structural deficit has been $1\frac{1}{2}$ percentage points of GDP, nearly triple the average of the three previous cycles. In contrast, state and local governments' deficits have widened by 0.2 percentage point of GDP, whereas their structural surpluses typically edge up by 0.1 percentage point of GDP.

21. The abrupt shifts in the first quarter of 1994 in this and other series referred to in this paragraph may be due to the break in the series with the new Current Population Survey which began at that point.

22. Some have argued that since the unemployed have been drawn increasingly from the ranks of white-collar workers in recent years longer search times and higher reservation wages may be explanatory factors.

23. This pattern is very similar to that observed in the previous cycle, except it has taken place later in the expansion: during 1984, the second year of the expansion, yields on ten-year notes rose by some $2\frac{1}{2}$ percentage points, before an unprecedented 5 percentage point decline got underway, aided by the reverse oil shock of 1986. This time the rise in yields was about the same size, but it occurred only in the fourth year of the expansion, and the subsequent rally took yields down no more than 1.9 percentage points.

24. Econometric studies indicate that changes in price inflation typically precede those in wage inflation in the United States – see Huh and Trehan (1995) and citations therein.

25. It should be noted that the Secretariat's estimates of the output gap and labour-market gap are not perfectly correlated because of the separate role of the capital stock in determining productivity growth.

26. Another reason for a single target is that the Federal Reserve has only a single instrument – the reserves it provides to the banking system. For a useful summary of the views of members of the Federal Open Market Committee on the objective of price stability see Pakko (1995). Note that over the years many legislators have attempted to reform the workings and/or objectives of the Federal Reserve: some of those efforts have been directed

toward making it more politically accountable; others have tried to restrict its brief to the single goal of price stability. The most recent legislation along the latter lines was introduced in September 1995. It calls for price stability to be the primary goal of the Federal Reserve and for it to set out its own definition of price stability and a time frame and a means for achieving it, taking into account any potential short-term effects on output and employment.

27. Even the Federal Reserve Governors and Reserve Bank presidents in January 1995 expected the consumer price index to rise by 3 to $3\frac{1}{2}$ per cent in the four quarters ending in 1995 Q4, up from 2.6 per cent in the previous year and a low of 2.3 per cent in the 12 months to April 1994, due in part to a temporary decline in the price of cigarettes. This was in line with the forecasts compiled by Blue Chip Economic Indicators.

28. In the six months to April 1994 the Blue Chip average forecast for real GDP growth in 1994 moved from 2.7 to 3.7 per cent.

29. There are a number of alternative ways of determining the restrictiveness of monetary policy settings. It is useful to look at these since interest rates themselves – even the rate on federal funds itself to some extent – are endogenously determined by demand and supply in the credit markets. The growth rate of nonborrowed reserves slowed through 1993 but remained at a double-digit pace. Moderate growth persisted only until the first quarter of 1994; in the four quarters ending in 1995 Q1 they fell by some 3 per cent, a deeper decline than occurred in 1989-90. Another approach is to estimate a central bank reaction function for the federal funds rate and then examine the pattern of residuals. Pakko (1995) did just that using a specification suggested by Bernanke and Blinder (1992). Estimating over the period 1959 to 1994 he proposed the cumulant of the residuals as revealing that policy became steadily more stimulative from early 1989 to the end of 1993 and that, even though the reversal during 1994 was sharp, the level of exogenous restraint applied was far less than that which had been imposed in 1988-89.

30. The mean forecast for average real GDP growth in 1994 compiled by Blue Chip Economic Indicators moved up from 3.6 per cent in September to 3.9 per cent in December.

31. The average Blue Chip forecast for 1995 jumped from 2.7 per cent as late as November 1994 to 3.2 per cent in March 1995.

32. DiClemente and Burnham (1995) review the literature on monetary policy rules and conclude that policy is tighter than would be implied by rules suggested by John Taylor on the one hand and John Judd and Brian Motley on the other and in line with that suggested by Bennett McCallum.

33. In July 1995, FOMC members predicted that CPI inflation in the year to the fourth quarter would fall from about $3\frac{1}{4}$ per cent in 1995 to about 3 per cent in 1996.

34. Alternatively, it might be argued that it was the 1994 bond market weakness that was exaggerated and that the subsequent rally was merely an unwinding of this excessive movement.

35. These figures are derived from multiple regressions using monthly data which specify the change in the note rate on two own lags and the current value and two lags of the change in the funds rate. The reported coefficients on the current value of the funds rate have t-ratios of 6.7 and 2.5 in the two samples.

36. One indicator of this is the evolution of a crude measure of the dispersion of short-term interest rate forecasts as compiled by Blue Chip Economic Indicators. The normal pattern during the year prior to the year which is the subject of the forecast is for dispersion to shrink: for example, the gap between the 10 highest forecasts for the three-month Treasury bill average in 1994 and the 10 lowest was about 1.6 percentage points in the first six monthly compilations of 1993 but had fallen to 0.8 percentage points by year end. But forecasts in 1994 for 1995 showed no tendency to converge whatsoever: indeed, the smallest gaps of the year were in March, April and May.

37. This explanation was much invoked during the strong bond-market rally of 1993 and, in reverse, during the plunge in bond prices in 1994. However, since so much of the refinancing was already done in 1993, it is unlikely that there remained a great deal of potential demand for it in recent months.

38. Refinancings boost liquid deposits, especially demand deposits, because the relevant funds are temporarily placed in such accounts. Another factor was the introduction by a few large banks of programmes available to retail clients which automatically sweep excess balances into more lucrative money market accounts excluded from M1. The Federal Reserve estimates that M1 growth in the first half of 1995 was over 1 percentage point lower as a result of such sweep accounts. If the availability of such accounts were to spread, the Federal Reserve fears it would lead to potential problems for the implementation of monetary policy, in particular instability in the aggregate demand for reserves.

39. This assumes that these increases are greater than the average experienced by trading partners, that is that differentials are moving in the same direction and are not offset by changing relative inflation expectations. There is some evidence that expected long-term differentials were moving against the dollar for much of 1994. Some recent research, however, finds that there is no high-frequency link between real interest-rate differentials and real exchange rate changes and that such a relationship is only manifest at business-cycle and longer frequencies (Baxter, 1994).

40. These figures exclude the market value of official gold holdings from the US international investment position and value foreign direct investment positions at current cost.

41. In 1994 Taiwan cut the dollar share of its reserves from 59 to 54 per cent, as did Indonesia (52 to 49 per cent) and China (90 to 75 per cent). They also sold dollars to cover yen-denominated liabilities. It seems clear that the dollar's use as the main reserve currency declined during the 1980s, but it appears that there has been some rebound thus far in the 1990s. Use of other currencies rather than the dollar in official reserves erodes US seigniorage saving. The interest saving to the United States from foreign governments holding reserves in US dollar securities has been estimated to be worth some $10 billion per year (Feldstein, 1995).

42. Other nations and institutions also participated in the rescue. A more detailed description of the package and its impact can be found in the recent OECD Survey on Mexico (OECD, 1995c).

43. The unified budget is used by the government for most policy discussions. Unlike the national accounts definition, the unified budget includes financial transactions such as asset sales.

44. These projections are similar to those obtained by W. Leibfritz *et al.* (1995) which used slightly different assumptions. Their results were for the general government sector and were based on more a favourable assumption regarding the future course of health care spending.

45. The methodology for constructing baseline budget projections has been a contentious issue in recent years because the baseline can define the debate when the debate is framed by the amount by which a programme is being cut or increased, instead of focusing on the appropriate magnitude of resources to allocate to a programme. The House Budget Committee, by contrast, used 1995 nominal spending levels for its recent baseline. The difficulty with this approach is that is fails to distinguish between spending growth due to inflation and other causes and does not indicate the magnitude of programmatic changes.

46. Congressional Budget Office (1995*a*), Board of Trustees, Federal Old-Age and Survivors Insurance and Disability Insurance Trust Funds (1995) and Board of Trustees, Federal Hospital Insurance Trust Fund (1994). The longer-term projections do not incorporate any impact of high budget deficits on interest rates or GDP growth.

47. Historically, the rise in the GDP deflator is lower because prices for investment goods have risen much more slowly than consumer prices, in part because of the dramatic fall in the price of computers. In addition, implicit deflators tend to rise more slowly than fixed-weight measures such as the CPI because substitution towards cheaper goods is captured by the deflator. Partially offsetting these factors is health care, whose measured prices have risen rapidly and which is weighted more heavily in the GDP deflator than in the CPI.

48. During the 1960s, many excise taxes were eliminated, such as those on automobiles. Currently fuels, alcohol and tobacco (about three-quarters of excise tax revenues) are taxed at specific rates, while long-distance telephone service and airfares (about 10 per cent of revenues) are taxed according to sales revenues.

49. The share of national income generated by the corporate sector (profits, interest, rent and wages) actually rose slightly from the 1950s to the 1980s. But the share of profits in income declined, offset by a rising share allocated to interest payments. Profits may be taxed both at the corporate level and again at the personal level, whereas interest payments are taxed only once. Thus, this shift has lowered corporate profits taxes, but may not have increased personal income taxes. Corporate income taxes are paid only by sub-chapter "C" corporations; sub-chapter "S" corporations and partnerships are subject to personal income taxation. From the 1970s to 1988 the share of sub-chapter "S" corporation income in total corporate income rose from 2 per cent to nearly 10 per cent (US Department of the Treasury, 1992).

50. For example, to maintain an armed forces of a constant size, real spending would have to increase so that military salaries would keep pace with real wages in the private sector, and real procurement would rise to maintain modern weapon systems. The size of the armed forces needed to keep a constant degree of deterrence would be more related to adversaries' strength than to the size of the domestic economy.

51. Currently the primary programmes are: federal employee retirement benefits (1.0 per cent of GDP), unemployment insurance benefits (0.3 per cent), Food Stamps and other nutrition programmes (0.5 per cent), Supplemental Security Income (0.4 per cent), Earned Income

Tax Credit (0.3 per cent), Aid to Families with Dependent Children (0.3 per cent), veterans' benefits (0.3 per cent) and agriculture subsidies (0.1 per cent).

52. This is the age for full benefits. It will be raised by two months every year over the periods 2000 to 2005 and 2017 to 2022, inclusive. Benefits will still be available for those who retire at age 62. Currently early retirees receive 80 per cent of full benefits; when the phase-in is complete the figure will be 70 per cent. These reductions keep the present value of benefits approximately constant, but as explained in Steuerle and Bakija (1994), they are not actuarially fair for the system because the adjustments do not account for the difference in contributions.

53. More specifically, a worker's primary insurance amount (that due to a single worker, retiring at the normal retirement age) is based on the worker's taxable earnings adjusted for inflation and real wage growth. Wages are indexed by multiplying each year's earnings by a factor equal to the ratio of the average national wage in the year the worker turned 60 to the average national wage in the year to be indexed. Only the best 35 years are used; thus, working more than 35 years boosts benefits only if income in the additional year is higher (after adjustment) than the lowest of the 35.

54. The internal rates of return will be higher for women because of their longevity and for single-earner couples because of the spousal benefit that boosts payments by 50 per cent. As highlighted in calculations by Steuerle and Bakija (1994), the internal rates of return and replacement rates do not indicate clearly who receives the largest transfers. Indeed, they estimate that the present value of benefits less taxes was substantially greater for high-wage workers than low-wage workers until the 1985 cohort.

55. See, for example, OECD (1993a) and Oxley and MacFarlan (1994) for OECD results and Newhouse (1992) for more extensive work regarding the United States.

56. The HI programme pays for in-patient hospital care. The SMI programme pays for doctor visits and other out-patient care. It is voluntary, but virtually all HI beneficiaries enrol. Premiums are set at about 25 per cent of costs ($41.10 per month in 1994), with the rest borne by the Treasury. Individuals are responsible for long-term care, drugs as well as an annual deductible and co-insurance payments. Medicare pays after any private insurance which some retirees carry from their firms; in addition, many retirees purchase so-called Medigap policies from private insurers to fill in the gaps.

57. In 1991 approximately 11 per cent of beneficiaries who were in the programme over the course of the year were elderly, and 14 per cent were disabled, while 32 per cent of the payments were for the elderly and 36 per cent for the disabled.

58. For example, in late 1990 the government tightened fiscal policy to stem the burgeoning deficits in the face of a weakening economy. This sort of procyclical action could have been avoided if the federal finances had been in better condition.

59. Typically, there are portions of the budget that are not subject to the balanced budget requirements, particularly capital budgets. But the restraints do bind. For example, Bayoumi and Eichengreen (1994) report that states with stringent statutory and constitutional controls experience less variance in their fiscal balance over the cycle.

60. Indeed there is a large literature investigating the proposition, known as Ricardian equivalence, that changes in deficits are offset by changes in private saving. The results for the

United States are mixed but generally negative (Bernheim, 1988; Nicoletti, 1988). Many studies show that there is little response by saving to changes in the rate of return [see, for example, OECD (1994c) and Engen, Gale and Scholes (1994)], but others indicate that it may be substantial. Some studies indicate potentially large shifts in saving behaviour in response to qualifying asset limits imposed by some federal programmes (Hubbard *et al.*, 1995).

61. Congressional Budget Office (1995b) cites this range for the offset by private saving when budget reduction is accomplished without "altering any of the tax factors that enter into the decision to save".

62. Eventually, the ratio of capital to labour would stabilise when the additional investment is offset by the higher level of depreciation owing to the larger capital stock. At that time productivity growth would return to its original rate.

63. This calculation assumes that one-quarter of the increased federal government saving is offset by lower private and state and local government saving.

64. The relative strength of these two channels is a subject of debate. A high degree of capital mobility may decouple national saving and domestic investment, allowing most of the adjustment to occur in the external accounts. However, the econometric evidence is mixed. For example, Feldstein and Horioka (1980) found that 85 per cent of a sustained increase in national saving remained in the country of origin. See Obstfeldt (1993) for a more recent overview. Figure 30 suggests that much of the additional saving would be invested domestically.

65. This assumes that real interest rates on US assets abroad and foreign investment in the United States average 1.5 percentage points above the growth rate of real GDP. As shown by calculations in Chapter I, returns on the different components of net foreign debt vary dramatically; the estimated returns for US direct investment abroad and on portfolio income are much higher than those on foreign direct investment in the United States.

66. For example, the Administration assumes real GDP growth averaging 2.5 per cent over the next five years, 0.2 percentage point more than the CBO projections, and the Administration assumes that the differential between the growth rate of the CPI and the GDP deflator will turn out 0.2 percentage point smaller than does the CBO. Among technical assumptions, the Administration projects that spending on health care will rise less rapidly than does the CBO. Both sets of assumptions seem plausible.

67. Data for discretionary spending are available only as from 1962; however, OECD Secretariat calculations indicate that the proposed level for domestic spending as a share of GDP in 2002 would be similar to those of the 1950s and that defence and international spending would be lower than at any point in the post-war period.

68. In fiscal year 2000, mandatory spending cuts of $107 billion and discretionary cuts of $73 billion are proposed by Congress relative to the CBO baseline. But the baseline already includes substantial cuts in real discretionary spending relative to 1995 levels (roughly $37 billion in 2000), reflecting further implementation of OBRA93.

69. International comparisons routinely show that the share of GDP devoted to public investment in the United States is low relative to other OECD countries (OECD, 1994e), which might indicate that this source is not ripe for further cuts. Some of the divergence, however,

probably reflects greater reliance on private-sector provision of goods and services. More importantly, studies examining the impact of public capital are quite inconclusive as to whether there is too little spending currently (Holtz-Eakin, 1994); but neither do they indicate that there is too much investment. Thus, the proposed reductions could move the United States into a position of under-investment. The federal government's direct role is quite small, and questions have been raised about the efficacy of its indirect role (grants-in-aid). Empirical work reviewed by Tresch (1981) suggests that increases in grants may be largely offset by lower use of own funds; thus, a portion of the proposed reductions may be offset by lower levels of government.

70. Last year's Survey (OECD, 1994e) recommended better targeting of funds to disadvantaged communities.

71. Total Medicaid medical assistance spending per beneficiary in 1993 varied from $2 362 in Mississippi to $9 590 in New Hampshire. While some of the inter-state variation is due to the different structure of enrollees – the elderly and the disabled cost several times what the non-disabled under 65s cost – the within-category differences are also of the order of four to one. Only a small part of this can be explained by cost differences.

72. For example, there is empirical evidence to support the notion that high welfare benefits act as a magnet and high payment states have responded by cutting payments in real terms (Peterson, 1995). Consider a situation where two states offer identical benefits and the marginal cost equals the marginal benefit. It would be utility-enhancing for either state to cut benefits owing to the additional savings that are generated by the emigration of some of the current beneficiaries. The steady-state solution is that benefits in both would be less than the socially desirable level, unless there is co-ordination across the states, possibly through federal regulation.

73. For example, it is proposed to restrict eligibility for the EITC by including a limit on income from assets as well as earned income to prevent those with substantial assets from receiving benefits. Proposals for the SSI programme include more narrowly targeting benefits to disabled children and requiring families sponsoring an immigrant to support that person for a greater number of years.

74. A more detailed examination of fiscal federalism is found in OECD (1995c).

75. Tresch (1981) provides an extensive discussion on the theoretical considerations and empirical evidence on grants-in-aid.

76. See Stigler (1957) and Oates (1972).

77. Increasing the minimum retirement age is a slightly different policy and would affect more harshly those whose work capacity has decreased (near-elderly with disabilities or obsolete job skills). Any change in the minimum retirement age should also examine whether unemployment insurance and disability programmes adequately meet the needs of these near-elderly. Changes in the statutory retirement age may boost labour force participation because they send signals about social norms for retirement.

78. Steuerle and Bakija (1994) calculate that a male worker earning the average wage who retires at age 62 and receives benefits equal to 80 per cent of normal benefits experiences a 0.5 per cent reduction in lifetime benefits and a 7.2 per cent reduction in lifetime contributions. The increase in the net transfer received creates incentives for early retirement.

Likewise, those who stay in the labour force beyond age 65 are currently hit with high effective marginal tax rates because the benefit computation rules typically give little weight to the extra years of work and there is a wage earnings test that directly reduces benefits.

79. The Congressional Budget Office (1995c) estimates that a 5 per cent VAT on consumption excluding food, housing and medical care would boost revenues by 1.2 percentage points of GDP.

80. Tax reform has been receiving increased attention this year. Proposals for a national sales tax, a single-rated tax on earned and pension income ("flat tax") and a progressive consumed income tax ("Unlimited Savings Allowance" or USA tax) have been advanced. But these have been promoted as revenue-neutral changes to the system, rather than as means to increase revenues.

81. In addition, even the requirement that new programmes cannot increase the deficit is only on a prospective basis. For example, the temporary unemployment benefits legislated at the end of the last recession cost more than expected because unemployment continued to rise. But there was no requirement to offset the unexpected additional spending with further tax increases or spending cuts.

82. This would allow forward looking legislators to build surpluses and run a balanced budget over the business cycle instead of each year. This strategy has been pursued at the state level.

83. Some versions of the balance-budget amendment require that actual budgets balance, while others require only that projected budgets at the time of enactment be balanced. The former may have harsh consequences and force draconian policy reactions if a precariously balanced budget deteriorated part way through a budget year. The latter would provide substantial budget discipline, while allowing for some effects from automatic stabilisers. Greater discipline would apply if unexpected deficit outcomes were carried forward to be offset in the following year.

84. Most recent bills have included an escape clause that could be activated by a vote of three-fifths of the members of both houses of Congress and approval by the President.

85. This would clearly be the case if each budget were required to balance *ex post* without an escape clause. Addition of these provisions makes the argument less persuasive. Clearly in 1987 and 1990 Congress availed itself of escape clauses by repealing the Gramm-Rudman-Hollings deficit targets when the targets were difficult to meet. However, these actions required only majority votes.

86. Opportunities to redefine outlays and revenues to eliminate the deficit are virtually limitless. For example, during the thrift crisis the government created Resolution Finance Corporation (REFCORP) to move outlays for the thrift resolution off the books. Indeed, nearly $30 billion of borrowing by REFCORP appeared as negative outlays. The scheme failed because the cleanup needs turned out to be much greater than anticipated, and funding from the Treasury became necessary.

87. Both houses of Congress have passed versions of such a veto this year, but important differences remain to be worked out. A fully-fledged line-item veto would have required a Constitutional amendment. The House of Representatives therefore took an "enhanced rescissions" approach that would significantly boost the President's rescissions authority,

while the Senate took a "separate enrolment" approach which would implicitly divide each spending bill into a multitude of separate bills. Both of these proposals limit the line-item veto to discretionary spending bills.

88. In Ornstein and Makin (1994), it is argued that the likely result would be an increase in overall spending.

89. The legislation requires that the CBO estimate the effects on state and local spending of draft bills expected to raise outlays by at least $50 million for all lower levels of government combined. (The bill exempts programmes involving federal grants and anti-discrimination laws; it is estimated that two-thirds of existing mandates would have been exempt if the bill had been in effect.) In addition, the mandate provision would be subject to a separate vote requiring a majority to pass. As the majority vote is not an additional hurdle, the only effect of the legislation stems from the greater awareness of the cost of proposed mandates, although CBO already provides much of this information.

90. Support for such standards has waned in part because of the controversial set of standards developed in the subject of history; these allegedly overemphasise multiculturalism, thereby better reflecting the views of certain academics than of either teachers or the general public. Those recommended for the subject of English were rejected as too superficial by the Department of Education.

91. These centres have, however, begun to be implemented and seem to have bipartisan support.

92. A similar idea had been twice rejected in legislative form by the Congress in recent years. This time the Senate tried unsuccessfully to overturn the Order, but it is being challenged before the courts.

93. Implementing legislation has been introduced into both houses of Congress, but a Presidential veto has been threatened. The Commission also supported a number of other items intended to favour union organising activities.

94. Traditionally, the Administration seeks so-called "fast-track authority" from the Congress in order to negotiate trade agreements which are then presented to the Congress for final approval without further modification.

95. Aside from seeking sectoral deals the United States government had hoped to move on to more structural questions under the Framework Talks with Japan. These were to deal with, for example, the effects of competition policy and regulations in keeping out foreign goods and investment. Indeed, in June 1995 the two countries came to a conclusion on measures to increase foreign direct investment in Japan.

96. Details on flat glass were actually finalised only in December.

97. The major Japanese auto manufacturers announced voluntary plans to increase their purchases of competitive auto parts in early 1992. The results for 1993 show that indeed Japanese transplants in the United States boosted their purchases of US-made parts significantly and that Japanese imports of cars and parts from the United States also rose by one-third from 1992 levels. The latter may have represented trade diversion as corresponding imports from OECD-Europe fell 8.2 per cent that year. Exchange rate movements may have also contributed to these different outcomes.

98. The resulting uncertainty disturbed these imports.

99. By way of comparison, second place goes to the European Union with only 120. However, it should be noted that this number may decline significantly in the future because the United States has adopted a five-year "sunset" provision for antidumping and counter-vailing orders: all new orders are now subject to this provision, and existing orders will be reviewed within the next five years.

100. According to a study just released by the US International Trade Commission, cases filed under the so-called "fair trade laws" (antidumping and countervailing duty cases) in 1991 alone (excluding steel sector voluntary export restraints) imposed a net cost on the economy of $1.6 billion that year. The cost today could be much higher because duties have since been imposed in at least 71 more cases.

101. According to the International Trade Commission, of all antidumping cases for which there was a final determination that dumping had actually occurred from January 1980 to Septem-ber 1993, it was ultimately decided that no material injury to US producers had occurred in 31 per cent of those cases. For example, in September 1994 the Commerce Department imposed preliminary duties of up to 85 and 36 per cent, respectively, on imports of roses from Ecuador and Columbia, although the preliminary duties were withdrawn, as in March 1995 the International Trade Commission ruled that US producers had not been materially injured. Nevertheless, even though any duties paid are refunded in such cases, some recent research has indicated that the effect of a typical antidumping investigation is to reduce imports during the investigation period by about half the reduction that could be expected if duties had been imposed at the beginning of the investigation (Staiger and Wolak, 1994).

102. It should be noted that an OECD Environmental Performance Review of the United States is forthcoming in early 1996.

103. This includes public and private enterprise expenditures. According to internationally com-parable data, this represents about 1.6 per cent of GDP, a share among the highest of major OECD countries. Under current regulations it is likely to rise to about 2.6 per cent in the year 2000. Note that federal expenditures are a small share of the total – about 15 per cent of the public share.

104. Although no doubt many regulations do achieve a useful social goal, their cost is hidden and possibly not widely appreciated. For example, some growth accountants believe that they have cut productivity growth and impeded competitiveness. However, a recent revisionist view holds that some regulations have been proven to stimulate technological innovation which has ultimately led to an international comparative advantage. The overall evidence is inconclusive (see Jaffe et al., 1995).

105. This Congressional Budget Office cost estimate is based on the Senate Republican proposal to eliminate liability prior to late 1980, when the original legislation was passed. Republican members of the House of Representatives, on the other hand, favour eliminating liability before 1987 which would boost estimated annual costs to $1.6 billion.

106. The PSE is a summary measure of the support provided to agricultural producers. It should be noted that product coverage is not complete, and that year-to-year changes do not necessarily reflect programmatic changes in incentives.

107. Individual states can opt out: Texas has already, and others are considering it.

108. The weakness of the case for the separation of investment from commercial banking even at the time of the passage of the legislation is pointed out by Benston (1990). Yet it should be recognised that in recent years the impact of the law has been diminished through regulatory, judicial, state legislative and technological changes.

109. Some in the House also wish to include insurance, but with the intent of rolling back banks' increasing insurance activities which have resulted from recent OCC regulation and court decisions. In a related bill to reduce regulatory burdens, a House Committee has attached the provision allowing banks to affiliate with insurance companies but preventing the Comptroller of the Currency from expanding banks' powers to sell insurance. This second bill also exempts most banks from the 1977 Community Reinvestment Act (CRA) which requires banks to lend to the communities where they take deposits. The Administration has expressed serious concerns about both the insurance fallback and CRA provisions of the second bill.

110. The Savings Association Insurance Fund has a balance of only $1.9 billion or 28 cents for every $100 in insured deposits and is in danger of becoming insolvent within two years, according to the Chairman of the Federal Deposit Insurance Corporation. In contrast, the Bank Insurance Fund has reserves of $1.25 per $100 in insured deposits.

111. The PBGC guarantees the pensions of some 41 million private-sector workers. The maximum guarantee, however, is about $30 700 per year.

112. These officials are, respectively, David Kearns, Chairman of Xerox Corporation, and James Burke, Chief Executive Officer of Johnson and Johnson. They are quoted on page 23 of National Centre on Education and the Economy (1990).

113. The US "system" is not so much a system as an array of institutions that are loosely bound together by the legal, cultural and economic environment in which they operate.

114. See, for example, Bishop (1994), US Department of Labor (1995), National Center on Education and the Economy (1990) and Freeman (1994).

115. The 1994 Survey showed that the performance of elementary and secondary education systems in terms of achievement and attainment has been approximately stable since the early 1970s. Achievement scores declined slightly during the 1970s and increased slightly during the 1980s; they are now at about their 1970 levels. Drop-out rates have declined in recent years, but they remain very high for some population groups. Hispanic males, for example, had a drop-out rate of about 40 per cent in 1991.

116. See the 1994 Economic Report of the President, Chapter 5, for an detailed discussion of earnings trends.

117. This evolution of relative compensation in favour of the highly educated or the highly skilled has not been a uniform trend over the entire post-war period, however. Mincer (1994) describes the historical pattern of post-war rates of return to education as follows: "They (grew) in the sixties, fell in the 1970s to reach a low of about 4 per cent, a decline which was labelled or diagnosed as 'over-education' at the time. They have since rebounded in the 1980s to reach new heights at 12 per cent or more in the past half a dozen years."

118. Relative job stability refers to the retention rate relative to another reference group. For example, the declining relative job stability of young workers means that their retention rate fell relative to that of older workers.

119. In fact, for the years reported in the table, the Australian job tenure average is lower only in 1979, 1985 and 1991.

120. These might include services – real estate, mortgage lending, long-distance air transport, long-distance telecommunications – that lower the various costs of inter-regional migration. Another contributing factor might be the lack of extensive rent controls or housing subsidies that, in some other countries, bind large sections of the workforce into particular living arrangements (OECD, 1994*b*).

121. Job rotation may enhance the worker's attachment to his firm by increasing job interest but can also serve as an internal substitute for the flexibility and diversity of experience provided through the external labour market in the United States.

122. Qualifying training is defined as the process by which the basic skills and knowledge required in an occupation are acquired. Retraining is a type of qualifying training that the worker undertakes in order to shift careers.

123. A small but growing number of firms have gone somewhat beyond simple contracting for training with institutions of higher education. A few large companies have created autonomous business units whose primary function is to meet the continuing education requirement of all the firms' employees and its suppliers. This generally involves planning and contracting out with the most appropriate training providers. Sometimes it involves designing and giving courses. This development, if it becomes more common, will further blur the distinction between in-firm training and formal institutions.

124. In addition to instructional services, universities and colleges also provide research services, library services, community services, extension, hospitals and publishing.

125. Because of strong reputation effects, competition on the high end of the adult education market has not come from "new entrants" so much as through internal evolution and repositioning of existing institutions in a process that alters their relative competitiveness in different market segments.

126. Since these charitable contributions are so unevenly distributed, the implicit subsidy given to individual institutions is quite large. The total market value of all reported endowments was $59.5 billion in 1989. The two institutions with the largest endowments (Harvard University and the University of Texas at Austin) accounted for $7.3 billion of this. The top five institutions in terms of endowments accounted for $13 billion. Thus, the tax expenditure may be a significant subsidy for the small number of institutions who are very successful in attracting such contributions.

127. These districts are analogous to the school districts that control primary and secondary schools discussed in last year's Survey. They almost always exist solely for the purpose of controlling one or more community colleges and would not generally be associated with a municipal or county government. It is interesting to note that local control of community colleges seems to generate somewhat lower disparity in service quality than similar arrangements do in primary and secondary education. This is presumably because community colleges draw students – who would in any case usually commute – from a larger and presumably more diverse array of surrounding communities.

128. Apparently though the returns to different "associate degree" course work are highly variable, depending on the subject matter. For women, for example, most of the positive

returns appear to be due to taking courses in a limited number of areas: health fields, communications and design (Grubb, 1994; Kane and Rouse, 1995).

129. The sub-baccalaureate market is defined as adult education services that are not oriented toward completion of a four-year college or university degree. Usually such programmes give certificates (for very short programmes) or associate degrees (for a two-year programme).

130. These wage gains are apparent for individuals who undertook training prior to obtaining their current job; enrolment in these courses has no significant effect on wages for students who were already employed in their current job before enrolling.

131. The four-year academic market is sufficiently large and the price paid by families sufficiently high that private vendors have for many years found it profitable to publish a great deal of information about their services and outcomes. Private information services have not gained a foothold in the sub-baccalaureate market, however.

132. The rise in the college wage premium appears to have been in large part responsible for the increase in enrolments from 8.5 million people in 1970 to 14.4 million people in 1991.

133. Stafford loans can be of two types: the so-called "subsidised" and "unsubsidised" loans. (In economic terms, both types are subsidised because both involve government guarantees extended free of charge.) The college, university or training institute is responsible for screening eligible students and for determining their credit worthiness. The subsidised loans are available to financially needy students. For these, the federal government pays interest on the loan amount to the bank while the student is in school as well as the difference between the competitive rate and the subsidised interest rate during the life of the loan. The unsubsidised loans do not require that the student show financial need and are "unsubsidised" only in the sense that interest owed accrues to loan principal while the student is in school. Given these arrangements and the type of loan being subsidised, it is not surprising that default costs on the loan components of federal assistance to higher education are large and growing.

134. The problems US industry encounters in trying to work together on such standards are precisely those one would expect to find as private parties attempt to come together to develop an asset for which property rights are not well defined. First, the coalition is threatened by free riders, who do not pay to maintain the system, but who employ the skilled workers who emerge from it. Second, problems of cost sharing arise among the participants who are actively involved in the standards-setting process (General Accounting Office, 1993).

135. Occupations for which industries have been able to organise on their own in the United States include automotive technicians, medical record technicians, medical laboratory technicians, welders, heating and refrigeration technicians, engineers operating construction equipment, carpenters, stone masons and printing technicians (General Accounting Office, 1993). Professional occupations, such as doctors, accountants and architects, also have well-developed skill standards.

136. A report on eight industry-sponsored voluntary standards and credentials systems found that the development time for such systems ranged between two and eight years without pay-

back. In addition to development time, it takes a number of years for the systems to gain national credibility and acceptance.

137. Half of the households headed by someone under the age of 25 in the United States have less than $746 in financial assets. Only 34 per cent of the households headed by someone under the age of 35 own their own home. These low levels of assets mean that the worker has little borrowing capacity and a higher incentive to default and declare bankruptcy when borrowing (Bishop, 1994).

138. The Departments of Defence, Agriculture, Energy, Health and Human Services and Interior all operate training programmes as well.

139. The discussion contained in the next two paragraphs is based mainly on General Accounting Office (1994b).

140. Random assignment studies attempt to eliminate selection biases by using a lottery to determine who will receive programme services from a group of people who have applied for such services. This method allows for near-perfect control of background and motivational variables that might influence a programme's outcomes. The significant self-selection biases that are present in the econometric approach to evaluation of training programmes – where the analyst attempts to control for non-programme variables by introducing measures (such as innate ability) into estimated equations – have been convincingly demonstrated (Lalonde, 1986). Note that these experimental studies typically measure the incremental impact of the programme rather than training versus no training. The control group is prohibited from receiving services through the programme being tested, but not prohibited from receiving other education and training services available in the community. In the experimental evaluation of Jobstart discussed below, 94 per cent of the experimental group received education and training services, while 56 per cent of the control group eventually received some type of education and training service (Cave et al., 1993). Nevertheless, a training impact can still be derived since a much larger proportion of participants than controls receive services.

141. The assessment presented in this paragraph is based mainly on a document summarising the results of studies of federal training and adult education programmes (US Department of Labor, 1995).

142. The study involves 20 601 JTPA applicants at 16 sites over the period November 1987 to September 1989. The study tracked the experimental and control groups' earnings and employment histories for 18 months. The average 18 month salaries of the adult women randomly assigned to the treatment group was 7.2 per cent higher than the control group's mean salary and their employment rate was 2.1 percentage points higher than the control group. The adult men in the programme showed similar differences vis-à-vis the control group, but the differences were not statistically significant. In contrast to the findings for adults, the programme had little or no effect on the average earnings of female youths and actually reduced the earnings of male youths, on average, as evidenced by a statistically significant loss of $854 or –7.9 per cent over the 18 month period relative to the control group (General Accounting Office, 1994b).

143. The GED is the United States' most common high school equivalence certification for adults. GEDs account for about 15 per cent of the flow of new high school graduates

nationally. Basic education programmes frequently have GED receipt as a major goal for their participants. GED recipients earn less on average than high school graduates, but earn 5 to 10 per cent more than high school drop-outs (US Department of Labor, 1995). These earnings differences may reflect inherent differences in the earnings potential of high school graduates, drop-outs and GED holders. Those unable or unwilling to finish high school may be expected to have worse employment outcomes than those who graduate, regardless of their educational status. It is difficult to control statistically for all the differences between graduates, drop-outs and GED holders. Studies that explore the effect of GED attainment on earnings over time for the same individuals tend to find substantial payoffs from the GED credential (Cave and Bos, 1995).

144. For people who participated in Jobstart but who did not earn the GED, however, the cumulative earnings effect was negative, due essentially to the opportunity cost of having participated in the programme instead of having worked.

145. New approaches to serving both adults and youths show some promise but need more testing. These include the Center for Employment Training (CET) Program, the Quantum Opportunities Program (QOP), and the Riverside Country Program for welfare recipients. Each of these programmes has been shown to be highly cost-effective in random assignment studies, and need to be tested on a wider scale. There is some optimism in the research field that more comprehensive models are gradually being developed that will be effective for youth.

146. The new system is envisioned as utilising state-of-the-art automation to provide information on labour market trends, job openings, career options, and training and education opportunities. Grants have so far been made to all states to develop improved occupational projects and expanded dissemination of information.

147. Recent EDRC surveys have explored both the advantages and the disadvantages of relying on carefully cultivated long-term relationships as a means of channelling transactions in various activities. Two recent surveys in which this emerged as an issue are Germany (1995) for corporate governance and Japan (1993) for competition policy (in particular, the discussion of industrial alliances). In both cases, the United States system of arms-length contracting – both in finance and in organising relationships between firms – provided a useful counter-example.

148. The Earned Income Tax Credit appears to be a much more efficient way of boosting the incomes of the working poor.

149. Reliable evidence on comparative minimum wage settings is difficult to obtain.

150. Various exclusions allow some employers to pay less than the minimum wage. Under federal minimum wage laws, most of the exemptions are for small businesses and for agriculture.

151. Among workers aged 25 and above in 1993, the proportion working at or below the federal minimum wage was 2.5 per cent for men and 5.4 per cent for women.

152. This statement refers only to the forces that are exogenous to the domestic supply of skills in US markets. With regard to endogenous adjustment, it is reasonable to expect that private households will properly evaluate the shifting incentives in favour of skills acquisition and

respond accordingly. Indeed, the long-term behaviour of the adult education market, at a very aggregate level, shows fairly clear adjustment to shifting skills premia.

153. The sections on performance by state and by ethnic grouping are particularly telling in this regard. Accompanying data shows a ranking of states and nations with regard to the mathematics proficiency of thirteen year-olds. These show variation which is as high among the states as among countries. At the bottom of the ranking are a number of southern states and the country of Jordan. Furthermore, because the "general" education track – an ill-defined programme, neither academic nor vocational, that is followed by most young people – places few demands on students, many do not acquire basic habits of relevance to the workplace (discipline, timeliness, rigour).

154. The conclusions of last year's report highlighted the importance of "greater intellectual investment in the design of school-to-work programmes (which is given additional impetus under the School-to-Work Opportunities Act) and in occupational skills certification" (p. 129). It also emphasised the need to experiment with educational innovations designed to meet the needs of disadvantaged communities (*e.g.* "pro-poor" variants of voucher systems).

155. For example, in the Jobstart experimental evaluation described earlier, the arrest rate during the first year of the programme was 10.1 per cent for Jobstart participants and 12.6 per cent for the control group (US Department of Labor, 1995).

156. Criminal supervision is defined as parole or incarceration.

157. This cost was calculated from data presented in US Bureau of Census (1994) concerning annual expenditure on corrections by state and federal governments in 1990. Expenditure is divided by the number of people who were in federal or state prisons at the end of 1990.

Bibliography

Abt Associates (1994), *The National JTPA Study*, January.

Baker, Dean (1994), "The Myth of the Investment-Led Recovery", *Challenge*, November-December.

Ball, Laurence, Douglas W. Elmendorf and N. Gregory Mankiw (1995), "The Deficit Gamble", National Bureau of Economic Research Working Paper No. 5015, February.

Baxter, Marianne (1994), "Real exchange rates and real interest differentials: Have we missed the business cycle relationship?", *Journal of Monetary Economics*, 33.

Bayoumi, Tamim and Barry Eichengreen (1994), "Restraining Yourself: Fiscal Rules and Stabilisation", Centre for Economic Policy Research Discussion Paper No. 1029, September.

Benston, George J. (1990), *The Separation of Commercial and Investment Banking: The Glass Steagall Act Revisited and Reconsidered*, Oxford University Press.

Berger, Allen N. and David B. Humphrey (1992), "Megamergers in banking and the use of cost efficiency as an antitrust defense", *Antitrust Bulletin*, 37, 3, Autumn.

Bernanke, Ben S. and Alan S. Blinder (1992) "The Federal Funds Rate and the Channels of Monetary Transmission", *American Economic Review*, 82, 4, September.

Bernheim, B.D. (1987), "Ricardian Equivalence: An Evaluation of Theory and Evidence", in S. Fischer (ed.), *NBER Macroeconomic Annual 1987*, MIT Press, Cambridge, Massachusetts.

Bishop, John (1994), "Employer Training in the United States: A Review of the Literature", Consultancy report submitted to the OECD.

Board of Governors of the Federal Reserve System (1995), "Monetary Policy Report to the Congress Pursuant to the Full Employment and Balanced Growth Act of 1978", 19 July.

Board of Trustees, Federal Old-Age and Survivors Insurance and Disability Insurance Trust Funds (1995), "1995 Annual Report", April.

Board of Trustees, Federal Hospital Insurance Trust Fund (1994), "1994 Annual Report", April.

Bosworth, Barry and George Perry (1994),"Productivity and Real Wages: Is There a Puzzle?", *Brookings Papers on Economic Activity*, 1.

Boulton, Leyla (1995), "Politics of Pollution", *Financial Times*, 3 May.

Campbell, John Y. (1995), "Some Lessons from the Yield Curve", National Bureau of Economic Research Working Paper No. 5031, February.

Card, David and Alan Krueger (1995), *Myth and Measurement: The New Economics of the Minimum Wage*, Princeton University Press, Princeton, New Jersey.

Cave, George, Hans Bos, Fred Doolittle and Cyril Toussaint (1993), *Jobstart: Final Report on a Program for School Dropouts*, Manpower Demonstration Research Corporation, October.

Cave, George and Hans Bos (1995), "The Value of GED in a Choice Based Experimental Sample", unpublished working paper.

Clark, Peter, Douglas Laxton and David Rose (1995), "Asymmetry in the US Output-Inflation Nexus: Issues and Evidence", IMF Working Paper, WP/95/76, July.

Clotfelter, C.T. *et al.*, (1991), *Economic challenges in higher education*, University of Chicago Press, Chicago.

Congressional Budget Office (1991), *The Experience of the Stafford Loan Programme and Options for Change*, December.

Congressional Budget Office (1995a), *The Economic and Budget Outlook: Fiscal Years 1996-2000*, January.

Congressional Budget Office (1995b), *An Analysis of the President's Budgetary Proposals for Fiscal Year 1996*, April.

Congressional Budget Office (1995c), *Reducing the Deficit: Spending and Revenue Options*, February.

Cramton, Peter C., Morley Gunderson and Joseph S. Tracy (1995), "The Effect of Collective Bargaining Legislation on Strikes and Wages", National Bureau of Economic Research Working Paper No. 5105, May.

Cramton, Peter C. and Joseph S. Tracy (1995), "The Use of Replacement Workers in Union Contract Negotiations: The US Experience 1980-1989", National Bureau of Economic Research Working Paper No. 5106, May.

DiClemente, Robert V. and Deborah Burnham (1995), "Policy Rules Shed New Light on Fed Stance", Salomon Brothers Monetary Policy Update, 26 June.

Diebold, Francis, David Neumark and Daniel Polsky (1994), "Job Stability in the United States", National Bureau of Economic Research Working Paper No. 4859, September.

Eichengreen, Barry, (1993), "Labour Markets and European Monetary Unification", in P. Masson and M. Taylor (eds.), *Policy Issues in the Operation of Currency Unions*, Cambridge University Press, Cambridge.

Engen, Eric, William Gale and John Karl Scholz (1994), "Do Savings Incentives Work?", *Brookings Papers on Economic Activity,* 1.

Feldstein, Martin (1995), "Stabilize Prices, Not the Dollar", *Wall Street Journal Europe*, 21 March.

Feldstein, Martin and Charles Horioka (1980), "Domestic Saving and International Capital Flows", *Economic Journal*, 90, June.

Finegold, David (1995), "Workforce Development in the United States: Creating a More Effective Training Market", Consultancy report submitted to the OECD.

Frazis, Harley J., Diane E. Herz and Michael W. Horrigan (1995), "Employer-provided training: results from a new survey", *Monthly Labor Review*, 118, 5, May.

Freeman, Richard (1994), "Lessons for the United States", in Richard Freeman (ed.), *Working under Different Rules*, Russell Sage Foundation, New York.

General Accounting Office (1993), "Skills Standards: Experience in Certification Systems Shows Industry Involvement to be Key", May.

General Accounting Office (1994*a*), "Multiple Employment Training Programs: Overlapping Programs Can Add Unnecessary Administrative Costs", January.

General Accounting Office (1994*b*), "Multiple Employment Training Programs: Most Federal Agencies Do Not Know If Their Programs Are Working Effectively", March.

General Accounting Office (1995), "Block Grants: Characteristics, Experience and Lessons Learned", February.

Greenspan, Alan (1995), Remarks before the 31st Annual Conference on Bank Structure and Competition, Federal Reserve Bank of Chicago, Chicago, 11 May.

Grubb, W. Norton (1994), "Post-secondary Education and the Sub-baccalaureate Labor Market: Corrections and Extensions", forthcoming in *Economics of Education Review*.

Harhoff, Dietmar and Thomas Kane (1995), "Is the German Apprenticeship System a Panacea for the US Labor Market?", unpublished Working Paper, May.

Hirsch, Albert A. (1994), "Residential Construction From a Long-Run Perspective", *Survey of Current Business*, 74, 6, June.

Holtz-Eakin, Douglas (1994), "Public Sector Capital and the Productivity Puzzle", *Review of Economics and Statistics*, 76, 1, February.

Hubbard, R. Glenn, Jonathan Skinner and Stephen P. Zeldes (1994), "Precautionary Saving and Social Insurance", National Bureau of Economic Research Working Paper 4884, October.

Huh, Chan G. and Trehan, Bharat (1995), "Modelling the Time-Series Behavior of the Aggregate Wage Rate", *Economic Review*, Federal Reserve Bank of San Fransicso, No. 1.

Ilg, Randy (1995), "The Changing Face of Farm Employment", *Monthly Labor Review*, 118, 4, April.

Jaffe, Adam B., Steven R. Peterson, Paul R. Portney and Robert Stavins (1995), "Environmental Regulation and the Competitiveness of US Manufacturing", *Journal of Economic Literature*, XXXIII, 1, March.

Kane, Thomas J. and Cecilia Elena Rouse (1995), "Labor-Market Returns to Two- and Four-Year College", *American Economic Review*, 85, 3, June.

Karim, Amin and Arthur Patton (1995), "Motorola-DeVry Partnership Customisation of the Technician Curriculum", *Learning Organisations for the 21st Century: Education on Demand*, Conference Proceedings, American Society of Engineering Education, College Industry Education Conference, 22-27 January.

Keltner, Brent (1994), "Relationship-Banking as a Competitive Response to Dynamic Financial Sector Markets: Evidence from the US and Germany", paper submitted to the *California Management Review*.

Lalonde, Robert (1986), "Evaluating the Econometric Evaluations of Training Programs with Experimental Data", *American Economic Review*, 76, 4, September.

Landefield, J. Steven and Robert P. Parker (1995), "Preview of the Comprehensive Revision of the National Income and Product Accounts: BEA's New Featured Measures of Output and Prices", *Survey of Current Business*, 75, 7, July.

Lasky, Mark J. (1995), "A Preview of the New Chain-Weighted GDP Measures", *Review of the US Economy*, Data Resources Incorporated, September.

Lee, William and Eswar Prasad (1994), "Changes in the Relationship Between the Long-Term Interest Rate and its Determinants", International Monetary Fund Working Paper WP/94/124, September.

Leibfritz, W. *et al.* (1995), "Ageing populations, pension systems and government budgets: how do they affect saving?", OECD Economics Department Working Paper 156.

Lynch, Lisa M. (1992), "Private Sector Training and the Earnings of Young Workers", *American Economic Review*, 82, 1, March.

Mangum, Steve and David Ball (1986), "Military Service, Occupational Training and Labor Market Outcomes: An Update", Centre for Human Resource Research, The Ohio State University, Columbus, March.

McLaughlin, Susan (1995), "The Impact of Interstate Banking and Branching Reform: Evidence from the States", *Current Issues in Economics and Finance*, Federal Reserve Bank of New York, 1, 2, May.

Meyer, John, Francisco Ramirez and Yasemin Nuhoglu Soysal (1992), "World Expansion of Mass Education, 1870-1980", *Sociology of Education*, 65, April.

Mincer, Jacob (1994), "Investment in US Education and Training", National Bureau of Economic Research Working Paper No. 4844, August.

Mishkin, Frederic S. (1976), "Illiquidity, Consumer Durable Expenditure, and Monetary Policy", *American Economic Review*, 66, 4, September.

National Center on Education and the Economy (1990), *America's Choice: High Skills or Low Wages*, June.

Neumark, David and William Wascher (1994), "Minimum Wage Effects on Employment and School Enrolment", National Bureau of Economic Research Working Paper No. 4679, March.

Neumark, David and William Wascher (1995), "Minimum Wage Effects on School and Transitions of Teenagers", *American Economic Review*, 85, 2, May.

Newhouse, J. (1992), "Medical care costs: how much welfare loss?", *Journal of Economic Perspectives*, 6, 3, Summer.

Nicoletti, Giuseppe (1988), "A cross-country analysis of private consumption, inflation and the debt neutrality hypothesis", *OECD Economic Studies*, 10, Spring.

Oates, Wallace (1972), *Fiscal Federalism*, Harcourt Brace Jovanovich, New York.

Obstfeldt, Maurice (1993), "International Capital Mobility in the 1990s", National Bureau of Economic Research Working Paper 4534, November.

OECD (1988), *Why Economic Policies Change Course*, Paris.

183

OECD (1993*a*), *Economic Survey of Iceland 1993*, Paris, May.

OECD (1993*b*), *Employment Outlook*, Paris, July.

OECD (1994*a*), *Employment Outlook*, Paris, July.

OECD (1994*b*), *Jobs Study, Part II, Evidence and Explanations*, Paris.

OECD (1994*c*), *Taxation and Household Saving*, Paris.

OECD (1994*d*), *Farm Employment and Economic Adjustment in OECD Countries*, Paris.

OECD (1994*e*), *Economic Survey of the United States 1994*, Paris, November.

OECD (1995*a*), *Education at a Glance*, Paris.

OECD (1995*b*), *Agricultural Policies, Markets and Trade in OECD Countries: Monitoring and Outlook*, Paris, May.

OECD (1995*c*), *Economic Survey of Mexico 1995*, Paris.

OECD (1995*d*), *Reviews of Foreign Direct Investment: United States*, Paris.

Ornstein, Norman and John Makin (1994), *Debt and Taxes,* Times Books, New York.

Osterberg, William P. and James B. Thomson (1995), ''SAIF Policy Options'', *Economic Commentary*, Federal Reserve Bank of Cleveland, June.

Oxley, Howard and Maitland MacFarlan (1994), ''Health care reform: controlling spending and increasing efficiency'', OECD Economics Department Working Papers No. 149, Paris.

Pakko, Michael R. (1995), ''The FOMC in 1993 and 1994: Monetary Policy in Transition'', *Federal Reserve Bank of St. Louis Review*, 77, 2, March/April.

Peterson, Paul (1995), ''Who Should Do What?'', *The Brookings Review*, Washington, DC, Spring.

Roberts, Kristin and Peter Rupert (1995), ''The Myth of the Overworked American'', *Economic Commentary*, Federal Reserve Bank of Cleveland, 15 January.

Rose, Stephen (1995), *Declining Job Security and the Professionalisation of Opportunity*, National Commission for Employment Policy, May.

Saunders, Lisa (1995), ''Relative earnings of black men to white men by region, industry'', *Monthly Labor Review*, 118, 4, April.

Schor, Juliet B. (1992), *The Overworked American: The Unexpected Decline of Leisure*, Basic Books, New York.

Snower, Dennis (1994), ''The Low-Skill, Bad-Job Trap'', Centre for Economic Policy Research Discussion Paper No. 999, September.

Staiger, Robert W. and Frank A. Wolak (1994), ''The Trade Effects of Antidumping Law: Theory and Evidence'' in Alan Deardorff and Robert Stern (eds.), *Analytical and Negotiating Issues in the Global Treading System*, pp. 231-261, cited in Staiger, Robert W. and Frank A. Wolak (1994), ''Differences in the Uses and Effects of Antidumping Law Across Import Sources'', National Bureau of Economic Research Working Paper No. 4846, September.

Steuerle, C. Eugene and Jon M. Bakija (1994), *Retooling Social Security for the 21st Century*, Urban Institute Press, Washington, DC.

Stigler, George (1957), "Tenable Range of Functions of Local Governments", *Federal Expenditure Policy for Economic Growth and Stability*, Joint Economic Committee, Subcommittee on Fiscal Policy, Washington, DC.

Tresch, Richard W. (1981), *Public Finance: A Normative Theory*, Business Publications, Plano, Texas.

Turner, David (1995), "Speed limit and asymmetric inflation effects from the output gap in the major seven economies", *OECD Economic Studies*, 24.

US Bureau of the Census (1994), *Statistical Abstract of the United States*.

US Department of Education (1992), *Digest of Education Statistics 1992*.

US Department of Labor (1995), *What's Working (and what's not): A Summary of Research on the Economic Impacts of Employment and Training Programs*, Office of the Chief Economist, January.

US Department of the Treasury (1992), *Integration of the Individual and Corporate Tax Systems*, US Government Printing Office, January.

US Senate Budget Committee (1995), "FY 1996 Concurrent Resolution on the Budget", US Government Printing Office, May.

Background material for Chapter II

This annex will briefly document the specification and estimation of equations describing the evolution over time of unemployment shares by reason for unemployment and by duration and of the average workweek. The intent of the empirical work is to extract underlying trends corrected for cyclical variations.

Unemployment shares by reason for unemployment

The US Department of Labor publishes monthly data on the reason why those unemployed were without a job. Three categories are given: job losers, job leavers (quits) and new entrants and re-entrants. To purge these series of their cyclical components the three shares were regressed against the aggregate unemployment rate and a quadratic trend term, along with a series of lagged dependent variables to proxy the relevant dynamic reactions. In addition, interaction terms between the trends and the unemployment regressor were admitted, thereby allowing for time-varying coefficients. To investigate the impact of the change in the Current Population Survey (from which these data are extracted) in 1994, additive and multiplicative dummies were originally included. Finally, lagged cross shares were also entered to see whether any patterns of interaction could be uncovered.

Estimation was undertaken using Ordinary Least Squares; cross-equation constraints (implicit in the share equation specification) were not explicitly imposed because of the inclusion of the lagged dependent variables. Adding-up is therefore violated, but this was deemed to be acceptable since the primary goal, as stated above, was to extract underlying trends. The preferred estimation results are given in Table A1. We see that higher unemployment boosts the job losers' share at the expense of the other two shares, as would be expected. The job losers' share also has a U-shaped trend, while the trend in the leavers' share is linear but related to the cycle (the trend is negative when the unemployment rate exceeds 5.8 per cent and *vice versa*) and that in the entrants' share is inverse U-shaped. In the final quarter of the sample, the first quarter of 1995, it can be seen that the trend is toward a rising share for job losers and a falling share for new entrants and re-entrants, with little change in the leavers' share.

	Job losers' share	Job leavers' share	New entrants' and re-entrants' share
Constant	−0.1221	0.0418	0.6025
	(1.17)	(3.99)	(3.47)
UNR	0.0455	−0.0106	−0.0331
	(9.82)	(5.45)	(8.98)
D94*UNR	−0.0079	−0.0020	0.0096
	(5.47)	(3.98)	(7.23)
UNR (−1)	−0.0270	0.0095	0.0166
	(5.44)	(5.03)	(3.64)
Trend	−0.1563E-2	0.3254E-3	0.8552E-3
	(2.18)	(3.34)	(3.01)
Trend**2	0.2661E-4		−0.1788E-3
	(2.98)		(4.48)
Trend*UNR	0.7733E-4	−0.5605E-4	
	(0.71)	(3.46)	
Trend**2*UNR	−0.1548E-5		0.1155E-5
	(1.43)		(3.28)
LDV1	0.5689	0.7018	0.5389
	(6.26)	(10.32)	(6.55)
LDV2	0.2619		0.3860
	(1.75)		(2.04)
LDV3		0.2638	
		(2.79)	
LDV4	−0.0967	−0.2380	
	(2.15)	(3.34)	
Entrants' share (−2)	0.3520		
	(2.62)		
RBSQ	0.9679	0.9535	0.9458
SEE	0.0109	0.0050	0.0101
Durbin h	0.90	−0.95	0.56
Sample period	68Q1-95Q1	68Q1-95Q1	68Q1-95Q1
Trend effect in 95Q1	0.20	0.00	−2.14

1. UNR = civilian unemployment rate; D94 is a dummy variable equal to one beginning in 1994.
Source: OECD.

Unemployment shares by duration

Along with data on the reason for unemployment, the Current Population Survey categorises the unemployed by the duration of their current spell. The categories are as follows: less than 5 weeks, 5-14 weeks, 15-26 weeks and 27 weeks and over. Share equations have again been estimated along the lines of the previous specification. Cyclical effects are purged by controlling for the aggregate unemployment rate and its lags, dynamics are allowed for by including a series of lagged dependent variables, and cross share effects were also permitted. Trends were again modelled by a quadratic specification, and no cross-equation constraints were imposed.

The regression results are reported in Table A2. Those unemployed for less than 5 weeks are seen to be less numerous when the unemployment rate is high, mainly at the expense of those unemployed for slightly longer duration. But higher overall unemploy-

Table A2. **Shares of joblessness by duration**

	Less than 5 weeks	5-14 weeks	15-26 weeks	27 weeks and over
Constant	0.1114	0.1234	−0.0739	−0.0231
	(2.99)	(4.67)	(4.66)	(3.90)
LDV1	0.8902	0.5778	0.4060	0.9484
	(10.16)	(7.84)	(6.41)	(11.00)
LDV2	−0.1986		0.2021	−0.2566
	(1.60)		(3.62)	(4.03)
LDV3	0.3100	0.1385		
	(2.84)	(1.57)		
LDV4	−0.1664	−0.1324		
	(2.65)	(1.75)		
UNR	−0.0164	0.0163		−0.0039
	(4.55)	(6.18)		(1.82)
UNR$_{-1}$	−0.0116	−0.0207	0.0170	0.0118
	(1.60)	(6.48)	(8.60)	(4.71)
UNR$_{-2}$	0.0209		−0.0116	−0.0065
	(4.05)		(4.99)	(1.97)
UNR$_{-4}$		0.0026		
		(1.78)		
Trend	0.4004E-3	0.4429E-3	−0.5331E-3	−0.7254E-3
	(2.07)	(2.81)	(4.33)	(4.77)
Trend**2	−0.3883E-5	−0.2820E-5	0.4160E-5	0.5810E-3
	(2.01)	(2.68)	(4.76)	(4.96)
5-14 week share$_{-1}$			0.3377	
			(6.18)	
15-26 week share$_{-1}$				0.3586
				(4.60)
15-26 week share$_{-2}$				−0.3203
				(3.19)
15-26 week share$_{-3}$				0.1635
				(2.04)
RBSQ	0.9812	0.7182	0.9340	0.9875
SEE	0.0094	0.0079	0.0056	0.0058
Durbin h	−0.00	−0.42	1.21	−0.92
Sample period	65Q2-95Q1	65Q2-95Q1	65Q2-95Q1	65Q2-95Q1
Mean residual, 91Q2-95Q1	−0.0019	0.0007	0.0012	0.0006
Trend analysis:				
Peak/trough quarter	76Q4	83Q3	79Q4	79Q2
Trend effect per quarter in 95Q1	−.003 points	−.008 points	.007 points	.013 points

Source: OECD.

188

ment eventually leads to an increase in longer-duration unemployment at the expense of shorter-duration unemployment. Most important for present purposes is the finding that both shorter-duration shares manifest inverted U-shaped trends, while both longer-term shares manifest U-shaped trends. All maxima/minima occur in the late-1970s or early 1980s. By the first quarter of this year therefore the shorter-duration shares were exogenously trending down, while the longer-duration shares were trending up, especially the 27 weeks and over share.

The average workweek

The monthly establishment survey of the US Department of Labor includes figures on the average workweek in hours, both for the total private sector as well as disaggre-

Table A3. **The average workweek over time**

	Total private sector	Goods-producing	Services-producing
Constant	1.5931	1.7441	0.8523
	(7.38)	(16.10)	(3.86)
LDV1	0.4447	0.3524	0.5801
	(5.81)	(imposed)	(6.25)
LDV2	0.1208		0.1848
	(1.68)		(2.08)
LDV3		0.1771	
		(5.43)	
Employment Growth		0.4705	
		(16.08)	
Deviations from trend	0.4298		0.1288
	(10.82)		(2.25)
Deviations lagged once	−0.4244		−0.1770
	(11.36)		(3.03)
Trend	−0.9023E-3	−0.4596E-3	−0.6673E-3
	(7.20)	(9.35)	(3.71)
Trend**2	0.3675E-5	0.4307E-5	0.2870E-5
	(7.14)	(10.92)	(3.84)
Dummy = 1 in each Q1		−0.0073	
		(9.57)	
RBSQ	0.997	0.940	0.998
SEE	0.0020	0.0036	0.0022
Sample period	65Q1-95Q1	65Q1-95Q1	65Q1-95Q4
Trend analysis: Peak/trough quarter	94Q3	77Q1	92Q4
Trend effect per quarter in 95Q1	0.03 minute	1.5 minutes	0.1 minute
(in per cent per year)	0.007	0.246	0.020

Source: OECD.

gated by sector. In order to discern underlying trends, equations were estimated for the aggregate as well as for goods-producing and services-producing sub-sectors. This time cyclical influences were found to be clearer when the control variable was either employment growth or deviations of employment from trend (as proxied by a Hodrick-Prescott procedure). Again, lagged dependent variables were allowed for, and trends were proxied by a quadratic specification. Finally, a seasonal pattern to the goods producing series was allowed for. The estimation results are given in Table A3.

The results show that when employment is above trend the workweek lengthens; this implies that in the short term hiring and lengthening the workweek are complementary strategies to increase labour inputs. However, this effect dissipates quite rapidly. In goods-producing sectors any growth at all in employment generates a lengthening of the workweek. The estimations also show U-shaped trends in the aggregate and in each component. The trend turns positive already in 1977 in the goods-producing industries but not until the 1990s in the services-producing sector and in the aggregate. The effect is quite large in the goods-producing equation: about ¼ per cent per year.

Annex II

Calendar of main economic events

1994

October

Agreement is reached to end the trade disputes with Japan in the areas of telecommunications equipment, medical technology, insurance and flat glass.

The federal government records a deficit of $203 billion for fiscal year 1994, 3 per cent of GDP, the lowest figures since 1989.

November

The Federal Reserve increases the federal funds rate to $5\frac{1}{2}$ per cent, 75 basis points above the rate that had prevailed since August. It also increases the discount rate by a similar amount to $4\frac{3}{4}$ per cent and issues a symmetric directive towards inter-meeting policy changes.

In mid-term elections, the Democratic party loses control of the House of Representatives and the Senate.

At the meeting of the Asia Pacific Economic Co-operation forum it is agreed to move further toward free and open trade and investment in the area by 2020.

December

In Miami, 34 western hemisphere nations agree to establish a free trade area by 2005.

The Federal Reserve leaves its short-term policy instruments unchanged but issues an asymmetric directive biased toward further tightening.

1995

January

The United States becomes a founding member of the World Trade Organisation.

Japan and the United States reach a trade agreement in the financial services area.

The Administration co-ordinates a $50 billion international relief package for Mexico.

February

The Administration's FY 1996 budget calls for $200 billion deficits, on average over the next five years.

- Under Administration policies, it is projected that the FY 1995 deficit will total $193 billion and the FY 1996 deficit $197 billion.
- The deficit-to-GDP ratio is projected to edge down from $2^3/_4$ per cent in FY 1995 to 2 per cent by 2000.
- Discretionary spending is projected to decline by about 3 per cent annually in real terms through agency restructuring and reductions in size and scope of programmes.
- Mandatory spending proposals reduce expenditures by an average of about $6 billion per year beginning in 1997.
- Net tax cuts totalling $10 billion in 1997 rising to $18 billion by 2000 are proposed. The two main elements are a tax credit for dependent children and tax incentives for education and training.

The Federal Reserve boosts the federal funds rate and the discount rate by $1/_2$ percentage point to 6 per cent and $5^1/_4$ per cent, respectively and adopts a symmetric directive. In semi-annual testimony before Congress, Chairman Greenspan states that increases and decreases in short-term rates are now equally likely.

An agreement is reached with China regarding intellectual property rights.

March

A balanced-budget amendment to the constitution fails to pass the Senate after having passed the House in January.

US dollar declines sharply against Deutschemark and yen. The slide continues into April, especially against the yen before the dollar stabilises and then recovers a bit. On a monthly basis, the dollar traded at 98, 91 and 84 yen and 1.50, 1.41 and 1.38 Deutschemark in February, March and April, respectively.

At its March meeting, the Federal Reserve leaves interest rates unchanged but issued a biased directive towards additional restraint.

House passes its welfare reform bill.

April

House passes tax bill which cuts taxes by $189 billion over 5 years.

May

The United States announces 100 per cent tariffs on Japanese luxury autos, as part of a Section 301 investigation, if agreements are not reached on trade issues related to US access to Japanese automobile and auto parts markets.

The Senate and House each develop outlines of programmes to balance the budget by 2002 through expenditure cuts. Both proposals also contemplate tax cuts.

At its May meeting the Federal Reserve leaves monetary policy unchanged.

June

United States and Japan agree to a resolution in auto dispute.

The Administration announces a program to balance the budget over 10 years based on more modest spending cuts and tax cuts than congressional proposals.

Congress passes FY 1996 Budget Resolution calling for a balanced budget by 2002.

The United States announces that it is unsatisfied with the offers of other countries in the multilateral financial services negotiations and will pursue bilateral negotiations in this area.

Senate passes a bill further deregulating the telecommunications sector.

July

The Federal Reserve cuts the Federal funds rate to 5¾ per cent, stating that "inflationary pressures have receded enough to accommodate a modest adjustment in monetary conditions", and issues a biased directive towards additional easing.

August

Federal Reserve leaves interest rates unchanged and issues an unbiased directive.

193

House passes telecommunications deregulation bill which is similar in scope but is different than the Senate-passed bill.

Aided by official intervention, dollar rallies against yen and Deutschemark and finishes the month near 97 yen and 1.46 Deutschemark.

September

Senate passes a welfare reform bill.

Federal government's fiscal year ends without enactment any of the thirteen annual appropriations bills for FY 1996; a continuing resolution is passed to fund the government until mid-November.

STATISTICAL ANNEX AND STRUCTURAL INDICATORS

Table A. **Selected background statistics**

	Average 1985-94	1985	1986	1987	1988	1989	1990	1991	1992	1993	1994
A. Percentage change from previous year at constant 1987 prices											
Private consumption	2.7	4.4	3.6	2.8	3.6	1.9	1.5	-0.4	2.8	3.3	3.5
Gross fixed capital formation	2.9	5.0	0.4	-0.5	4.2	0.1	-1.8	-7.6	5.5	11.3	12.3
Residential	1.9	1.3	12.0	-0.4	-1.1	-3.8	-9.2	-12.9	16.2	8.2	8.6
Non-residential	3.4	6.4	-4.1	-0.5	6.6	1.7	1.2	-5.7	2.0	12.5	13.7
GDP	2.6	3.2	2.9	3.1	3.9	2.5	1.2	-0.6	2.3	3.1	4.1
GDP price deflator	3.3	3.6	2.7	3.2	3.9	4.5	4.3	3.8	2.8	2.2	2.1
Industrial production	2.4	1.7	0.9	5.0	4.4	1.5	0.0	-1.7	3.3	4.1	5.3
Employment	1.6	2.0	2.3	2.6	2.3	2.0	0.5	-0.9	0.6	1.5	3.1
Compensation of employees (current prices)	6.1	7.0	5.9	6.9	8.3	6.1	6.4	3.3	5.5	5.3	5.9
Productivity (GDP/employment)[1]	0.8	0.5	1.2	0.4	0.8	0.1	-0.1	0.3	2.6	1.2	1.2
Unit labour costs (compensation/GDP)	3.4	3.7	2.9	3.7	4.2	3.5	5.1	3.9	3.1	2.1	1.8
B. Percentage ratios											
Gross fixed capital formation as per cent of GDP at constant prices	15.7	16.9	16.5	15.9	16.0	15.6	15.1	14.1	14.5	15.7	16.9
Stockbuilding as per cent of GDP at constant prices	0.4	0.5	0.2	0.6	0.4	0.6	0.1	0.0	0.0	0.3	0.9
Foreign balance as per cent of GDP at constant prices	-1.9	-3.4	-3.5	-3.1	-2.2	-1.5	-1.1	-0.4	-0.6	-1.4	-2.1
Compensation of employees as per cent of GDP at current prices	59.4	59.0	59.1	59.4	59.6	59.0	59.5	59.5	59.7	59.6	59.4
Direct taxes as per cent of household income	12.0	12.0	11.8	12.5	11.9	12.5	12.3	11.8	11.6	11.7	12.0
Household saving as per cent of disposable income	4.9	6.6	6.2	4.5	4.5	4.1	4.3	5.1	5.2	4.6	4.2
Unemployment as per cent of total labour force	6.4	7.2	7.0	6.2	5.5	5.3	5.5	6.7	7.4	6.8	6.1
C. Other indicator											
Current balance (billion dollars)	-108.5	-124.2	-150.9	-166.3	-127.1	-103.8	-92.7	-7.4	-61.6	-100.2	-151.2

1. Ratio of business sector GDP to business sector employment.
Source: US Department of Commerce, Survey of Current Business, and OECD.

Table B. National product and expenditure

Seasonally adjusted, percentage changes from previous period, annual rates, 1987 prices

	Average 1984-94	1984	1985	1986	1987	1988	1989	1990	1991	1992	1993	1994
Private consumption	2.9	4.8	4.4	3.6	2.8	3.6	1.9	1.5	-0.4	2.8	3.3	3.5
Public expenditure	2.0	3.1	6.1	5.2	3.0	0.6	2.0	3.1	1.2	-0.7	-0.8	-0.8
Gross fixed investment	4.1	15.9	5.0	0.4	-0.5	4.2	0.1	-1.8	-7.6	5.5	11.3	12.3
Residential	3.0	14.4	1.3	12.0	-0.4	-1.1	-3.8	-9.2	-12.9	16.2	8.2	8.6
Non-residential	4.6	16.5	6.4	-4.1	-0.5	6.6	1.7	1.2	-5.7	2.0	12.5	13.7
Final domestic demand	2.9	6.2	4.8	3.4	2.3	3.1	1.7	1.3	-1.2	2.5	3.7	4.1
Stockbuilding[1]	0.1	1.6	-1.1	-0.3	0.4	-0.1	0.2	-0.5	-0.1	0.1	0.3	0.6
Total domestic demand	3.0	7.8	3.6	3.0	2.7	3.0	1.8	0.8	-1.3	2.5	3.9	4.7
Exports of goods and services	7.9	6.9	1.2	6.6	10.5	15.8	11.9	8.2	6.3	6.7	4.1	9.0
Imports of goods and services	7.8	25.0	6.3	6.6	4.6	3.7	3.8	3.6	-0.5	8.7	10.7	13.4
Foreign balance[1]	-0.1	-1.7	-0.6	-0.2	0.3	0.9	0.6	0.4	0.7	-0.3	-0.8	-0.7
GDP	2.9	6.2	3.2	2.9	3.1	3.9	2.5	1.2	-0.6	2.3	3.1	4.1

	1994 levels (1987 $ billions)	1992 Q4	1993 Q1	Q2	Q3	Q4	1994 Q1	Q2	Q3	Q4	1995 Q1	Q2
Private consumption	3 579.6	5.6	1.6	2.6	3.9	4.0	4.7	1.3	3.1	5.1	1.6	3.4
Public expenditure	922.8	0.9	-5.9	1.2	1.1	-0.1	-4.9	-1.2	6.7	-4.1	-0.7	0.2
Gross fixed investment	903.8	11.7	12.3	8.9	11.4	22.9	10.6	8.6	8.6	13.6	15.0	4.9
Residential	231.4	23.8	5.3	-7.6	9.4	28.2	10.0	7.0	-6.0	2.3	-3.4	-13.7
Non-residential	672.4	7.5	15.1	15.6	12.2	21.1	10.9	9.2	14.1	17.6	21.5	11.3
Final domestic demand	5 406.2	5.6	1.7	3.3	4.5	6.0	3.9	2.0	4.6	4.8	3.4	3.1
Stockbuilding[1]	47.8	0.0	0.2	0.0	-0.1	0.0	0.3	0.6	0.0	-0.1	0.0	-0.3
Total domestic demand	5 454.0	5.7	2.7	3.3	4.0	5.8	5.0	4.6	4.4	4.2	3.5	1.9
Exports of goods and services	657.0	7.2	-1.0	7.7	-3.2	21.7	-3.5	16.6	14.8	20.2	4.8	6.6
Imports of goods and services	766.9	6.5	11.6	14.9	7.4	16.0	9.5	18.9	15.6	11.4	10.1	9.9
Foreign balance[1]	-109.9	0.0	-0.4	-0.2	-0.3	0.1	-0.4	-0.1	-0.1	0.2	-0.2	-0.2
GDP	5 344.1	5.7	1.2	2.4	2.7	6.3	3.3	4.1	4.0	5.1	2.7	1.3

1. Changes as a percentage of previous period GDP.
Source: US Department of Commerce, *Survey of Current Business.*

Table C. Labour market

Seasonally adjusted

	1986	1987	1988	1989	1990	1991	1992	1993	1994	1994 Q2	1994 Q3	1994 Q4	1995 Q1	1995 Q2
1. Number of persons, millions														
Population of working age[1,2]	180.6	182.8	184.6	186.4	188.0	189.8	192.0	194.8	196.8	196.5	197.1	197.6	197.9	198.3
Civilian labour force[1]	117.8	119.9	121.7	123.9	124.8	125.3	126.9	128.0	131.0	130.7	131.1	131.7	132.3	132.1
Unemployment[1]	8.2	7.4	6.7	6.5	6.9	8.4	9.4	8.7	8.0	8.1	7.8	7.3	7.3	7.5
Employment[1]	109.6	112.4	115.0	117.3	117.9	116.9	117.6	119.3	123.1	122.6	123.2	124.4	125.0	124.6
Employment[3]	99.3	102.0	105.2	107.9	109.4	108.3	108.6	110.7	114.0	113.6	114.5	115.3	116.1	116.4
Federal government	2.9	2.9	3.0	3.0	3.1	3.0	3.0	2.9	2.9	2.9	2.9	2.9	2.8	2.8
State and local	13.8	14.1	14.4	14.8	15.2	15.4	15.7	15.9	16.2	16.2	16.3	16.4	16.4	16.4
Manufacturing	18.9	19.0	19.3	19.4	19.1	18.4	18.1	18.1	18.3	18.3	18.3	18.4	18.5	18.5
Construction	4.8	5.0	5.1	5.2	5.1	4.7	4.5	4.7	5.0	5.0	5.0	5.1	5.2	5.2
Other	58.9	61.0	63.4	65.5	66.9	66.8	67.4	69.1	71.6	71.3	71.9	72.5	73.1	73.4
2. Percentage change from previous period (s.a.a.r.)														
Population of working age[1,2]	1.3	1.2	1.0	1.0	0.9	0.9	1.2	1.5	1.0	0.9	1.1	1.1	0.6	0.8
Civilian labour force	2.1	1.7	1.5	1.8	0.8	0.4	1.3	0.8	2.3	-0.1	1.2	2.0	1.9	-0.5
Employment[1]	2.3	2.6	2.3	2.0	0.5	-0.9	0.6	1.5	3.1	1.6	2.1	3.8	2.1	-1.2
Employment[3]	2.0	2.6	3.2	2.6	1.4	-1.1	0.3	2.0	3.0	3.6	3.0	3.0	2.6	1.0
Federal government	0.8	1.5	0.9	0.6	3.3	-3.8	0.1	-1.8	-1.5	-2.4	-1.5	-1.1	-3.1	-0.1
State and local government	2.0	0.3	2.5	2.6	2.9	1.4	1.5	1.6	2.0	2.6	2.3	1.7	0.7	0.6
Manufacturing	-1.5	0.3	1.7	0.4	-1.6	-3.5	-1.6	-0.2	1.3	1.9	1.5	2.3	1.8	-1.1
Construction	3.1	3.1	2.8	1.5	-0.9	-9.2	-3.5	3.8	7.3	11.0	5.1	6.9	7.3	-0.2
Other	3.2	3.6	4.0	3.4	2.1	-0.2	0.8	2.6	3.6	4.0	3.5	3.4	3.2	1.8
3. Unemployment rates														
Total	7.0	6.2	5.5	5.3	5.5	6.7	7.4	6.8	6.1	6.2	6.0	5.6	5.5	5.7
Married men	4.4	3.9	3.2	3.1	3.4	4.4	5.0	4.4	3.7	3.7	3.5	3.2	3.2	3.4
Females	7.1	6.2	5.6	5.4	5.5	6.3	7.3	7.3	6.0	6.2	5.9	5.6	5.5	5.7
Youths	18.4	16.9	15.3	15.0	15.5	18.7	20.3	20.3	17.6	18.1	17.5	16.7	16.8	17.2
4. Activity rate[4]	60.7	61.5	62.3	62.9	62.7	61.6	61.2	61.2	62.6	62.4	62.5	63.0	63.2	62.8

1. Household survey. Data from the household survey for 1994 are not directly comparable to data for 1993 and earlier years because of the implementation in January 1994 of a major redesign of the survey and the introduction of 1990 Census-based population controls, adjusted for the estimated undercount.
2. Non-institutional population aged 16 and over.
3. Non-agricultural payroll.
4. Employment as percentage of population aged from 16 to 64.
Source: US Department of Labor, Monthly Labor Review.

Table D. Costs and prices

Percentage changes from previous period, s.a.a.r.

	1986	1987	1988	1989	1990	1991	1992	1993	1994	1994 Q2	1994 Q3	1994 Q4	1995 Q1	1995 Q2
Rates of pay														
Major wage settlements[1]	2.3	3.1	2.6	3.2	3.5	3.5	3.0	2.9	2.7	3.2	3.6	2.4	1.2	3.2
Hourly earnings index[2]	2.3	2.5	3.3	4.0	3.7	3.1	2.5	2.4	2.7	2.1	2.8	3.8	2.3	3.0
Wages and salaries per person	4.1	4.6	4.8	3.4	4.7	3.4	5.6	1.6	3.4	4.6	2.5	3.8	3.6	3.5
Compensation per person	3.6	4.2	5.9	4.0	5.8	4.2	4.8	3.8	2.7	4.5	2.4	3.3	4.0	3.7
Productivity, non-farm business														
Hourly	2.0	0.8	0.9	-0.9	0.5	1.5	2.7	1.3	1.9	-1.4	2.7	4.3	2.5	4.8
Per employee	0.8	1.4	1.2	-0.9	-0.8	0.1	2.2	2.1	2.3	-0.2	1.1	4.6	1.9	1.4
Unit labour cost, non-farm business	3.0	2.5	3.3	4.3	5.0	3.5	2.3	1.7	0.7	2.8	0.0	-0.4	1.6	-1.2
Prices														
GDP deflator	2.7	3.2	3.9	4.5	4.3	3.8	2.8	2.2	2.1	3.0	2.1	1.2	2.0	1.6
Private consumption deflator	3.1	4.2	4.2	4.9	5.1	4.2	3.2	2.5	2.1	3.3	3.2	1.6	2.4	2.2
Consumer price index	1.9	3.7	4.1	4.8	5.4	4.2	3.0	3.0	2.6	2.6	3.6	1.9	3.3	3.6
Food	3.2	4.2	4.1	5.8	5.8	2.9	1.2	2.1	2.5	1.9	4.9	2.9	1.8	3.7
Wholesale prices	-2.9	2.6	4.0	5.0	3.6	0.2	0.6	1.5	1.3	2.3	3.1	1.6	6.8	5.1
Crude products	-8.4	6.7	2.5	7.4	5.7	-7.0	-0.8	2.0	-0.7	1.6	-8.1	-7.7	12.1	5.5
Intermediate products	-3.5	2.4	5.5	4.6	2.2	0.0	0.2	1.4	2.0	3.1	7.0	4.2	9.0	6.6
Finished products	-1.4	2.1	2.5	5.1	4.9	2.1	1.2	1.2	0.6	1.8	2.4	0.0	2.7	3.4

1. Total effective wage adjustment in all industries under collective agreements in non-farm industry covering at least 1 000 workers, not seasonally adjusted.
2. Production or non-supervisory workers on private non-agricultural payrolls.

Source: US Department of Labor, Bureau of Labor Statistics, *Monthly Labor Review;* US Department of Commerce, *Survey of Current Business.*

Table E. Monetary indicators

	1986	1987	1988	1989	1990	1991	1992	1993	1994	1994 Q2	1994 Q3	1994 Q4	1995 Q1	1995 Q2
Monetary aggregates (percentage changes from previous period s.a.a.r)														
M1	13.5	11.6	4.3	1.0	3.6	6.0	12.4	11.6	6.2	2.7	2.4	-1.2	0.0	-0.9
M2	8.3	6.6	5.2	4.0	5.3	3.2	2.1	1.3	1.9	1.7	1.0	-0.3	1.7	4.4
M3	8.3	7.0	6.4	4.5	2.7	1.7	0.6	0.2	1.6	1.3	2.2	1.7	4.4	7.2
Velocity of circulation														
GDP/M1	6.4	6.1	6.3	6.7	6.8	6.7	6.2	5.9	5.9	5.8	5.9	6.0	6.1	6.1
GDP/M2	1.6	1.6	1.6	1.7	1.7	1.7	1.7	1.8	1.9	1.9	1.9	1.9	1.9	1.9
GDP/M3	1.3	1.3	1.3	1.3	1.4	1.4	1.4	1.5	1.6	1.6	1.6	1.6	1.6	1.6
Federal Reserve Bank reserves ($ billion)														
Non-borrowed	33.6	38.6	37.8	38.7	39.9	42.7	50.0	57.2	59.8	60.0	59.4	59.1	58.8	57.5
Borrowed	0.8	0.8	2.4	1.1	0.9	0.4	0.2	0.2	0.3	0.2	0.5	0.3	0.1	0.2
Total	34.5	39.4	40.1	39.8	40.9	43.1	50.2	57.4	60.1	60.2	59.9	59.4	58.9	57.7
Required	33.5	38.4	39.1	38.9	39.9	41.9	49.2	56.3	59.0	59.1	58.9	58.4	57.8	56.8
Excess	0.9	1.0	1.0	1.0	1.0	1.2	1.0	1.1	1.1	1.1	1.0	1.0	1.1	0.9
Free (excess – borrowed)	0.1	0.3	-1.3	-0.2	0.0	0.8	0.8	0.9	0.8	0.9	0.5	0.7	1.0	0.7
Interest rates (%)														
Federal funds rate	6.8	6.7	7.6	9.2	8.1	5.7	3.5	3.0	4.2	3.9	4.5	5.2	5.8	6.0
Discount rate[1]	6.3	5.7	6.2	7.0	7.0	5.4	3.3	3.0	3.6	3.3	3.8	4.4	5.1	5.3
Prime rate[2]	8.3	8.2	9.3	10.9	10.0	8.5	6.3	6.0	7.1	6.9	7.5	8.1	8.8	9.0
3-month Treasury bills	6.0	5.8	6.7	8.1	7.5	5.4	3.4	3.0	4.2	4.0	4.5	5.3	5.7	5.6
AAA rate[3]	9.0	9.4	9.7	9.3	9.3	8.8	8.1	7.2	8.0	7.9	8.2	8.6	8.3	7.7
10-year Treasury notes	7.7	8.4	8.8	8.5	8.6	7.9	7.0	5.9	7.1	7.1	7.3	7.8	7.4	6.6

1. Rate for Federal Reserve Bank of New York.
2. Prime rate on short-term business loans.
3. Corporate Bonds, AAA rating group, quoted by Moody's Investors Services.
Source: Board of the Governors of the Federal Reserve System, *Federal Reserve Bulletin*.

	1982	1983	1984	1985
Exports, fob[1]	211 157	201 799	219 926	215 915
Imports, fob[1]	247 642	268 901	332 418	338 088
Trade balance	–36 485	–67 102	–11 2492	–122 173
Services, net[2]	42 118	40 384	33 330	19 751
Balance on goods and services	5 633	–26 718	–79 162	–102 422
Private transfers, net	–8 738	–9 066	–9 756	–9 545
Official transfers, net	–8 338	–8 676	–10 853	–13 406
Current balance	–11 443	–44 460	–99 771	–125 373
US assets abroad other than official reserves	–117 370	–57 539	–31 787	–35 368
US private assets, net[3]	–111 239	–52 533	–26 298	–32 547
Reported by US banks	–111 070	–29 928	–11 127	–1 323
US government assets[4]	–6 131	–5 006	–5 489	–2 821
Foreign assets in the United States				
Liabilities to foreign official monetary agencies[5]	3 593	5 845	3 140	–1 119
Other liabilities to foreign monetary agencies[6]	88 826	77 534	110 792	142 301
Reported by US banks	65 633	50 342	33 849	41 045
Allocation of SDR's	–	–	–	–
Errors and omissions	41 359	19 815	20 758	23 415
Change in reserves (+ = increase)	4 965	1 196	3 131	3 858
a) Gold	–	–	–	–
b) Currency assets	1 040	–3 305	1 156	3 869
c) Reserve position in IMF	2 552	4 435	995	–909
d) Special drawing rights	1 372	65	979	897

1. Excluding military goods.
2. Services include reinvested earnings of incorporated affiliates.
3. Including: Direct investment financed by reinvested earnings of incorporated affiliates; foreign securities; US claims on unaffiliated foreigners reported by US nonbanking concerns; and US claims reported by US banks, not included elsewhere.
4. Including: US credits and other long-term assets; repayments on US credits and other long-term assets, US foreign currency holdings and US short-term assets, net.

1986	1987	1988	1989	1990	1991	1992	1993	1994
223 344	250 208	320 230	362 116	389 303	416 913	440 361	456 866	502 729
368 425	409 765	447 189	477 365	498 336	490 981	536 458	589 441	669 093
−145 081	−159 557	−126 959	−115 249	−109 033	−74 068	−96 097	−132 575	−166 364
18 055	15 513	23 742	38 563	50 948	60 429	60 253	60 796	44 812
−127 026	−144 044	−103 217	−76 686	−58 085	−13 639	−35 844	−71 779	−121 552
−10 112	−10 544	−11 958	−12 700	−13 043	−13 811	−13 297	−13 712	−15 344
−14 064	−12 508	−13 019	−13 434	−20 619	20 498	−18 745	−18 405	−18 778
−151 202	−167 096	−128 194	−102 820	−91 747	−6 952	−67 886	−103 896	−155 674
−105 131	−80 591	−95 447	−143 451	−68 205	−57 275	−65 411	−146 519	−131 042
−103 109	−81 597	−98 414	−144 710	−70 512	−60 175	−63 759	−146 213	−130 755
−59 975	−42 119	53 927	58 160	16 027	4 763	22 314	32 238	−2 033
−2 022	1 006	2 967	1 259	2 307	2 900	−1 652	−306	−287
35 648	45 387	39 758	8 503	33 910	17 199	40 858	71 681	38 912
190 463	197 596	200 507	209 987	88 282	80 935	105 646	159 017	275 702
76 737	86 537	63 744	51 780	−3 824	3 994	15 461	18 452	106 189
−	−	−	−	−	−	−	−	−
29 908	−4 443	−12 712	53 075	39 919	−39 670	−17 108	21 096	−33 255
−312	−9 149	3 912	25 293	2 158	−5 763	−3 901	1 379	−5 346
−	−	−	−	−	−	−	−	−
942	−7 589	5 065	25 229	2 697	−6 307	−4 277	797	−5 293
−1 501	−2 070	−1 024	−471	−731	367	2 692	44	−494
246	509	−127	535	192	177	−2 316	537	441

5. Including: US Government securities and other US Government liabilities, US liabilities reported by US banks not included elsewhere and other foreign official assets.
6. Including direct investment; US Treasury securities; other US securities; US liabilities to unaffiliated foreigners reported by US non-banking concerns; US liabilities reported by US banks not included elsewhere.

Source: US Department of Commerce, *Survey of Current Business*.

	1960	1970	1980	1990	1992	1993	1994
A. Budget indicators:							
General government accounts (% GDP)							
Current receipts	27.0	29.7	30.5	30.8	30.7	31.0	31.5
Non-interest expenditures	25.0	29.6	30.6	31.2	32.9	32.6	31.6
Primary budget balance	2.0	0.1	-0.1	-0.4	-2.2	-1.5	-0.1
Net interest	-1.3	-1.2	-1.2	-2.1	-2.1	-1.9	-1.9
General government budget balance	0.7	-1.1	-1.3	-2.5	-4.3	-3.4	-2.0
of which:							
Central government	0.7	-1.3	-2.2	-2.9	-4.7	-3.8	-2.4
Excluding Social security	-0.8	-1.7	-2.1	-4.0	-5.5	-4.5	-3.3
B. The structure of expenditure and taxation (% GDP)							
Government expenditure							
Transfers	5.7	8.3	11.7	12.3	14.2	14.3	14.2
Subsidies	-0.1	0.3	0.2	0.1	0.1	0.1	0.0

	United States			OECD average		
	1991	1992	1993	1991	1992	1993
Tax receipts (% GDP)						
Income tax	10.3	10.1	10.2	11.3	11.4	11.3
Social security tax	8.8	8.8	8.7	9.7	9.9	10.2
Goods and services tax	5.0	5.1	5.1	11.5	11.7	11.6

C. Tax rates (%)	
Top rate	39.6
Lower rate	15.0
Social security tax rate	
Employer	7.15
Employee	7.15

	1960	1970	1980	1990	1992	1993	1994
D. Government debt (% GDP)							
General government gross debt	60.3	45.4	37.7	55.6	62.5	64.6	64.7
Net debt	46.6	28.5	18.8	31.5	36.2	38.1	40.1

Source: Economic Report of the President, February 1995; Department of Treasury, Office of Tax Analysis; *Revenue Statistics of OECD Member Countries, 1965-1994*, OECD 1995.

Table H. Financial markets

	1970	1975	1980	1990	1991	1992	1993	1994
A. Financial and corporate flows								
Share of private financial institutions' financial assets in national net assets (%)[1]	49.0	43.9	41.0	67.2	73.3	78.7	83.9	83.2
Market value of equities including corporate farm equities (billions of dollars)[1]	0.631	0.635	1.256	3.011	4.126	4.609	5.127	5.003
Debt-to-equity ratio in non-financial corporate business excluding farms (%)[1]	56.5	87.6	70.5	82.0	59.5	54.2	46.9	53.5
Ratio of market value to net worth[1]	77.8	39.0	41.3	73.2	106.8	126.3	136.1	126.8
B. Foreign sector (billions of dollars)								
Net foreign assets outstanding[1,3]	68.7	81.4	278.6	-266.9	-346.0	-472.5	-632.6	-886.3
Changes in net foreign investment[2]	3.0	24.0	25.7	-51.8	-46.4	-85.0	-82.8	-188.9
of which net financial investment of:								
Private sector	17.1	93.3	81.2	202.3	270.7	306.9	204.5	51.3
Public sector	-22.2	-80.0	-63.3	-217.6	-306.3	-389.1	-339.4	-285.9
Foreign purchases of US corporate equities[2]	0.7	3.1	4.2	-16.0	10.4	-5.8	20.5	0.3
US purchases of foreign equities[2]	1.1	-0.9	2.4	7.4	30.7	30.7	60.6	43.0
C. Net worth (billions of dollars)[1]								
Total, all sectors	3.070	5.558	10.666	18.323	18.459	18.500	19.052	20.014
Private, consolidated	3.488	6.203	11.689	20.941	21.321	21.592	22.336	23.287
Household	3.349	5.109	9.666	19.059	20.900	21.879	23.054	23.714
Total owner-occupied real estate	0.867	1.572	3.289	6.016	6.484	6.709	7.010	7.390
Home mortgages as a per cent of owner-occupied real estate	31.5	27.9	27.5	40.8	40.3	41.5	42.4	42.7
D. Debt to net worth ratios, private sector (%)[4]								
Household	13.5	14.3	14.4	19.0	18.1	18.3	18.6	19.6
Non-farm non-corporate business	38.3	46.5	42.5	64.5	65.5	64.8	63.8	61.8
Farm business	18.3	16.8	17.6	16.9	17.0	16.8	16.5	16.4
Non-financial corporate business excluding farms	44.0	34.2	29.1	60.1	63.6	68.5	67.9	67.9
Private financial institutions	65.2	73.9	77.3	114.7	108.5	109.6	109.1	124.0

1. Data are year-end outstandings.
2. Data are annual flows.
3. Net foreign assets exclude US holdings of foreign equities and foreign holdings of US equities.
4. Debt is credit market debt.
Source: Board of Governors of the Federal Reserve System, *Balance Sheets for the US Economy, 1945-94.*

Table I. Labour market indicators

	Peak	Trough	1990	1991	1992	1993	1994
A. Evolution							
Standardised unemployment rate	1982: 9.6	1969: 3.4	5.4	6.7	7.3	6.7	6.0
Unemployment rate							
Total	1982: 9.5	1969: 3.4	5.4	6.6	7.3	6.7	6.0
Male	1983: 9.7	1969: 2.7	5.5	6.9	7.6	7.0	6.1
Female	1982: 9.4	1969: 4.7	5.4	6.3	6.9	6.5	6.0
Youth[1]	1982: 17.0	1969: 7.4	11.1	13.4	14.2	13.3	12.5
Share of long-term unemployment[2]	1983: 13.4	1969: 1.9	5.6	6.3	11.2	11.7	12.2
Productivity index, 1987 = 100[3]			102.9	103.2	104.9	106.6	107.5

	1970	1980	1990	1991	1992	1993	1994
B. Structural or institutional characteristics							
Participation rate[4]							
Global	60.4	63.8	66.4	66.0	66.1	65.7	66.6
Male	79.7	76.0	74.9	74.4	74.4	74.1	75.0
Female	43.3	51.4	57.4	57.3	57.7	57.8	58.8
Employment/population between 16 and 64 years	57.4	59.2	62.7	61.6	61.2	61.2	62.5
Employment by sector							
Agriculture – per cent of total	4.5	3.6	2.8	2.9	2.9	2.7	2.9
– per cent change	−3.6	0.6	−0.5	1.0	−0.3	−3.5	10.1
Industry – per cent of total	34.3	30.5	26.2	25.3	24.6	24.0	24.0
– per cent change	−1.8	−1.9	−1.2	−4.3	−2.1	−0.9	2.9
Services – per cent of total	61.1	65.9	71.0	71.8	72.5	73.2	73.1
– per cent change	3.0	1.7	1.2	0.3	1.6	2.4	3.0
of which:							
Government – per cent of total	0.2	0.2	0.2	0.2	0.2	0.2	0.2
– per cent change	3.0	1.8	2.9	0.6	1.3	1.1	1.5
Voluntary part-time work[5]	13.9	14.2	13.7	13.7	13.4	13.4	14.7
Social insurance as a per cent of compensation	10.8	16.3	16.8	17.3	17.2	18.5	18.1
Government unemployment insurance benefits[6]	12.3	12.6	9.9	10.9	13.6	12.3	9.0
Minimum wage:							
as a percentage of average wage[7]	49.6	46.6	36.8	40.1	40.2	39.2	38.2

1. People between 16 and 24 years as a percentage of the labour force of the same age group.
2. People looking for a job since one year or more as a percentage of total unemployment.
3. Production as a percentage of employment.
4. Labour force as a percentage of the corresponding population aged between 16 and 64 years.
5. As a percentage of salary workers.
6. Value of the unemployment benefits per unemployed divided by the compensation per employee.
7. Private non-agricultural sector.

Source: US Department of Labor, Bureau of Labor Statistics, Data Resources Incorporated, and OECD.

BASIC STATISTICS

BASIC STATISTICS:

INTERNATIONAL COMPARISONS

	Units	Reference period [1]	Australia	Austr
Population				
Total	Thousands	1992	17 489	7 8
Inhabitants per sq. km	Number	1992	2	
Net average annual increase over previous 10 years	%	1992	1.4	0
Employment				
Civilian employment (CE)[2]	Thousands	1992	7 637	3 54
Of which: Agriculture	% of CE		5.3	7
Industry	% of CE		23.8	35
Services	% of CE		71	57
Gross domestic product (GDP)				
At current prices and current exchange rates	Bill. US$	1992	296.6	186
Per capita	US$		16 959	23 61
At current prices using current PPPs[3]	Bill. US$	1992	294.5	14
Per capita	US$		16 800	18 01
Average annual volume growth over previous 5 years	%	1992	2	3
Gross fixed capital formation (GFCF)	% of GDP	1992	19.7	2
Of which: Machinery and equipment	% of GDP		9.3	9
Residential construction	% of GDP		5.1	5
Average annual volume growth over previous 5 years	%	1992	–1	5
Gross saving ratio[4]	% of GDP	1992	15.6	25
General government				
Current expenditure on goods and services	% of GDP	1992	18.5	18
Current disbursements[5]	% of GDP	1992	36.9	46
Current receipts	% of GDP	1992	33.1	48
Net official development assistance	% of GNP	1992	0.33	0
Indicators of living standards				
Private consumption per capita using current PPPs[3]	US$	1992	10 527	9 95
Passenger cars, per 1 000 inhabitants	Number	1990	430	38
Telephones, per 1 000 inhabitants	Number	1990	448	58
Television sets, per 1 000 inhabitants	Number	1989	484	47
Doctors, per 1 000 inhabitants	Number	1991	2	2
Infant mortality per 1 000 live births	Number	1991	7.1	7
Wages and prices (average annual increase over previous 5 years)				
Wages (earnings or rates according to availability)	%	1992	5	5
Consumer prices	%	1992	5.2	
Foreign trade				
Exports of goods, fob*	Mill. US$	1992	42 844	44 36
As % of GDP	%		14.4	23
Average annual increase over previous 5 years	%		10.1	10
Imports of goods, cif*	Mill. US$	1992	40 751	54 03
As % of GDP	%		13.7	2
Average annual increase over previous 5 years	%		8.6	10
Total official reserves[6]	Mill. SDRs	1992	8 152	9 00
As ratio of average monthly imports of goods	Ratio		2.4	

* At current prices and exchange rates.
1. Unless otherwise stated.
2. According to the definitions used in OECD *Labour Force Statistics*.
3. PPPs = Purchasing Power Parities.
4. Gross saving = Gross national disposable income minus private and government consumption.
5. Current disbursements = Current expenditure on goods and services plus current transfers and payments of property income.
6. Gold included in reserves is valued at 35 SDRs per ounce. End of year.
7. Including Luxembourg.

		Spain	Sweden	Switzerland	Turkey	United Kingdom	United States
45	)	39 085	8 668	6 875	58 400	57 998	255 610
29	r	77	19	166	75	237	27
).2	)	0.3	0.4	0.6	2.2	0.3	1
24	)	12 359	4 195	3 481	18 600	25 175	117 598
2.6	)	10.1	3.3	5.6	43.9	2.2	2.9
7.7	)	32.4	26.5	33.9	22.1	26.5	24.6
).7	)	57.5	70.2	60.6	34	71.3	72.5
).9	)	576.3	247.2	240.9	159.1	1 042.8	5 937.3
91		14 745	28 522	35 041	2 724	17 981	23 228
.5	)	500.2	143.3	152.8	297.3	941.1	5 953.3
71		12 797	16 526	22 221	5 019	16 227	23 291
.1		3.3	0.6	1.7	3.7	0.9	1.9
.1	)	21.8	17	23.7	23	15.6	15.6
.6		6.8	6.2	8	8.5	7.2	7.2
.6		4.3	5.9	15.7 [10]	7.6	3	3.7
7.1		6.2	−0.6	1.5	4.6	0.6	0.7
.3		19.1	14.1	29.7	23.1	12.8	14.5
.7		17	27.8	14.3	12.9	22.3	17.7
.6		..	64.6	35.1	..	42.1	36.7
).7		..	59.6	34.7	..	38	31.6
39		0.26	1	0.47	..	0.31	0.2
.20		8 083	8 907	13 043	3 206	10 397	15 637
.87	)	307	418	441	29	361	568
46		323	681	905	151	434	509
47		389	471	406	174	434	814
3.6		3.9	2.9	3	0.9	1.4	2.3
.4		7.8	6.1	6.2	56.5	7.4	8.9
.1		7.7	7.3	..	..	8.3	2.9
2.7		6	6.8	4.1	66.6	6.3	4.3
.64 [7]	1)	64 509	55 980	65 478	14 853	190 103	448 033
5.8		11.2	22.6	27.2	9.3	18.2	7.5
8.2		13.7	4.8	7.5	7.5	7.8	12
33 [7]	1:	99 659	49 916	65 587	23 267	220 994	531 070
6.6		17.3	20.2	27.2	14.6	21.2	8.9
8.4		15.3	4.2	5.3	10	7.5	5.5
.37 [7]		33 094	16 454	24 185	4 480	26 648	43 831
1		4	4	4.4	2.3	1.4	1

November 1994

ncluded in fig
Refers to the p
ncluding non-
ces: Populatio
Accounts,
Indicator
Financial

EMPLOYMENT OPPORTUNITIES

Economics Department, OECD

The Economics Department of the OECD offers challenging and rewarding opportunities to economists interested in applied policy analysis in an international environment. The Department's concerns extend across the entire field of economic policy analysis, both macroeconomic and microeconomic. Its main task is to provide, for discussion by committees of senior officials from Member countries, documents and papers dealing with current policy concerns. Within this programme of work, three major responsibilities are:

- to prepare regular surveys of the economies of individual Member countries;
- to issue full twice-yearly reviews of the economic situation and prospects of the OECD countries in the context of world economic trends;
- to analyse specific policy issues in a medium-term context for the OECD as a whole, and to a lesser extent for the non-OECD countries.

The documents prepared for these purposes, together with much of the Department's other economic work, appear in published form in the *OECD Economic Outlook, OECD Economic Surveys, OECD Economic Studies* and the Department's *Working Papers* series.

The Department maintains a world econometric model, INTERLINK, which plays an important role in the preparation of the policy analyses and twice-yearly projections. The availability of extensive cross-country data bases and good computer resources facilitates comparative empirical analysis, much of which is incorporated into the model.

The Department is made up of about 80 professional economists from a variety of backgrounds and Member countries. Most projects are carried out by small teams and last from four to eighteen months. Within the Department, ideas and points of view are widely discussed; there is a lively professional interchange, and all professional staff have the opportunity to contribute actively to the programme of work.

Skills the Economics Department is looking for:

a) Solid competence in using the tools of both microeconomic and macroeconomic theory to answer policy questions. Experience indicates that this normally requires the equivalent of a Ph.D. in economics or substantial relevant professional experience to compensate for a lower degree.

b) Solid knowledge of economic statistics and quantitative methods; this includes how to identify data, estimate structural relationships, apply basic techniques of time series analysis, and test hypotheses. It is essential to be able to interpret results sensibly in an economic policy context.

c) A keen interest in and extensive knowledge of policy issues, economic developments and their political/social contexts.

d) Interest and experience in analysing questions posed by policy-makers and presenting the results to them effectively and judiciously. Thus, work experience in government agencies or policy research institutions is an advantage.

e) The ability to write clearly, effectively, and to the point. The OECD is a bilingual organisation with French and English as the official languages. Candidates must have excellent knowledge of one of these languages, and some knowledge of the other. Knowledge of other languages might also be an advantage for certain posts.

f) For some posts, expertise in a particular area may be important, but a successful candidate is expected to be able to work on a broader range of topics relevant to the work of the Department. Thus, except in rare cases, the Department does not recruit narrow specialists.

g) The Department works on a tight time schedule with strict deadlines. Moreover, much of the work in the Department is carried out in small groups. Thus, the ability to work with other economists from a variety of cultural and professional backgrounds, to supervise junior staff, and to produce work on time is important.

General information

The salary for recruits depends on educational and professional background. Positions carry a basic salary from FF 305 700 or FF 377 208 for Administrators (economists) and from FF 438 348 for Principal Administrators (senior economists). This may be supplemented by expatriation and/or family allowances, depending on nationality, residence and family situation. Initial appointments are for a fixed term of two to three years.

Vacancies are open to candidates from OECD Member countries. The Organisation seeks to maintain an appropriate balance between female and male staff and among nationals from Member countries.

For further information on employment opportunities in the Economics Department, contact:

Administrative Unit
Economics Department
OECD
2, rue André-Pascal
75775 PARIS CEDEX 16
FRANCE

E-Mail: compte.esadmin@oecd.org

Applications citing ''ECSUR'', together with a detailed *curriculum vitae* in English or French, should be sent to the Head of Personnel at the above address.

MAIN SALES OUTLETS OF OECD PUBLICATIONS
PRINCIPAUX POINTS DE VENTE DES PUBLICATIONS DE L'OCDE

ARGENTINA – ARGENTINE
Carlos Hirsch S.R.L.
Galería Güemes, Florida 165, 4° Piso
1333 Buenos Aires   Tel. (1) 331.1787 y 331.2391
Telefax: (1) 331.1787

AUSTRALIA – AUSTRALIE
D.A. Information Services
648 Whitehorse Road, P.O.B 163
Mitcham, Victoria 3132   Tel. (03) 9873.4411
Telefax: (03) 9873.5679

AUSTRIA – AUTRICHE
Gerold & Co.
Graben 31
Wien 1   Tel. (0222) 533.50.14
Telefax: (0222) 512.47.31.29

BELGIUM – BELGIQUE
Jean De Lannoy
Avenue du Roi 202 Koningslaan
B-1060 Bruxelles   Tel. (02) 538.51.69/538.08.41
Telefax: (02) 538.08.41

CANADA
Renouf Publishing Company Ltd.
1294 Algoma Road
Ottawa, ON K1B 3W8   Tel. (613) 741.4333
Telefax: (613) 741.5439

Stores:
61 Sparks Street
Ottawa, ON K1P 5R1   Tel. (613) 238.8985
211 Yonge Street
Toronto, ON M5B 1M4   Tel. (416) 363.3171
Telefax: (416)363.59.63

Les Éditions La Liberté Inc.
3020 Chemin Sainte-Foy
Sainte-Foy, PQ G1X 3V6   Tel. (418) 658.3763
Telefax: (418) 658.3763

Federal Publications Inc.
165 University Avenue, Suite 701
Toronto, ON M5H 3B8   Tel. (416) 860.1611
Telefax: (416) 860.1608

Les Publications Fédérales
1185 Université
Montréal, QC H3B 3A7   Tel. (514) 954.1633
Telefax: (514) 954.1635

CHINA – CHINE
China National Publications Import ·
Export Corporation (CNPIEC)
16 Gongti E. Road, Chaoyang District
P.O. Box 88 or 50
Beijing 100704 PR   Tel. (01) 506.6688
Telefax: (01) 506.3101

CHINESE TAIPEI – TAIPEI CHINOIS
Good Faith Worldwide Int'l. Co. Ltd.
9th Floor, No. 118, Sec. 2
Chung Hsiao E. Road
Taipei   Tel. (02) 391.7396/391.7397
Telefax: (02) 394.9176

CZECH REPUBLIC – RÉPUBLIQUE TCHÈQUE
Artia Pegas Press Ltd.
Narodni Trida 25
POB 825
111 21 Praha 1   Tel. (2) 2 46 04
Telefax: (2) 2 78 72

DENMARK – DANEMARK
Munksgaard Book and Subscription Service
35, Nørre Søgade, P.O. Box 2148
DK-1016 København K   Tel. (33) 12.85.70
Telefax: (33) 12.93.87

EGYPT – ÉGYPTE
Middle East Observer
41 Sherif Street
Cairo   Tel. 392.6919
Telefax: 360-6804

FINLAND – FINLANDE
Akateeminen Kirjakauppa
Keskuskatu 1, P.O. Box 128
00100 Helsinki
Subscription Services/Agence d'abonnements :
P.O. Box 23
00371 Helsinki   Tel. (358 0) 121 4416
Telefax: (358 0) 121.4450

FRANCE
OECD/OCDE
Mail Orders/Commandes par correspondance:
2, rue André-Pascal
75775 Paris Cedex 16   Tel. (33-1) 45.24.82.00
Telefax: (33-1) 49.10.42.76
Telex: 640048 OCDE
Internet: Compte.PUBSINQ @ oecd.org
Orders via Minitel, France only/
Commandes par Minitel, France exclusivement :
36 15 OCDE

OECD Bookshop/Librairie de l'OCDE :
33, rue Octave-Feuillet
75016 Paris   Tel. (33-1) 45.24.81.81
(33-1) 45.24.81.67

Dawson
B.P. 40
91121 Palaiseau Cedex   Tel. 69.10.47.00
Telefax : 64.54.83.26

Documentation Française
29, quai Voltaire
75007 Paris   Tel. 40.15.70.00

Economica
49 rue Héricart
75015 Paris   Tel. 45.78.12.92
Telefax : 40.58.15.70

Gibert Jeune (Droit-Économie)
6, place Saint-Michel
75006 Paris   Tel. 43.25.91.19

Librairie du Commerce International
10, avenue d'Iéna
75016 Paris   Tel. 40.73.34.60

Librairie Dunod
Université Paris-Dauphine
Place du Maréchal de Lattre de Tassigny
75016 Paris   Tel. 44.05.40.13

Librairie Lavoisier
11, rue Lavoisier
75008 Paris   Tel. 42.65.39.95

Librairie des Sciences Politiques
30, rue Saint-Guillaume
75007 Paris   Tel. 45.48.36.02

P.U.F.
49, boulevard Saint-Michel
75005 Paris   Tel. 43.25.83.40

Librairie de l'Université
12a, rue Nazareth
13100 Aix-en-Provence   Tel. (16) 42.26.18.08

Documentation Française
165, rue Garibaldi
69003 Lyon   Tel. (16) 78.63.32.23

Librairie Decitre
29, place Bellecour
69002 Lyon   Tel. (16) 72.40.54.54

Librairie Sauramps
Le Triangle
34967 Montpellier Cedex 2   Tel. (16) 67.58.85.15
Tekefax: (16) 67.58.27.36

A la Sorbonne Actual
23 rue de l'Hôtel des Postes
06000 Nice   Tel. (16) 93.13.77.75
Telefax: (16) 93.80.75.69

GERMANY – ALLEMAGNE
OECD Publications and Information Centre
August-Bebel-Allee 6
D-53175 Bonn   Tel. (0228) 959.120
Telefax: (0228) 959.12.17

GREECE – GRÈCE
Librairie Kauffmann
Mavrokordatou 9
106 78 Athens   Tel. (01) 32.55.321
Telefax: (01) 32.30.320

HONG-KONG
Swindon Book Co. Ltd.
Astoria Bldg. 3F
34 Ashley Road, Tsimshatsui
Kowloon, Hong Kong   Tel. 2376.2062
Telefax: 2376.0685

HUNGARY – HONGRIE
Euro Info Service
Margitsziget, Európa Ház
1138 Budapest   Tel. (1) 111.62.16
Telefax: (1) 111.60.61

ICELAND – ISLANDE
Mál Mog Menning
Laugavegi 18, Pósthólf 392
121 Reykjavik   Tel. (1) 552.4240
Telefax: (1) 562.3523

INDIA – INDE
Oxford Book and Stationery Co.
Scindia House
New Delhi 110001   Tel. (11) 331.5896/5308
Telefax: (11) 332.5993

17 Park Street
Calcutta 700016   Tel. 240832

INDONESIA – INDONÉSIE
Pdii-Lipi
P.O. Box 4298
Jakarta 12042   Tel. (21) 573.34.67
Telefax: (21) 573.34.67

IRELAND – IRLANDE
Government Supplies Agency
Publications Section
4/5 Harcourt Road
Dublin 2   Tel. 661.31.11
Telefax: 475.27.60

ISRAEL
Praedicta
5 Shatner Street
P.O. Box 34030
Jerusalem 91430   Tel. (2) 52.84.90/1/2
Telefax: (2) 52.84.93

R.O.Y. International
P.O. Box 13056
Tel Aviv 61130   Tel. (3) 546 1423
Telefax: (3) 546 1442

Palestinian Authority/Middle East:
INDEX Information Services
P.O.B. 19502
Jerusalem   Tel. (2) 27.12.19
Telefax: (2) 27.16.34

ITALY – ITALIE
Libreria Commissionaria Sansoni
Via Duca di Calabria 1/1
50125 Firenze   Tel. (055) 64.54.15
Telefax: (055) 64.12.57

Via Bartolini 29
20155 Milano   Tel. (02) 36.50.83

Editrice e Libreria Herder
Piazza Montecitorio 120
00186 Roma   Tel. 679.46.28
Telefax: 678.47.51

Libreria Hoepli
Via Hoepli 5
20121 Milano   Tel. (02) 86.54.46
                                Telefax: (02) 805.28.86
Libreria Scientifica
Dott. Lucio de Biasio 'Aeiou'
Via Coronelli, 6
20146 Milano   Tel. (02) 48.95.45.52
                                Telefax: (02) 48.95.45.48

JAPAN – JAPON
OECD Publications and Information Centre
Landic Akasaka Building
2-3-4 Akasaka, Minato-ku
Tokyo 107   Tel. (81.3) 3586.2016
                                Telefax: (81.3) 3584.7929

KOREA – CORÉE
Kyobo Book Centre Co. Ltd.
P.O. Box 1658, Kwang Hwa Moon
Seoul   Tel. 730.78.91
                                   Telefax: 735.00.30

MALAYSIA – MALAISIE
University of Malaya Bookshop
University of Malaya
P.O. Box 1127, Jalan Pantai Baru
59700 Kuala Lumpur
Malaysia   Tel. 756.5000/756.5425
                                   Telefax: 756.3246

MEXICO – MEXIQUE
OECD Publications and Information Centre
Edificio INFOTEC
Av. San Fernando no. 37
Col. Toriello Guerra
Tlalpan C.P. 14050
Mexico D.F.
        Tel. (525) 606 00 11 Extension 100
              Fax : (525) 606 13 07

Revistas y Periodicos Internacionales S.A. de C.V.
Florencia 57 - 1004
Mexico, D.F. 06600   Tel. 207.81.00
                                Telefax: 208.39.79

NETHERLANDS – PAYS-BAS
SDU Uitgeverij Plantijnstraat
Externe Fondsen
Postbus 20014
2500 EA's-Gravenhage   Tel. (070) 37.89.880
Voor bestellingen: Telefax: (070) 34.75.778

NEW ZEALAND
NOUVELLE-ZÉLANDE
GPLegislation Services
P.O. Box 12418
Thorndon, Wellington   Tel. (04) 496.5655
                                Telefax: (04) 496.5698

NORWAY – NORVÈGE
Narvesen Info Center – NIC
Bertrand Narvesens vei 2
P.O. Box 6125 Etterstad
0602 Oslo 6   Tel. (022) 57.33.00
                                Telefax: (022) 68.19.01

PAKISTAN
Mirza Book Agency
65 Shahrah Quaid-E-Azam
Lahore 54000   Tel. (42) 353.601
                                Telefax: (42) 231.730

PHILIPPINE – PHILIPPINES
International Booksource Center Inc.
Rm 179/920 Cityland 10 Condo Tower 2
HV dela Costa Ext cor Valero St.
Makati Metro Manila   Tel. (632) 817 9676
                          Telefax : (632) 817 1741

POLAND – POLOGNE
Ars Polona
00-950 Warszawa
Krakowskie Przedmieácie 7   Tel. (22) 264760
                          Telefax : (22) 268673

PORTUGAL
Livraria Portugal
Rua do Carmo 70-74
Apart. 2681
1200 Lisboa   Tel. (01) 347.49.82/5
                             Telefax: (01) 347.02.64

SINGAPORE – SINGAPOUR
Gower Asia Pacific Pte Ltd.
Golden Wheel Building
41, Kallang Pudding Road, No. 04-03
Singapore 1334   Tel. 741.5166
                                   Telefax: 742.9356

SPAIN – ESPAGNE
Mundi-Prensa Libros S.A.
Castelló 37, Apartado 1223
Madrid 28001   Tel. (91) 431.33.99
                             Telefax: (91) 575.39.98

Mundi-Prensa Barcelona
Consell de Cent No. 391
08009 – Barcelona
                                Tel. (93) 488.34.92
                             Telefax: (93) 487.76.59

Llibreria de la Generalitat
Palau Moja
Rambla dels Estudis, 118
08002 – Barcelona
             (Subscripcions) Tel. (93) 318.80.12
             (Publicacions) Tel. (93) 302.67.23
                             Telefax: (93) 412.18.54

SRI LANKA
Centre for Policy Research
c/o Colombo Agencies Ltd.
No. 300-304, Galle Road
Colombo 3   Tel. (1) 574240, 573551-2
                          Telefax: (1) 575394, 510711

SWEDEN – SUÈDE
CE Fritzes AB
S–106 47 Stockholm   Tel. (08) 690.90.90
                             Telefax: (08) 20.50.21

Subscription Agency/Agence d'abonnements :
Wennergren-Williams Info AB
P.O. Box 1305
171 25 Solna   Tel. (08) 705.97.50
                             Telefax: (08) 27.00.71

SWITZERLAND – SUISSE
Maditec S.A. (Books and Periodicals - Livres
et périodiques)
Chemin des Palettes 4
Case postale 266
1020 Renens VD 1   Tel. (021) 635.08.65
                             Telefax: (021) 635.07.80

Librairie Payot S.A.
4, place Pépinet
CP 3212
1002 Lausanne   Tel. (021) 320.25.11
                             Telefax: (021) 320.25.14

Librairie Unilivres
6, rue de Candolle
1205 Genève   Tel. (022) 320.26.23
                             Telefax: (022) 329.73.18

Subscription Agency/Agence d'abonnements :
Dynapresse Marketing S.A.
38 avenue Vibert
1227 Carouge   Tel. (022) 308.07.89
                             Telefax: (022) 308.07.99
See also – Voir aussi :
OECD Publications and Information Centre
August-Bebel-Allee 6
D-53175 Bonn (Germany)   Tel. (0228) 959.120
                            Telefax: (0228) 959.12.17

THAILAND – THAÏLANDE
Suksit Siam Co. Ltd.
113, 115 Fuang Nakhon Rd.
Opp. Wat Rajbopith
Bangkok 10200   Tel. (662) 225.9531/2
                             Telefax: (662) 222.5188

TURKEY – TURQUIE
Kültür Yayinlari Is-Türk Ltd. Sti.
Atatürk Bulvari No. 191/Kat 13
Kavaklidere/Ankara   Tel. 428.11.40 Ext. 2458
Dolmabahce Cad. No. 29
Besiktas/Istanbul   Tel. (312) 260 7188
                             Telex: (312) 418 29 46

UNITED KINGDOM – ROYAUME-UNI
HMSO
Gen. enquiries   Tel. (171) 873 8496
Postal orders only:
P.O. Box 276, London SW8 5DT
Personal Callers HMSO Bookshop
49 High Holborn, London WC1V 6HB
                             Telefax: (171) 873 8416
Branches at: Belfast, Birmingham, Bristol,
Edinburgh, Manchester

UNITED STATES – ÉTATS-UNIS
OECD Publications and Information Center
2001 L Street N.W., Suite 650
Washington, D.C. 20036-4910 Tel. (202) 785.6323
                             Telefax: (202) 785.0350

VENEZUELA
Libreria del Este
Avda F. Miranda 52, Aptdo. 60337
Edificio Galipán
Caracas 106   Tel. 951.1705/951.2307/951.1297
                          Telegram: Libreste Caracas

Subscriptions to OECD periodicals may also be
placed through main subscription agencies.

Les abonnements aux publications périodiques de
l'OCDE peuvent être souscrits auprès des
principales agences d'abonnement.

Orders and inquiries from countries where Distribu-
tors have not yet been appointed should be sent to:
OECD Publications Service, 2 rue André-Pascal,
75775 Paris Cedex 16, France.

Les commandes provenant de pays où l'OCDE n'a
pas encore désigné de distributeur peuvent être
adressées à : OCDE, Service des Publications,
2, rue André-Pascal, 75775 Paris Cedex 16, France.

                                           10-1995

OECD PUBLICATIONS, 2 rue André-Pascal, 75775 PARIS CEDEX 16
PRINTED IN FRANCE
(10 95 02 1) ISBN 92-64-14667-9 - No. 48349 1995
ISSN 0376-6438

ADVANCE PRAISE FOR THE JOY OF GEOCACHING

"Here is an excellent introduction to this emerging sport. Longtime tech writer Paul Gillin and his wife, Dana, are the perfect ambassadors for geocaching. This is a lively and well-written introduction to a sport that is rapidly gaining followers. It makes a fine source for instruction—its clear writing and personable tone far surpass similar instruction books—but it is also simply an interesting read for all curious about the phenomenon."
—*Library Journal*

"*The Joy of Geocaching* is perfectly titled. With all the great information included, it is an excellent introduction to geocaching; or for those who have been involved for a long time, it reminds us of many of the reasons we still love it. It gives a well-informed snapshot of this great activity/sport/obsession and blends the personal and the technical aspects perfectly. Having just entered my ninth year of geocaching, I still learned plenty from this book. This book is by cachers, about cachers, and for cachers. Three thumbs up! Peace."
— **Darrell Smith (Show Me The Cache)**

"Geocaching is not for dummies. Finally, here's the definitive book about it written by experienced and enthusiastic geocachers!"
—**Elin Carlson (EMC of Northridge, CA)**

"This is a superb resource not only for the new geocacher, but also those cachers who have thousands of finds. It is the most comprehensive, up-to-date discussion of various geocaching tips, techniques, and tales that I have read in my more than seven years being a geocacher. It will enhance your geocaching experience as well as your fun. Many thanks to Paul and Dana for devoting a year of their life researching and writing this book. It will sit proudly and prominently on my bookshelf."
—**Bert Carter (WE4NCS)**

"This book is much more than just a how-to guide. It's an insight into the passion and enjoyment many of us get from geocaching. I love the way the book captures the energy and enjoyment my fellow geocachers get from the sport through a great collection of stories that demonstrate the many different types and styles of geocaching. How will you play the game?"
— **Steve O'Gara (ventura_kids)**

"*The Joy of Geocaching* is a joy to read. The book captures the unexpected social aspect of the sport. The gathering of like-minded knuckleheads was a joy we never anticipated."
—Gary & Vicky Hobgood (Gary&Vicky)

"*The Joy of Geocaching* captures the adventure and spirit of geocaching that causes so many of us to ignore housework, forego our work and/or school responsibilities, and shirk our family and friends to be the first to hunt for new cache sites and solve that next puzzle cache. A must-read for any and all geocachers from newbie to grizzled old pro!"
—Wade Mauland (Ecorangers)

"*The Joy of Geocaching* is the only book I've seen that combines the how-to, the folklore and the excitement of geocaching all in one place. It's a highly readable book full of valuable information for geocachers of all skill levels."
—Dave Grenewetzki (dgreno)

"*The Joy of Geocaching* is the ultimate fuel to turn the smallest spark of geocaching curiosity into the roaring flames of addiction that we geocachers cherish. It reveals the passion and experiences of geocachers while clearly explaining everything you need to know to play. As soon as you start reading you're hooked. So save yourself some time and go ahead and get the GPSr while you're shopping."
—InfiniteMPG (Scott Veix)

"The caching stories reminded me why geocaching has risen above a hobby to become a way of life for me. The book explains geocaching so well that even the most disinterested muggle will understand it. Thank you for a well-written chronicle of our sport."
— Mark Wilcoxson (Deermark)

"This book is a great read for both the novice and experienced geocacher. A comprehensive compendium of geocaching information, written in a style that is entertaining and easy to read. A definite must-have!"
—Clyde England (clydee), developer of the Geocaching Swiss Army Knife

"*The Joy of Geocaching* captures the spirit of geocaching and the players like no book before it. A fun and interesting read that tells all one needs to know to enjoy geocaching and the websites and tools that we use."
—Ed Manley (TheAlabamaRambler)